Letters to Friends of the Spirit

Martinist Views & Others

Also by Rémi Boyer

THE WAYS OF AWAKENING TRILOGY

Freemasonry as a Way of Awakening

Mask Cloak Silence:
Martinism as a Way of Awakening

Beneath the Veil of Elias Artista
The Rose-Croix as a Way of Awakening:
An Oral Tradition
(with Lima de Freitas and Manuel Gandra)

The Rectified Scottish Rite:
From the Doctrine of Reintegration
to the Imago Templi

WITH SYLVIE BOYER-CAMAX

The Way Without Masters

Letters to Friends of the Spirit

Martinist Views & Others

Sylvie Boyer-Camax
and Rémi Boyer

Rose Circle Publications
Bayonne NJ
2022

Letters to Friends of the Spirit
Martinist Views & Others

Copyright © 2022 by Rémi Boyer
English translation copyright © 2022 by Michael Sanborn

ISBN: 978-1-947907-21-8
Library of Congress Control Number: 2022908174

Paintings and illustrations by Lima de Freitas courtesy of Helle Hartvig de Freitas

Photograph on p. 233 by Einsamer Schütze, CC-BY-SA-3.0 (http://creativecommons.org/licenses/by-sa/3.0), via Wikimedia Commons.

Book design and layout by Michael Sanborn, TextArc LLC. michael@textarc.net

All rights reserved. No part of this publication may be reproduced, distributed, or transmitted in any form or by any means, including photocopying, recording, or other electronic or mechanical methods, without the prior written permission of the publisher, except in the case of brief quotations embodied in critical reviews and certain other non-commercial uses permitted by copyright law. For permission requests, write to the publisher at the address below.

Rose Circle Publications
P.O. Box 854
Bayonne, NJ 07002, U.S.A.
www.rosecirclebooks.com

To the Sisters and Brothers of the *Grand Order Sébastianiste*
Who Recognized the *Hidden King*

CONTENTS

Preface • xi

FIRST SERIES • 1
I A Few Points on Prayer • 3
II Trees in the Garden of Eden • 5
III The Holy Spirit • 9
IV Wisdom • 11
V Prophecies • 15
VI Rhély • 21
VII The Old and the New • 25
VIII Anointing • 29
IX Grace • 33
X Chivalry • 37
XI The Sword and the Lance • 41
XII The Armor of the Knight • 45
XIII The Letter Shin • 53
XIV Meta-Initiation • 57
XV The Lady • 61
XVI The *Shekinah* • 65
XVII 515 • 69
XVIII Revelation • 79
XIX The Essene Cross • 83
XX The Covenants • 87
XXI The Letter A • 91
XXII The Letter K • 97

LITTLE TREATISE ON THE
CHRISTIFICATION OF BEINGS • 101

SECOND SERIES • 123
    I The Secret Grammar • 125
   II The Order of Knight-Masons
        Élus Coëns of the Universe • 131
   III Sacraments • 139
   IV The Way of Bread and Wine • 143
   V The Baptism of the Spirit • 149
   VI Transmission • 153
   VII The Cryptic Doctrine • 157
   VIII Saint Paraskeva • 161
   IX Saint Isabella • 167
   X Crocodile • 173
   XI A Chivalry of the Spirit • 179
   XII The Way of Elias Artista • 183
   XIII The Superior Geometry of the Builders • 193
   XIV The Point and the Line • 201
   XV Alchemy and Initiation • 207
   XVI The *Arcana Cœlestia* and Swedenborg • 215
   XVII Woman, Muse and Initiator • 221
   XVIII Black Virgins • 231
   XIX The *Arcana Arcanorum* • 237
   XX Death, an Old Friend • 251
   XXI Joy • 255
   XXII From the People of Letters
        to the People of Being • 261

BIBLIOGRAPHIES AND MALLARMÉ • 281

The *Letters to Friends of the Spirit* were sent in the form of "Briefs," on a weekly basis, during the periods of restricted freedoms in 2021, to members of initiatory, Masonic, Martinist, Gnostic, Pythagorean, Rose-Croix, Swedenborgian, and other organizations to support practice.

It is a meandering through the traditional world, the unique golden thread of which is nonduality. A stroll through a labyrinth of doors.

The Great Door is the door to nonduality, always open and so vast that, from moment to moment, we walk past it without seeing it.

Some doors are ajar. You need only nudge them open to discover gardens of knowledge. Other doors are merely indicated, designated simply as landmarks to remember, and some, finally, are only mentioned, because it is useless to know their location without having sought them out for a long time.

Rather than a teaching, which it is not, this book can be seen as a set of footnotes referring to the knowledge that each of us carries within. Everyone is the best expert of their own realization. It's just a matter of attention.

As for the rest, it's not nothing. It is companionship, spiritual friendship, and shared regard.

> *We are scientific because we lack subtlety.*
> — Roland Barthes, *The Pleasure of the Text*

PREFACE

It is relatively rarely that we discover information in precious teachings that offers us the light of that most beautiful of Roses, the one that opens the doors of the Light to us.

The following "Letters" to Friends of the Spirit are, symbolically, the vision or inner contemplation of a diamond in its esoteric Light, the companion Light of the evoked Rose.

The student of Sacred Science will discover in these distilled pages many keys relating to the opening of the secret knowledge inherent in the human soul in its quest for eternity in the light of perpetual becoming.

These letters are a friendly and fraternal dispatch, opening a way to the disciples of the Way of the Heart, in an ineffable love evoking "I am the way, the truth, and the life"—an important reminder.

In each paragraph, these clarified details are assurances of deep meditations, becoming clearer in fruitful interior images, in subtle responses to many questions, including those of Martinez de Pasqually de La Tour's predecessors. This is perhaps the moment to recall who his predecessors were…

Martinez traveled widely and certainly consulted a great many documents in the monasteries of Europe. When he talks about "his predecessors" there is no indication of whom he means. *"La Chose"* is complex, both mysterious and political.

During the separation from the Order of the Knights of Christ—the Templars—into the Order of the Teutonic Knights for "xenophobic" reasons (i.e., the link between the Templars and the Saracen Sufis), the Templars who had become Teutonics kept the original theurgic operative rituals of the Knights of Christ very secret. In the Teutonic Order, four knights had to induct four other knights of their choosing, without the hierarchical structure knowing. Some ritual texts were deposited in convents in France, in Orléans and Blois. Martinez de Pasqually consulted them, copied them, noted them down, worked them, and transmitted them without revealing their origin. Then one day, the Teutonic transmission could no longer be accomplished in the Order and the documents alone, subsequently withdrawn by the Benedictines, returned to the Vatican. Furthermore, Martinez entered into a "post mortem" relationship with the Teutonics/Templars through theurgic working to authenticate the uncovered documents and validate the Operations.

Where does this information come from?

From cryptic communications in the 1960s resulting from evocations in Arginy and Dévoluy (among others).

We are under no obligation to believe it. Nevertheless, these contemporary "Letters" are in the directly actualized lineage of Louis-Claude de Saint-Martin and Martinez de Pasqually de La Tour.

The initiatory content of the texts opens up new avenues, completes the old teachings, distills information which is both from the past and certainly of the present, a present which prepares for a future that may pose multiple, even frightening, difficulties.

Thus, therefore, hope is present in the inner reality of those who turn to the light (of the seven companions) at the opening of the cave.

To readers in search of Wisdom, Strength, Beauty...
Take courage,
    Gird your souls, and
        Lift up your Hearts!

To all who have RECOGNIZED *the* HIDDEN KING,

September 10, 2021
Guy Thieux

FIRST SERIES

O milagre das rosas
Painting by Lima de Freitas

A FEW POINTS ON PRAYER

FIRST LETTER TO FRIENDS OF THE SPIRIT • FIRST SERIES

*HE NATURE OF GOD:* GOD IS. NOTHING IS EXTERNAL to Him. He is Absolute Will, Absolute Love, and Absolute Freedom. It is the exercise of this freedom that leads Him to stretch into duality and to contract into an infinity of more or less self-conscious forms, such as we are, in order to recognize Himself, each time on a different sabbatical.

The nature of the illusion of separation: What we call error is the result of this false separation within duality. The oppositions are born from this separate posture that nourishes polarizations: good/bad, light/shadow, etc.

Upon awakening, we can take a conscious action to extract ourselves from duality and reduce the feeling of separation. This prepares us for meditation in the very heart of everyday life. By becoming aware of the movement of separation that is "consciousness of," we become disidentified from the subject-object relationship and leave more room for Being within Appearance itself. God is the only actor, spectator, creator, and producer. We have nothing to do, other than to preserve the free space. To observe the play of identifications by polarization and separation is enough to ensure the porosity between the worlds and to distinguish the intervals. "Inter-vals," between two vales, we have the mountain, the Greatest Height of Self, God.

The nature of prayer: Addressing a prayer to a god experienced as exterior in order to obtain is a mistake. It assumes that God is not the whole, Is not. This creates duality between a world where God is present and a world where God is absent. It is to deny the omnipresence, omniscience, and omnipotence of God.

His Presence is absolute, here and now, in the situation that is ours. To pray is to become aware of this silent Presence. The only prayer is silence, which takes place through self-remembering. Here the Presence reigns.

"I Am, available to the Grace of God, I hear the Word of God, I do not pray for any of the things of this world. In silence, I make myself Prayer."

The use of this formula, ten times a day, while becoming fully aware of the words, is enough to transform the dualistic posture into an openness to nonduality. This prayer, which lets God operate, realizes us as Christ.

"Except the Lord build the house, they labour in vain that build it" (Psalm 127).

In the restored silence, the free and natural turning of the soul towards the altar of the Spirit carries away the body, which becomes that "of Glory." Physical limits are blurred in the Christic sabbatical of non-separation. This is what we sense as being love, not "love of," conjoined with "consciousness of," but Love without an object, a quality of Consciousness without an object that makes Law.

Transparency, Silence, and Recognition are all words that designate mystical marriage, the abolition of the illusion of separation, and the reestablishment of the Natural State of God. We are that designated state within duality itself as Christ. The gifts of God are that very State, always present no matter what the situation in Appearance.

TREES IN THE GARDEN OF EDEN

SECOND LETTER TO FRIENDS OF THE SPIRIT • FIRST SERIES

HE MYTH OF THE GARDEN OF EDEN ALLOWS FOR multiple interpretations. Let's look at some of the myths from the perspective of arousal pathways.

In the Garden of Eden, there is talk of two singular trees, named by Moses the Tree of Life and the Tree of the Knowledge of Good and Evil. God would have forbidden Adam and Eve to eat the fruits of the Tree of Good and Evil before those of the Tree of Life.

"And out of the ground made the Lord God to grow every tree that is pleasant to the sight, and good for food; the tree of life also in the midst of the garden, and the tree of knowledge of good and evil" (Genesis, 2:9).

The Tree of the Knowledge of Good and Evil is the Tree of duality. To eat of its fruit is to exist, literally "to be thrown out" into the game of oppositions. With duality are born time, separation, comparison, fragmentation, language… It is the proliferation of diaboles[1] which, in medieval thought, signify scattering. The first pair of Good/Evil opposites breaks down into an infinity of pairs of opposites, polarities which are inscribed in the Aristotelian structure of language (if proposition A exists, proposition non-A does not exist): man/woman, peace/war, life/death, etc. Everything is an object of "consciousness of," including "me" since I am aware of myself as an entity separate from others.

The Tree of Life is the Tree of nonduality. It is significantly in the Center of the Garden. We do not know where the Tree of Knowledge of Good and Evil is located, but it is necessarily off-center, on a periphery.

Before tasting the fruit of the Tree of Knowledge of Good and Evil, Adam and Eve live naked. They are without "persona," without masks woven by the games within duality. They are not separate, not identified with any object, qualifier, or attribute. They are "I I." It is the experience of the initial separation that generates duality.

Before exiling into duality, the Adam-Eve couple, universal Father-Mother, who is God, Absolute, Total Consciousness, is neither mortal nor immortal. It lives. By eating the fruit of dual knowledge, Adam and Eve live apart and become mortal. Through the play of oppositions, they therefore seek immortality, their first and ultimate state, their natural state.

The Absolute thus exercises its Total Freedom by forgetting itself in duality in order to better recognize itself as being the Lord. Existence is a game of recognition with infinite variations and not the result of a "mistake." The snake represents the energy which will be the material for the weaving of forms but also the fire of the Reintegration of the Garden.

The serpent is called *Nachash* in Hebrew: Nun, Chet, Shin; the fish, the barrier, the divine fire. It is the serpent who, at each step, assesses the ability to pass, to engage in verticality, to take the path of Reintegration into the Garden of Eden. Let us observe the kinship between *Nachash*, the serpent, and *Nechoshet*, the brass. The brass serpent of Moses preserves poison by sublimating it. The serpent of Aaron that destroys the snakes of the Egyptian magi is a vertical serpent of serpents which redirects the energy of the serpentine powers that weave the horizontal peripheral realities. This evokes the "coiled," the energy located at the base of the spine to which it is advisable to restore its ascending freedom by directing it to a "Higher Sense" so that it goes, symbolically, from wood to Gold, from nature to Light.

Since the diabole itself is an object, it has an opposite, the symbol, which unites pairs of opposites and creates a dynamic continuum between them. The symbol conveys the primary intention and memory of the Garden and its Middle Tree.

The fruit of the Tree of Life makes one immortal. It establishes or restores a conscious nonduality. Eating the fruit of the Tree of Life before tasting the fruit of the Knowledge of Good and Evil inscribes Eternity in Consciousness. To bite into the fruit of the Knowledge of Good and Evil without having tasted the fruit of the Tree of Life leads one to seek immortality by reversing mortality and not by the sensing of one's Eternity. The quest for a lasting immortality will remain dualistic until the illusion of this temporary immortality is grasped.

In fact, whenever we get carried away with object identification, we bite into the fruit of the Tree of Duality. Whenever we recall ourselves into Silence and Presence, we taste the fruit of the Tree of Nonduality.

In the Center, we are all the peripheries. Lost in the peripheries, however, they never cease to point out the Center to us.

THE HOLY SPIRIT

THIRD LETTER TO FRIENDS OF THE SPIRIT • FIRST SERIES

F THE HOLY SPIRIT DID NOT EXIST, THE discourses of wisdom and knowledge would not be in the Church: "For to one is given by the Spirit the word of wisdom; to another the word of knowledge" (1 Corinthians 12:8).

We mean here the interior Church according to Louis-Claude de Saint-Martin, the New Church according to Swedenborg, and the invisible Church of those who have received the Holy Spirit.

"If the Spirit were not present, the Church would not form a consistent whole. The consistency of the Church manifests the presence of the Spirit."[2]

The members of this invisible Assembly constitute the manifestation of Spirit within duality. This is also indicated by the Torch of the Past Masters.

The French word "esprit" translates both the Greek word *pneuma* and the Hebrew word *ruach*. However, the Greek word and the Hebrew word are not equivalent. The Greek word *pneuma* is opposed to "body" in an immaterial-material duality while the Hebrew word *ruach* is opposed to "flesh" in an incorruptible-corruptible duality.

We will not enter into the theological, dogmatic, legal, or other quarrels that have torn Christianity apart for centuries so that we can focus on the essentials. The Holy Spirit remains a mystery; it is in essence indefinable.

Ruach is a feminine noun. Originally, the verbal root of *ruach* evoked space, especially the space between heaven and earth. Subsequently, the word referred equally well to wind, respiration, and the human spirit. The wind can be good or destructive, light and subtle or violent.

A process of interiorization shifts from the wind to the breath, then from the breath to the internal movement of energy. With each breath we are born (inhalation), we return to the divine Source (interval), we die (exhalation). Or again: we exist (inhalation), we return to the divine Source (interval), we reintegrate the Source (exhalation). At the end of the exhalation, we are Christ. This is why some of our exercises are based on thinning air. According to Martinez de Pasqually, there are only three elements: Earth, Water, and Fire—Air being rarefied Water. By prolonging the process of rarefaction of the breath until the end of the breath, we pass from Water to Fire, or to Spirit. The breath of respiration comes from the Source, God (cf. Genesis 6:3; Job 33:4) and returns there after death (cf. Ecclesiastes 12:7; Song of Solomon 15:11).

We see that interiorization coincides with rarefaction. What actually becomes scarce along with the breath is the identification with duality, giving way to nonduality. The nature of Spirit is nondual.

God animates creation with his breath, just as he enters into a particular individual. The Spirit then teaches.

When we divide the attention between the senses (cf. *The Quadrant of Awakening*), we become aware of the breath in a heightened way and, naturally, the breathing slows down until it becomes slight, suspended, deathlike. At the same time, thoughts fade away. There is only the nondual Spirit left. It is by the Spirit that the New Man arises and, when reified, he exercises the Ministry of the Spirit-Man.

WISDOM

FOURTH LETTER TO FRIENDS OF THE SPIRIT • FIRST SERIES

OR WISDOM, WHICH IS THE WORKER OF ALL THINGS, *taught me: for in her is an understanding spirit, holy, one only, manifold, subtil, lively, clear, undefiled, plain, not subject to hurt, loving the thing that is good, quick, which cannot be letted, ready to do good, kind to man, steadfast, sure, free from care, having all power, overseeing all things, and going through all understanding, pure, and most subtil, spirits. For wisdom is more moving than any motion: she passeth and goeth through all things by reason of her pureness.*

For she is the breath of the power of God, and a pure influence flowing from the glory of the Almighty: therefore can no defiled thing fall into her. For she is the brightness of the everlasting light, the unspotted mirror of the power of God, and the image of his goodness.

And being but one, she can do all things: and remaining in herself, she maketh all things new: and in all ages entering into holy souls, she maketh them friends of God, and prophets. For God loveth none but him that dwelleth with wisdom. For she is more beautiful than the sun, and above all the order of stars: being compared with the light, she is found before it. For after this cometh night: but vice shall not prevail against wisdom. Wisdom reacheth from one end to another mightily: and sweetly doth she order all things. (Wisdom of Solomon 7:22–8:1)

This text, dated to the 1st century and written in Greek, is part of the wisdom literature of the Old Testament. It is considered the essential text of the Old Testament on Wisdom.

The text emphasizes the unifying dimension of the Spirit which naturally tends towards non-separation. It also emphasizes its intimate presence in each of us. Finally, Spirit is the operator of all enlightenment or liberation.

The text qualifies the Spirit twenty-one times. 3 × 7. 21 dynamics of perfection. The two Hebrew letters together, Gimel and Daleth, carry the numerical value of seven (3 + 4), that of the seventh letter Zain whose shape evokes a sword. The 3 is the balance of form, or space. It evokes a perfection in duality, a holiness, as Isaiah points out: *"Holy, holy, holy is the Eternal..."* The number 4 refers us to the sacred Tetragrammaton. The initiation invites us to get out of the repetition of forms (3, 3 × 3...), creation, by the 4. Graphically, the Hé presents three dimensions (3) and an opening (1). In this quaternary of the Tetragrammaton, there is a double Hé, one male, the other female. Wisdom, Sophia, is a manifestation of the Divine Feminine, of the Absolute characterized by non-separation and inclusion.

We operatively summon Wisdom whenever we seek to include rather than separate. She is associated with Silence, which brings together, while discourse separates, compares, distinguishes, ranks, classifies... The sword of 7 slices the before and the after to constitute the interval of Silence. The sword of 7 slices *chronos.* The number 7 designates a time beyond the six days of creation, a non-time. The spelling of Zain (7) represents a crowned Vau (6). The 7 in the hexagram (the Martinist seal *par excellence*) is the center of the two triangles. Remember that this seal represents the path of Reintegration (according to Martinez de Pasqually) to the abode of Adam that we join at the Center, as the "new Christ."

Sophia, archetype of the Eternal Feminine, of the Absolute, is the nondual work within the heaviest duality. She is a figure of Redemption or Reintegration, absolutely inclusive of the visible and the invisible, the gross and the divine. This Wisdom, twenty-one times characterized, 3 × 7, contemplates three centers of perfection, one per septenary: the center of forms, the center of energies, and the center of essences.

The 7, the sword, refers both to death, destruction of forms, and to awakening when it directs the serpentine powers within verticality. As the association of Wisdom with the Breath of God, the Spirit leads us again to respiration. The letter Hé represents the *ruach elohim*, the breath of God.

Let us connect respiration with the Breath and the Wisdom.

Inhalation: Existence (life of separation). Interval: Returning. Exhalation: Reintegration (death to the dual world). Interval: Source.

Inhalation: Hé fertilizing, the lower world. Interval: Vau, conversion. Exhalation: Hé, the upper world. Interval: Yod, God transcendent.

But the Yod is also double, like the Hé, it is the mirror-game of Reintegration. Yod, transcendent god; Yod, immanent god.

Breathing is going from Yod to Yod: Yod, Hé, Vau, Hé, Yod. From immanence to transcendence.

To breathe *wisely*, to breathe with Spirit, is to breathe *consciously*.

PROPHECIES

FIFTH LETTER TO FRIENDS OF THE SPIRIT • FIRST SERIES

HAT ARE PROPHECIES? THEY ARE NOT MERE intuitions or the fruit of a work of divination, of some kind of augury. They arise from a vision in the Imaginal, from an access to the divine ideas which need to be precipitated in temporality not as possibility, but as a truth.

Raymond Abellio tells us of the adjusted bearing to establish with prophecies:

> All initiation leads to prophetism, this last word not at all signifying this or that capacity of "prediction" of more or less minor events, but a general aptitude to project, in terms of meaning, into the unfolding of history, the capacity for inspiration and integration of what I have called the "second memory," which in fact inserts the "events" in a process of transfiguration where they in turn become "useless intermediaries."[3]

It's about "speaking the truth" and writing what Antonio Vieira would call a "History of the Future." We are a long way from the sense we commonly attribute to the word "prophecy" today.

To speak of prophecy, and of prophets, several criteria must be gathered:

1. The reality of the prophecy depends on the authenticity of the vision of the prophet within the Imaginal. The prophet "sees." This is a choice by God who gives vision. Doubt is absent from the experience of the prophet. Kant would say that these judgments are assertoric, that the affirmation refers to a reality, not a mere possibility.
2. The proof of the prophetic spirit lies in the realization of the prophesied events.
3. Prophecy is by definition enigmatic. The prophet may be oblivious to the scope of his visions and his words. Some prophets are aware, understanding what they prophesy, others are not.
4. The prophets go in pairs. There is a redoubling of the prophecy. For example, the prophecies of the prophet Bandarra (1500–1556) duplicate and update those of Daniel relating to the Fifth Empire. He inscribes Portugal as a vector for the advent of the "Quinto Império," an empire of light, peace, and justice. We can also consider Martinez de Pasqually and Louis-Claude de Saint-Martin as a prophetic couple.

So we see that one who is inhabited by the prophetic spirit or, more simply, who respects the prophetic spirit, can take hold of the prophecies as a divine plan to be followed in building the future. Antonio Vieira would later say that the history of the future is more certain than the history of the past.

The Cistercian monk Joachim de Fiore (c. 1135–1202) announced three ages:

- The era of the Old Testament, age of the Father, which begins with Abraham and ends with the birth of Christ. The Time of Thorns.

- The era of the New Testament, age of the Son, the Time of Grace, which begins with the last king of Israel, Hosea (732–724 BC) and develops with Saint John the Baptist and Jesus. The Time of Roses.
- The era of the coming World, age of the Holy Spirit,[4] or the Time of Lilies, underlying the other two, but explicit with the return of the Prophet Elijah to continue until the Last Judgment.

These three ages become five times according to Antonio Vieira (1608–1697) who, after the disappearance of King Sebastião in 1578, revisited and revived, in the perspective of a Fifth Empire, the prophecies of Bandarra from the dream of Nebuchadnezzar reported in the prophecy of Daniel. Father Vieira announced the advent of the Fifth and last Empire of a thousand years succeeding the Assyrian, Persian, Greek, and Roman (extending into the Holy Roman) empires. The Assyrian Empire is that of the Father, the Persian Empire is that of the Father and the Son, the Greek Empire that of the Son, the Roman Empire that of the Son and the Holy Spirit. The Portuguese or Lusitanian Empire marks the reign of the Spirit, represented by Sebastião who assumes a function of the priest-king of Christ, similar to that of the mythical Prester John, whom certain missions in the Age of Discoveries sought in Africa and then in India. Vieira places this Empire under a double authority, that of the King of Portugal and that of the Pope.

The process takes up the cyclical theory of the *translatio imperii,* a Latin expression which translates a concept in vogue in the Middle Ages of the transfer of spiritual and temporal power at the same time as the succession of empires. This concept incorporates the emperor's privileged relationship with a god inherited from antiquity. This is the function of hierophany that certain initiatory orders took up later.

If we examine the way Vieira extends Joachim de Fiore's approach, we see more of a continuum, rather than a sequence. This is a process. If we consider this process as initiatory, internal rather than external or temporal, we become aware that the three ages perceived by Joachim de Fiore are three states of consciousness that determine a relationship to time.

The Time of Thorns corresponds to a state of total identification with duality. It is *chronos,* the time of the Man of the Stream of Louis-Claude de Saint-Martin, of the man-machine totally identified and conditioned.

The Time of Roses indicates nondual awareness within duality, by reversal, or conversion. This is the time of the *aion,* the time of the Man of Desire who remembers what he is, where he came from, and what his destiny is.

The Time of Lilies is a matter of nondual consciousness. It is the *kairos,* the interval, the non-time of awakening, of the New Man who realizes his state of Christ and can exercise the ministry of the Spirit-Man.

Note that in Appearance, we can pass in a few seconds from one time to another, from one state to another, depending on our degree of adherence to duality, to existence.

A ritual passes from the Time of Thorns, profane time, to the Time of Roses, through ceremony, then to the Time of Lilies through the rite, the invocation of Presence in the presentation.

For Louis-Claude de Saint-Martin "all men are prophets, since all men are made to manifest the Divinity." Everyone can access the divine plan and follow it in order to return to their original, ultimate, and permanent state, to recognize themselves as being the Lord himself, I AM. This "already and not yet," Christ, is being fulfilled "here and now."

If we adhere to this Joachimite conception introducing three ages and three states, the third being characterized by the Spirit, we are considered by Catholic or Orthodox institutions as heretics through "excess of the Holy Spirit," sometimes qualified as "enthusiasts" or "fanatics" and denounced as were the Cathars, the Alumbrados, or the illuminated Franciscans who supported the Cult of the Holy Spirit in Portugal developed by Queen Isabella and King Denis, at the same time as they welcomed the Templarism repudiated by Philippe le Bel in the Order of Christ, newly founded at the very beginning of the 14th century.

Jesus is for the Christian world the prophet of the prophets, as Spinoza is the philosopher of the philosophers. He says in Matthew 5:17, "Think not that I am come to destroy the law, or the prophets: I am not come to destroy, but to fulfill." He takes in himself the Time of Thorns, characterized by the prophets of the Old Testament, to fulfill the prophecies and the law of the Old Testament. He grows the roses: with Abel, he is killed; with Isaac he is bound to wood; with Jacob he experiences exile; with Moses, he borders on death; with David, he suffers persecutions; with all the prophets, he is despised... He fully integrates duality by including all the prophets and the sufferings that arise from duality. Nonduality is not opposed to duality but integrates it and includes it in the process of non-separation which, alone, liberates.

The Time of Lilies includes the Time of Roses which includes the Time of Thorns. The fall into existence (the "cast out"), into duality, reveals successive separations which dissolve during the dis-appearing, the Reintegration of nonduality.

RHÉLY

SIXTH LETTER TO FRIENDS OF THE SPIRIT • FIRST SERIES

ARTINEZ DE PASQUALLY EVOKED THE MYSTERIOUS figure of Rhély, who is said to be the Holy Spirit of Christ. It was discussed on July 26, 1775 in a class of the Order of Knight-Masons Élus Coëns of the Universe led by Jean-Jacques du Roy d'Hauterive and Louis-Claude de Saint-Martin:

> Without Christ, who came to stand between the Creator and man, man would have been no more than an object of justice. Instead, he became an object of mercy by obtaining from this same Christ in the form of Rhély the method of his religion of atonement and reconciliation.[5]

La Chose is Rhély which is also the Holy Spirit, which is also Christ, Martinez used the Hebrew word *Messias*. Saint-Martin went in the same direction by saying that *la Chose* is the Repairer, Christ-Wisdom, mediator between God and the world. It is also Sophia, Wisdom, or the universal spirit of the alchemists.[6]

In the Greek versions of the Old Testament and the New Testament, the word *Pneuma,* equivalent to the Hebrew *ruach,* is impersonal, which reinforces the mystery of the nature and the function of the Spirit that theology, far from clarifying, just walked away from. This impersonality is essential for the understanding of that which is beyond any concept or simplification. There is never any assertion of the divinity of the Spirit in the New Testament, while the divinity of Christ is well affirmed. The Spirit could be seen as a divine force or power or as God in manifestation and action, hence its association with the Feminine in the works of those like Leon Bloy. The Spirit perceives itself indirectly, through its effects. Its effects through overshadowing can be many: of prophecy, of healing, of knowledge… "The Holy Ghost shall come upon thee, and the power of the Highest shall overshadow thee: therefore also that holy thing which shall be born of thee shall be called the Son of God." (Luke 1:35). There is fertilization, a begetting, a birth.

Pneuma is associated either with God or with Christ (Spirit of God or of the Father, Spirit of Christ) and, fundamentally, it is identical in both cases even if the meanings vary according to its use: Absolute Spirit, Holy Spirit (interventional, especially in Luke), or of Holiness (*pneuma hagiosunes* that we find in invocations), or Spirit without any other qualifier.

The Spirit is essential for the union of the two Natures, human and divine, dear to Jean-Baptiste Willermoz. This union is what founds Christification, rebirth in God and by the Spirit. Death, on the contrary, is giving up the Spirit before receiving it again. "The Son of God was established in his power by his resurrection from the dead through the Spirit of holiness" (Romans 1:4). In each conscious breath, both external and internal, both formal and energetic, in the movement of life, death, and rebirth, we give back the Spirit ("to expire" in Greek is associated with *ex* which evokes the origin and *pneuma*, the Spirit) before it restores us in all our Christic, essential, and pneumatic fullness…

Note that the Latin expresses the moment when Jesus returns the Spirit through his last breath (traditionally in three steps, three expirations, hence the word *"trépas"*)[7] by the word *"tradidit"* which evokes transmission but, as we know, one of the formal modalities of transmission common in initiations is the voluntary breath, the vehicle, symbolic or operative, of the Spirit.

What characterizes the relationship with the divine is the circulation of the Spirit, the gift of the Spirit even in Christ's injunction to the future apostles to baptize "in the name of the Father, and of the Son, and of the Holy Spirit" (Matthew 28:19). Non-separation, nonduality contradicted by conceptual language, is marked by the singular "in the name" instead of "in the names." Some ancient Gnostic currents, in a very relevant but disturbing way for institutions, preferred the formula "in the name of the Father of the Son and in the Holy Spirit," indicating that any operation can really only be accomplished in the Holy Spirit or Free Spirit who re-unites what is separated in Appearance. We could still go further, at the risk of shocking more, with the formula "in the name of the Father, in the name of the Son, and in the Holy Spirit." However, it is in the name of the son, by the addition of Shin (with three or four branches), that we operate, Yod-Hé-Shin-Vau-Hé. Finally, with the Kabbalah, we could say "in the name of the Father, of the Daughter, and of the Spirit" because according to the *Zohar,* the Father, the thought, gives birth to the Daughter, the word.

THE OLD AND THE NEW

SEVENTH LETTER TO FRIENDS OF THE SPIRIT • FIRST SERIES

OLD TESTAMENT AND NEW TESTAMENT.
Old Covenant and New Covenant.
Language and its Aristotelian structure tend to separate, oppose, and prioritize. It is the natural game of the dualistic diabole from which we must free ourselves by traversing form.

In the first pages of his book *Man, His True Nature & Ministry,* Louis-Claude de Saint-Martin offers the alternative orientation:

> I have been equally explicit as to sacred traditions, in saying that everything must make its own revelation; so that, instead of proving religion merely by traditions, written or unwritten, which is all our ordinary teachers attempt, we have a right to draw directly from the depths which we have within us, since facts, how marvelous soever they may be, must be posterior to Thought; that we ought to have begun with the Spirit-Man and thought, before going to events, especially such as are only traditional; that thereby we might cause to germinate or reveal themselves, both the healing balm, of which we all feel so much need, and religion itself, which should be nothing but the mode or preparation of this sovereign remedy, and never be substituted for it, as it so often is, in passing through the hands of men.[8]

This can be a relationship to Tradition, to texts and their commentaries considered inspired, revealed, and sacred, to rites and to their interpretations, that liberates instead of imprisoning. Everything that presents itself within consciousness is an object, a form that we have to pass through, a mirror that sends us back to the deepening of ourselves, without which the object does not exist. Let's take a look at what the Old Testament (OT) and New Testament (NT) can say regarding the search for nonduality.

We are aware that the Gospels are a late construction that does not reflect the true teaching of Jesus. What historical and archaeological research shows is that the beliefs of first-century Christians were largely incompatible with the Christian beliefs and dogmas of today. However, the editors were careful in their writing to respect the OT and its promises.

The OT and the NT, far from opposing each other, are intertwined. The apparent opposition between the God of the OT and the God of the NT, which is almost an inverted reflection of their qualities, is an invitation to seek "God beyond God" according to Meister Eckhart. The NT can only be understood by the Old, so the references to the OT are numerous.

In Matthew 5:17, Jesus says "Think not that I am come to destroy the law, or the prophets: I am not come to destroy, but to fulfill." It refers to the law of Moses. He comes to fulfill the promise of the OT. What is new extends the old to bring it to fullness. There is only one Testament, one Covenant that unfolds in time yet is already fulfilled.

The past announces the future and the future realizes the expectation of the past. There is a double causality, past ↔ future, which justifies the prophetic oracle. The past prophesies the future through myths. The future fulfills the prophecies passed through the mythemes. What we have to observe is the permanence of the mythemes and their slips in time because they indicate the operations of deepening and completion.

The Old and the New

Let us follow the tracks of some mythemes, projections of archetypes from the Imaginal:

Like Moses, Jesus climbed a mountain to comment on Mosaic Law, to extend it, and to deepen it. He is the new Moses. Both are mediators of the Covenant. The mytheme of the mountain, of verticality, and that of the prophetic word born from the axis of silence (we seek solitude and silence in the heights) reminds us that there is only one principal Prophet (the Self), which manifests itself through all historical prophets.

The crossing of the Red Sea conveys the myth of the passage from one world to another, which is death, a liberation. The mytheme of liberation, of all liberation, is found in the Resurrection. The sea forming a wall to the right and to the left indicates the Interval. It is about deciding before and after, getting out of linear and temporal causalities, and dying to duality in order to access nonduality, Eternity.

The same mytheme works in the episodes of the gift of manna, the meal with the disciples in Emmaus, and the last meal of Jesus with the disciples that founded the Eucharist. The permanence of the Eucharist invites us to actualize it here and now (the way of immortality, the way of the Body of Glory…).

The myth of progression, of time for explanation or conversion, is found among the disciples in Emmaus as in the episode of the eunuch who needs explanations from Philip. Metanoia is permanent, already there but not yet, hence this apparent time of integration.

The Temple mytheme moves from the Temple of Solomon to the Temple of Jerusalem in which Jesus reveals himself as the New Temple, each being called to build himself as a New Temple.

Several myths of Elijah's life are found in the life of Jesus: retreat in the desert, elevation to the top of the mountain to meet God, powers (transformation of food, resurrection of a dead man, mastery of fire, etc.), double recognition of disciples, the indirect form of teaching…

Jesus teaches the disciples as Elijah teaches Elisha. Jesus, like Elijah, is an awakener. The function of mediator and facilitator is inseparable from that of awakener.

What is hidden must be unveiled, what is lost must be found, and what is dark must be illuminated. The temporal path of the mythemes is a path of augmented understanding, deepening, and accomplishment until fullness. This path operates in us, in consciousness, and nowhere else. But there is a form of retrocausality: it is the ending (the Resurrection) that gives meaning to all that precedes and announces the Resurrection. It is Awakening and nothing else that gives meaning to any initiatory quest. What gives meaning to the initiatory journey and its unpredictability and total originality in each of us, what illuminates it and fully reveals it, is the ultimate agreement, the total Reintegration, of our own Awakening or Liberation.

All the themes common to the OT and NT (revelation, liberation, election, alliance…) only lead to this ultimate agreement. The promise and fulfillment of it secures the unity of the OT and NT. They express the original intention and the ultimate direction which absolutely coincide. If revelation is progressive in Appearance, it is to express recognition (*anagnorisis*) of oneself as being the Lord. The unfolding and fulfillment in each of their true state is gradual or immediate, it makes no difference.

ANOINTING

EIGHTH LETTER TO FRIENDS OF THE SPIRIT • FIRST SERIES

The Spirit of the Lord is upon me, because he hath anointed me...
LUKE 4:18

IN THE OLD TESTAMENT, THE HEBREW ROOT *MShCh* represents anointing. We find this root in *mashiach* or *masiah*, which we translate by the word messiah.

However, another Hebrew word designates anointing, the word *semikhah*, which refers to the idea, or rather to the ancient gesture, of support, of supporting something. This same Hebrew word designates ordination.

As support, anointing indicates the gesture made on the sacrificed animal, a form of laying on of hands that sanctifies the offered animal.

As a gesture of ordination, support operates differently depending on whether it is applied to the king or the priest in Jewish tradition. A circle is drawn for the king, an X for the priest. Note that some initiatory transmissions associate the two with the X inscribed in a circle (referring to the crown or to the protective power). The X evokes the 515, the messenger of God in Dante to which we will return and which is a key, if not the essential operative key.

In the New Testament, the Greek word for anointing is *christos* which gives us Christ. Christ is the anointed, the divine anointing. In the New Testament, the word refers to the gesture of anointing someone with olive oil.

Anointing can be for therapeutic purposes. The oil can be scented or combined with other elements. The perfume evokes what is present but invisible: the divine, the Spirit. It is interesting that the word "Messiah" is associated in Hebrew with "Light." "Let there be…" teaches us that the Light precedes creation according to the principle that the remedy preexists evil, nonduality preexists duality, awakening preexists illusion or ignorance…

From this follows the presentation of any initiatory path, such as "return" (Ulysses), "remembrance" (Hermes), "reintegration" (Martinez de Pasqually), recognition (Abhinavagupta)… Anointing can be performed on an object as well: sanctified, consecrated, for worship or initiation rituals. Extreme unction is a special case of the therapeutic function of anointing since it is to promote the return or Reintegration to the original state.

The Messiah, the one who received anointing, who is the anointing, is the "Son of God," which means He lives in an unseparated state with God, the All. He is thus associated with Spirit, with the divine Breath, which manifests through Him. Whoever receives anointing thus has access to the prophetic office. He is also in the vertical passage between the visible world and the invisible world and in the horizontality between the present world and the next (approaching) world. At the heart of the individual on the Way, He is a conduit between the present individual and their neighbor. The one who approaches is the Self, the New Man, the Other Christ. "Love your neighbor as yourself," also means, axially, love the one who approaches (the Self, the New Man) as being yourself. Recognize Him!

The association between kingship, the priesthood, and the Messiah, Christ, invites us to consider that we must, by God's anointing, the permanent anointing, bring about — or better, let arise — in us and through us: the Hidden King, the Self, the Hidden Priest, the Self, the unique meditator, the Self…

Anointing

Note that in Hebrew the same letter *Mem* begins the words *mashiach*, messiah, *Moshe*, Moses, and *mayim*, water, while baptism is an anointing performed with water, which can have the same function as oil. Baptism by water introduces the baptism of fire and the baptism of Spirit. Rather than a sequence, we should see here an operational continuum.

These few considerations should alert us to the sense of touch. In Chinese tradition, touch is the only sense. It develops into smell and taste, into hearing and sight, to thought which is but an extension of touch. This is the construction of the world. Words touch us, they caress or hurt us, sights as well, and sounds… Perfumes and smells entrance us or repel us.

Everything in duality touches. As soon as we touch someone, or even an object, it is not trivial. Becoming aware of what touch is—the possibility of an anointing, of a permanent anointing—by setting our gestures in a conscious breath, is to set the very world that we create from moment to moment within transcendence. It is to summon nonduality within duality and illuminate it. Within the rites, each word, each look, each sound, each gesture, each perfume, and each touch can be an anointing.

GRACE

NINTH LETTER TO FRIENDS OF THE SPIRIT • FIRST SERIES

EONARDO COIMBRA ONCE SAID THIS MAGNIFICENT sentence: "Grace is the body of freedom."

Let's see what these few words can teach us.

God, the Absolute, the Lord, the Self… is absolute Freedom. This is what, more than anything, "defines" God, by nature indefinable. God's unlimited exercise of this Freedom goes so far as to forget His true Nature.

God generates duality in order to get lost in it, to forget Himself in the multiple and in temporality, even to ignore His own possibility, in order to have the pleasure of Recognizing Himself, each time in a totally original way, through each separate form of life.

What we refer to as Awakening is the Recognition by God of Himself as a separate individual within the heaviest duality. Each of us is God, contracted in duality.

The Man of the Stream knows nothing about his divine origin, his divine nature, and his divine purpose. He is tossed around in the eddies of duality and simply tries not to be swallowed up in self-oblivion.

The Man of Desire remembers, rarely at first, and then more and more, his divine nature. He has an intuition of what he really is, God himself, and that intuition points him to Recognizing himself as the Lord. This Recognition generates the New Man, the God-Being. As soon as the desire for God arises, God-the-All and God-the-part communicate and then commune until Absolute Recognition.

Grace is this self-communication of God, self-communion of God, self-Recognition of God, through every being and every form generated in duality. This Recognition is a nondual enjoyment, a unique and incomparable Joy. The Greek word for "grace," *charis,* is close to the word "joy," *chara.* The nature of God is revealed to us, as God, by grace.

Recognition can be gradual or sudden. It makes everyone a Christ, an absolutely free being, by the grace of God, by the self-communication of God who reveals Himself to Himself. This is why grace can be understood as the body of freedom. The old man gives way to the New Man by grace. Grace is always total and unconditional. God-the-All plays endlessly with God-the-part. Each of us is the divine Game until Recognition is accomplished unreservedly.

In the New Testament, in Titus 2:11, it is said "For the grace of God that bringeth salvation hath appeared to all men." Salvation is Recognition. And God's self-communication manifests in everyone. Even if the sound of the stream covers the Word, the communication, the Word is there. There will always be a lull, an interval in the agitated flow of the stream that will allow it to be heard and to be remembered.

Once the self-communication of God is consciously affirmed in the individual, the gifts of grace can be manifested: wisdom, teaching, prophecy, healing… even within duality. This is the work of nonduality within duality. Non-separation is an operating power even in duality because it can suspend or cancel temporal causalities.

The rites of alliance or of communion, of teaching or of elevation, like the sacraments, seek to recall grace or to renew it in order to awaken or strengthen the dynamic of Recognition.

As we can see, this nondualistic approach differs from the common approaches of Christianity and Judaism, which are too dualistic, which see in particular in grace a gift from God to those who have not deserved it—a very reductive conception. Grace is permanent, like a gift that is free and spontaneous, always a gift of Spirit, a gift of Freedom, a fullness.

But, again, the use of Hebrew and Greek, despite the ambiguities and multiple meanings, can enlighten us. The Hebrew word for "grace" is *chen*. Its initials are those of *chokhmah nisteret,* the kabbalah, or more exactly, "hidden wisdom."[9] Kabbalah is knowledge. We indeed find the Re-cognition. Grace, in Greek *charis,* is also associated with *apodidonai,* "to return," or *apodosis,* "return." *Charis* also conveys the idea of "benevolence" and "beneficence." In Hebrew "to do well" is to reintegrate. The whole question of grace points to a return to God, to the Self, to Reintegration or Recognition. In reality, what is reintegrating? What is recognizable? God, our true nature in the mirror game of nested creations from the infinitely small to the infinitely large.

The Hebrew word for "grace," *chen,* also introduces the operative notion of covenant, *beriyth,* qualified by election, *bakhir.* Now, he who has received the Spirit is elected. Thus, everything draws us towards the free circulation of the Spirit between God-the-All and God-the-part, the breath of God, in existence as in Reintegration. Note that Recognition is characteristic not only of Reintegration, it begins with existence. In other words, Recognition begins with the fall, the exile of God in duality, because separation calls for non-separation. Forgetting calls for remembrance.

There is nothing without the grace that is initiation itself.

CHIVALRY

TENTH LETTER TO FRIENDS OF THE SPIRIT • FIRST SERIES

CHIVALRIC (OR SO-CALLED) ORDERS ARE LEGION, but there is only one Chivalry. Just like the Temple and its *imago templi,* Chivalry is above all an archetype grasped in the Imaginal that manifests itself in duality in multiple forms, some attuned to the archetype, others deformed, sometimes to the point of monstrosity, like the SS of Hitler's Third Reich.

Any being who wants to be a Knight inscribes in their daily life ethical values, criteria of achievement, and beliefs that tend towards the archetype and are the basis of their behavior.

Here we are not going to take up the complex history of Chivalry, in its Western, Middle Eastern, and Far Eastern modalities, but will simply focus on the essentials. Let us just remember that it is important not to confuse the state of the Knight with belonging to an order, however prestigious. The most prestigious of them have distanced themselves from the archetype of Chivalry by falling into worldliness, the dualistic identification with the world. The Knights Templar became the first multinational enterprise with special forces in history, and the order of the black cross, the Order of Teutonic Knights, in a similar drift, evolved into a totalitarian expansionist state.

We initially distinguish three chivalries, or four: terrestrial chivalry, spiritual chivalry, celestial chivalry, and possibly an essential chivalry corresponding to the principle "neither duality nor nonduality" of which nothing can be said. Celestial chivalry is a matter of nonduality. Spiritual chivalry, which interests us here, is a nondual engagement that unites, makes an alliance, in duality. Terrestrial chivalry concerns the reduction of dualistic oppositions through reconciliation. Here we see the alliance as vertical and reconciliation as horizontal.

Mythemes associated with Western chivalry are primarily Christ and Our Lady, the Temple and the Crypt, the Grail and what it contains. Then come a series of secondary mythemes such as the sword, the lance, the pieces of armor, the coat of arms, the spurs, the horse…[10] They are secondary because they are second to the primary mythemes which merge with their archetypes, but particularly important because they participate in the understanding of the constitution (or liberation) of the Body of Glory, the body of immortality.

For each type of chivalry, or more precisely, for each manifestation of the archetype at different levels of density, the mythemes will operate differently to increasingly subtle degrees, moving away from dualistic and worldly sway.

Thus, for the member of terrestrial chivalry, Christ and Our Lady are external to them, venerated, prayed to, and replied to as pertaining to an ideal to be attained or, often, as inaccessible. The Temple is external, it must be rebuilt, a temple of stone or/and a temple of paper (doctrine, teaching…). The Crypt remains a mystery. The Grail receives the wine, symbol of the blood of Christ. But the symbols only represent, they are not operative, and do not orient. In a way, everything is body because the soul is turned entirely towards the body, ignoring the spirit, hence the need for a code of chivalry, of a morality. This chivalry is always ephemeral and doomed to deteriorate.

Spiritual chivalry is characterized by the turning of the soul towards the spirit, which opens the way for the Reintegration of the Man of Desire, because the desire is always desire for God, for non-separation, desire for the One. In this movement, the soul does not move away from the body but pulls it along. In Reintegration, the body reintegrates into the soul which reintegrates into the spirit which reintegrates into God. Institutional Christianity pays dearly for the dualistic fault of Saint Paul who, by rejecting the body, and consequently the woman, rejects the very material of the work of Reintegration or of Christification. Within the Body of Glory there is a body, both raw material and the crucible of the work, as evidenced by the crucial episode of the emergence from the tomb of Jesus. This body is no longer separated from the world, it is the body-world. The contents of the sacred cup are alchemical. Christ and Our Lady are no longer external but two internal principles, or better, two polarities of a single internal principle, polarities which tend to unite rather than separate, God as our true nature. The Crypt opens, that is to say the Center, the inexhaustible Imaginal Source of teaching which weaves a religion of the spirit, not subservient to traditional forms. A Temple without a Crypt is sterile.

In a way, dubbing into terrestrial chivalry is done by the sword, in spiritual chivalry by the paten, and in celestial chivalry by the direct anointing of the Spirit. In Hebrew, the letter Zain means "sword" and has the graphic form of it. This letter evokes both combat and nourishment. It's also a crowned Vau. Vau, the sixth letter, is represented by the hexagram. Crowned, the hexagram pointed at its center represents Christ or the New Man begotten by the path of Reintegration symbolized by the hexagram. Zain, the seventh letter, consists of a Vau crowned by Christ who is the Word.

The sword of the member of terrestrial chivalry is used in the fight between good and evil, the stream of oppositions, in the service of the weakest, or, with the point planted in the ground and made into a cross, to call for prayer. But, with the coronation, the sword points to the heaven of Spirit and typifies spiritual chivalry. It operatively orients the terrestrial energies, grasped in the horizontal peripheries of manifestation, towards the center, the nondual axis. The fight becomes "holy."

The various chivalric rituals merely stage this vertical orientation that signifies the quest. It begins in the duality of the stream to axialize desire, thus freeing itself from worldly identifications, and rejoins, absolutely conscious, the ocean of nonduality. If chivalry is an aristocracy, it does not want to be. It is naught but of the Spirit.

THE SWORD AND THE LANCE

ELEVENTH LETTER TO FRIENDS OF THE SPIRIT • FIRST SERIES

THE SWORD IS A SYMBOL AND AN OPERATIONAL vector very present in the Western initiatory paradigm. It is associated with Chivalry, as is the lance, which is an integral part of chivalric armament.

The sword and the lance are two fundamental myths of the Chivalric Quest and especially of Grail literature. It is interesting to consider in the Grail cycle that there is only one Knight throughout the figures of the quest. Gawain, Lancelot, Percival, Bors, and Galahad are the same Knight; we could include all the protagonists, including Arthur, in what represents different stages of the Quest, different states on the path that leads from the duality of combat to nonduality, or even different requisite qualifications.

Just as there is only one Knight, consider only one sword, one horse, one coat of arms, one queen, etc. Such a reading of mythemes allows us to decipher certain operativities conveyed in the arcana of the Chivalric Quest, especially one that refers to an internal alchemy, to the question of the vessel and what it contains.

Note first that the sword and the lance are phallic symbols,[11] but that the former finds its place in a scabbard while the lance remains naked. The lance can thus refer to raw phallic power (not necessarily brutal) unbalanced by feminine power. Moreover, it allows you to hit the opponent from a distance without requiring hand-to-hand combat. It depends on the bond with the horse and the channeling or orientation of the power of the horse, which is known to be characterized by extreme emotional sensitivity. This power must be left free in order to be directed, not by constraint but by fusion. An archetype of the Knight is the centaur. Chiron is immortal and he is dedicated to training young heroes. The heroic path begins with the capacity for presence here and now, an unidentified consciousness at the peripheries.

The lance will be used in fights at crossings of fords or bridges. The horse is a "courier"; the lance extends its power. These passages are a part of wandering; we remain in the terrestrial horizontality. It is in the fight with the dragon that the passage appears vertical. There is a reversal. The iconography of Saint George slaying the dragon indicates how the lance fixes the head of the dragon and directs its energy, through the lance, into verticality. More generally, Western or Eastern iconographies featuring characters holding lances often indicate a change in the weaving of the fabric of reality. It is an exit from the peripheries, an access to the center, to the axis, that we find in representations of Mary when she puts her foot on the head of the dragon. It is not a question of destroying but of inscribing in the axiality. In certain operations of the Élus Coëns, we find this operative gesture of pinning down the dragon (in this case it is a dagger and a serpent) to remind the center of the serpentine powers disoriented in dual manifestation.

The Knight's lance naturally evokes that of Longinius piercing the side of Christ. By "side," we should understand the heart from which emerge two substances, blood and water, which have an essential function in the alchemy of the Body of Glory. Blood and water are red and white, two colors which are mythemes to follow in the matter of the Grail. The blood and the water in this Christian version of the mystery are inseparable from the action of the Spirit: "It is expedient to you that I go: for if I go not, the Paraclete will not come to you" (John 16:7).

Let us look at the sword that brings the protagonists together, promotes touch, and therefore reduces duality. In martial arts, two-man sword duels or saber katas appear as dances.

The Sword and the Lance

Consider, for the example, the single sword in three episodes.

Of course we immediately think of Arthur's sword, the sword that makes him king. Until this episode which sees him seizing the sword fixed in the rock, Arthur is a Hidden King. His kingship is present but not actualized. The sword is sealed in rock, nature, which is dual. By freeing it from nature's grip, he can point it towards the sky, signaling that God and nature are the same. The rock is also symbolically the mountain. It is only at the top of the mountain, at the top of ourselves, that we can establish or actualize our kingship, the nondual nature of the Self.

But another famous sword, Excalibur, will be offered to Arthur in a particular episode. After a fight against a giant, a fight that would have been lost without Merlin's intervention, Arthur is invited by the latter to go to the center of a lake where a beautiful young woman awaits him: the Lady of the Lake, dressed all in white, who emerges from the water brandishing a shining sword towards the sky. Arthur sees this woman walking on the water of the lake, who evokes the nature of the Spirit. We find in this episode all the symbolism of the center or island. It is on a boat with two oars that Arthur will travel to the center of the lake, that is to say, by coordinating and balancing the action of the opposites symbolized by the oars.

A third episode, less known, is particularly revealing.

After a tournament, which therefore puts the lances into action, the protagonists feast at Camelot with King Arthur. A young woman walks into the great hall to everyone's amazement. She is wrapped in a large red coat over which her golden hair floats. She says she is from the Isle of Avalon and asks the Knights to deliver her from a gem-encrusted sword that she wears on her belt. One after another, the Knights try to extract the sword from the scabbard — without success. It's the same mytheme as the episode of Arthur pulling the sword out of the rock, a gesture that marks him as king, but on another logical level. Eventually, Balin, a Knight far less experienced than his peers, attempts half-heartedly to withdraw the sword. To everyone's surprise, he easily seizes it.

Immediately, the sword withdrawn from its scabbard, the young woman invites Balin to return the sword to her. Balin refuses. She reminds him that she is from Avalon, the Isle of Women, but also the Isle of the Immortals, and that if he does not return the sword he will face many misfortunes. First, he causes the death of two lovers. Despite his desire to repair his mistake, Balin generates a series of dramas. He kills the invisible knight, who is King Pellam's brother Garlon. In this episode, he doesn't recognize Garlon; he doesn't see the bond of brotherhood that unites him to the king. Later, he also doesn't recognize his own brother, Balan, until the two have killed each other in the water of a river. They die on the shore which they return to while holding onto each other.

The sword and the scabbard have a strong sexual and alchemical dimension. By not putting the sword back in the scabbard, Balin makes the Quest, which cannot be accomplished without the Lady, impossible. It remains incomplete. Alchemical nuptials are inaccessible. He does not recognize in the other a brother: he separates to the point of no longer seeing the mirror play of duality. It is only at the approach of death that he recognizes himself in the other, that he sets out on the path of Recognition. The episode also directs us to the subject of the double (the brother). The recognition of the double (of the serpentine energetic duality that lives us and which we must overcome by leaving the fight of the opposites for the dance that unites) is at the heart of this little preserved passage of the literature of the Grail.

If we consider these three swords as a single sword at three different times of the Quest, if we take these episodes in detail, very summarized here, we will discover many operational elements and the keys to an alchemy of the couple, whether external or internal.

THE ARMOR OF THE KNIGHT

TWELFTH LETTER TO FRIENDS OF THE SPIRIT • FIRST SERIES

E TAKE UP HERE A WORK BY ARMAND TOUSSAINT originally published as a brochure intended for members of the Martinist Order of the Knights of Christ and presented in the work *Mask Cloak Silence: Martinism as a Way of Awakening.*[12]

Through this work, Armand Toussaint envisaged using the letters of the Hebrew alphabet as dynamic materials for a spiritual armor or Christ body, a body of immortality. We extended his proposal by associating the letters with body parts and the pieces of armor that protect them. It is not about affirmed truths but about entry into the various levels of the Hebrew language, living letters that constitute us.

We can work from the letter itself, from its shape, from the sister letter with which it couples, from the way of representing the letter with the different parts of the body, from the letters which themselves make up the name of the letter, from the associated numbers... We can work from the different parts of the body and their correspondence with the pieces of the Temple of Solomon,[13] their symbolism, and their measurements. All of these views, and more, are legitimate for seeking the answer to the question, "How can I become God (Christ)?" Behind the subject of self-deification is the art of the ways of the Body of Glory that emerges in endless deepening.

ALPHA: "Know thyself…"
The initiate seeks his Unknown within himself.

ALEPH 1 — The will of unity (Alchemical Salt).
Aleph evokes the body in its totality, the one. It is therefore related to the armor as a collection of pieces that form a unit.

BETH 2 — The science of the inner binary.
Beth evokes the legs. In armor, it refers to the greaves.

GIMEL 3 — The positive inner synthesis.
Gimel also evokes the legs but in motion, race, or pursuit. The correspondence in the armor is the cuisses.

DALETH 4 — The quaternary of realization:
Sta – Solve – Coagula – Multiplica.
Daleth corresponds to the back. Often associated with poverty and the outstretched hand of the beggar who begs but in a hidden way. It is also a door. Daleth is represented by the back plate of the armor, sometimes called the backrest, which protects the back by being attached to the breastplate that protects the torso.

HÉ 5 — The inspired will, the era of the Popes.
Hé corresponds to the body in prayer, the body on its knees to pray.

The praying knight plants his sword in the ground to make a cross and places the helm next to him. He is "headless," that is to say without thought, pure silence. It is the armor without the helm that corresponds to this letter.

VAU 6 — The choice of the Path between spiritual Clarity and Darkness.

Vau is associated with the diaphragm that separates the waters above (air, rarefied water in the lungs) from the waters below (kidneys, the reproductive system). The associated piece of armor is the plastron (breastplate) or cuirass.

ZAIN 7 — The triumph or failure of spirit over matter.

Zain is the top of the head that evokes the crown. On the armor, it corresponds to the cimier (the crest on the helm). Recall that it is the woman who crowns the man.

CHETH 8 — The search and acquisition of inner balance.

Cheth evokes life. We think of the blood which is life itself, one of the contents of the Grail. The associated piece is the gorget which protects the neck and the carotid artery. Some transmissions are bestowed with two fingers on the carotid artery.

TETH 9 — The integration of enriching experiences through mystical techniques: *Look to see — Listen to hear — Make the inner Silence: "Vide, Audi, Tace."*

Teth corresponds to the belly where the serpent is coiled. The belly is associated with pregnancy. The piece of armor that protects the belly is the lower part of the cuirass or the plackart. Teth can also suggest the shield which is both a piece of protection and a weapon.

DELTA: "…you will know the others…"
The initiate in manifestation in the world, its habits and customs, learns to live there by experiencing the attacks that strengthen it. He dwells in the world, but he does not identify with the world, nor with worlds.

YOD   10 — The time, the opportunity to experiment in the vortices of the world.

Yod refers to the hand and also to power. The corresponding piece of armor is the gauntlet. The original dubbing of knights was made by a strike with the gloved hand.

KAPH   11 or 20 — The occult force.

The letter Kaph corresponds to the palm of the hand, dedicated to receiving, also associated with the gauntlet.

LAMED   12 or 30 — The sacrifice that the initiate makes by accepting constraints to make them serve his spiritual progression.

The letter Lamed refers to the heart. It is the upper part of the plastron that protects the heart but also the upper part of the backrest.

MEM   13 or 40 — The conquest of death or the division of consciousness, the change of dimension (Alchemical Sulfur).

The letter Mem evokes the water of the body. It is associated with the armor as a whole but above all with what guarantees the fluidity of movement, therefore the joints (the epaulette or spaulder, the couter, and others) and the leather ties that connect the different pieces.

The Armor of the Knight

NUN   14 or 50 — Energetic recapitulation, new associations, the creation of favorable future karma.

Nun means "fish" and symbolizes what is hidden. Fish are invisible in the water. When the water recedes, the land appears, opening a passage (the episode of the Red Sea). It is then possible to pass on foot. The corresponding pieces are therefore the sabotons.

SAMEKH   15 or 60 — The attack of Baphomet, emotional reactions.

Samekh evokes sustainment, that which supports. We think of the pelvis which allows the verticality of the spinal column and is supported on the columns that are legs. The corresponding part of armor is the tasset.

AYIN   16 or 70 — The shelter or the ruin.

Ayin is the eye, which allows you to see. It is associated with the visor of the helmet.

PÉ   17 or 80 — The star of hope.

Pé evokes the mouth and speech. The corresponding part of the armor is the lower part of the face of the helmet or helm, sometimes called a bevor, which protects the mouth and chin.

TZADDI   18 or 90 — The disappointment caused by treacherous attacks.

Tzaddi refers to justice. *Tzadik* is the righteous man. We are talking about the "mighty arm of righteousness." The letter is associated with the arm and the corresponding pieces of armor: the gardbrace and rerebrace.

OMEGA: "...and the Gods."
The initiate projects his love of the Beautiful, the True, and the Good into the world.

QOPH   19 or 100 — The inner light has come into being by the inner silence.

Qoph numerically hides within it the Tetragrammaton, which explains one of its meanings which is "holiness." Another meaning is "to surround." We can surround with our arms to signify an inner void or to hug a person. We thus connect this letter to the arms but on the inner side. The pieces of armor concerned are then the rondels under the armpits, the vembrace at the elbow, and others.

RESH   20 or 200 — Time, Rebirth, Renewal, Longevity, Immortality.

Resh means "head" and the associated piece of armor is of course the helmet or helm.

SHIN   21 or 300 — Victory in the very Kingdom of the Prince of this world. The Initiate, Fool of Spiritual Light, pursues his Way in his mystical intoxication, indifferent to the attacks of evil: he is the Mat of the Tarot of the visionaries of the Middle Ages, dead to the world.

The letter Shin presents three branches (incomplete shin) or four (complete shin). The letter corresponds to the teeth, protected by the bevor, the lower part of the helm.

TAU   22 or 400 — The Great Alchemical and Spiritual Work or the reward of the Man-God, replica of the God-Man, the New Man, Christ, the Panacea, the Philosopher's Stone.

According to Ezekiel, the righteous man (the New Man) wears the letter Tau on his forehead. We recall the upper part of the helmet, the front of the helmet.

The Armor of the Knight

We do not associate the final letters with body parts and armor here. Kaph final, Mem final, Nun final, Pé final, and Tzaddi final correspond to the essences.

While some correspondences are imposed (the eye, mouth, teeth…) others depend on more subtle associations or explorations, sometimes simple echoes, to which others could be opposed or related. There is not just one possibility, as the letter Shin indicates. Indeed, the thirty-two teeth of the human being correspond to the thirty-two ways of wisdom of the Kabbalists.

It does not matter which door is opened as long as the discovery of what it hides brings it closer to oneself and allows one to traverse form.

THE LETTER SHIN

THIRTEENTH LETTER TO FRIENDS OF THE SPIRIT • FIRST SERIES

THE LETTER SHIN PLAYS A CENTRAL ROLE IN THE ritualistic operativity of certain currents of illuminism, including ritualistic Martinism.

We have seen that the letter Shin means "tooth." We have thirty-two teeth just as there are thirty-two paths of wisdom in the Kabbalah. On the other hand, the tooth is innervated by the trigeminal nerve. Here we have the ternary.

Graphically the Shin can be drawn by three Vaus or even three Yods. In addition, this nerve has a mixed or dual function because it is both sensitive and motor, a binary.

The letter comes in either a three-pointed or four-pointed form. It is considered complete only when it has four branches. With four branches, it evokes the New Man, the accomplished human being, in fullness, realized, the Christ. With three branches, it represents the potential Christ, already present (we are born Christ) but who asks to be actualized.

The ternaries can be understood as: *Body – Soul – Spirit, Water – Earth – Fire, Mercury – Sulfur – Salt,* or *terrestrial world – celestial world – super-celestial world,* among others. The fourth branch will represent, for example, the Philosopher's Stone for the ternary *Mercury – Sulfur – Salt* or the divine world for the ternary *terrestrial world – celestial world – super-celestial world.*

If the letter Shin represents the ternary *form – energy – essence,* with the possible fourth branch relating to the *beyond-essence,* the point will be placed on the first branch of the Shin or the third, depending on the ingress of the energy from the right cerebral hemisphere or the left cerebral hemisphere.[14]

The tooth teaches us that to get out of duality, symbolized by the double function of the nerve, we must take into account the ternary (trigeminal) to achieve the quaternary. In other words, to free us from identification with duality (the body—sensitive and motor), we need the soul (the ternary) which, by turning towards the spirit, re-establishes the quaternary.

The word "trigeminal" itself is ambiguous since it can be understood as three sets of two, or six. We find the hexagram. Or again: there are two trigeminal nerves which are found in the brain, two times three, the hexagram, which form a pair, the fifth paired cranial nerve, relating to the letter Hé, letter of fertility and repeated knowledge in the Tetragrammaton, Yod Hé Vau Hé.

To go from the ternary to the quaternary, it is necessary to conquer the center of the triangle, to change dimension by a leap into the void. It is by changing dimension in this way that, geometrically, the hexagram becomes in three dimensions the *merkabah,* symbol of the Body of Glory.

The hexagram can be represented by two Shin with three branches, that is to say, one Shin that projects the archetypal powers of the Word and a second that actualizes them. Perfected by the Center, these two Shin become complete, with four branches. We find the seven and the eight, the number of Christ.

Behind the teeth we have the tongue, *lashon* in Hebrew, a word in which we find Shin. The (anatomical) tongue produces speech, hence the link with the Word, but it also produces hissing, especially when the tongue touches the front teeth.

The letter Shin is also associated with fertility. It is thus linked to the letter Teth which evokes both the belly (the cave below) and the serpent.

Hissing is a sound that epitomizes the snake and, operatively, hissing is used in a practice to raise serpentine energy. We find the three letters Shin (tooth), Pé (mouth), and Hé in the word *saphah,* relating to the spoken language. We find the letter Hé twice in the Tetragrammaton, once for the divine, nondual world and once for the created, dual world. One is considered "male," the other "female." Hé also refers to the air needed in the mouth (the upper cave) to speak or hiss.

We see that the letter Shin, which metaphysically means the Word, refers us physically to the teeth, used in the expression of speech as in hissing, both of which are operatively essential to Reintegration.

Hence the importance of the addition of Shin.

META-INITIATION

FOURTEENTH LETTER TO FRIENDS OF THE SPIRIT • FIRST SERIES

*HE HEROES IN ANCIENT GREEK TRAGEDIES WERE NO more or less than Dionysus's scattered limbs, clashing among themselves. They clashed because they were fragments. Each represented only one part of the deity; they were not an intact god. Dionysus, the intact god, stood invisible in the center of the tragedy and governed the story's birth, development, and catharsis. For the initiated spectator, the god's scattered limbs, though battling against one another, had already been secretly united and reconciled within him. They had composed the god's intact body and formed a harmony.* (Nikos Kazantzakis, *Report to Greco*)

If we consider initiation as the movement that leads consciousness from duality to nonduality, meta-initiation would be nondual in nature, i.e., free from identification with subject-object relationships, free from all form. Just as nonduality is not opposed to duality (despite what language implies in its limits) but includes it, meta-initiation is not opposed to initiation. In a way, it animates it and justifies it.

The real initiation begins when there is no more person. Meta-initiation is the innate consequence, born from the recognition of the formless within initiatory and traditional forms.

From a dualistic point of view, we hear about formal initiation, potential initiation, virtual initiation, actualized initiation, essential initiation... so many qualifiers that demonstrate a process, a process that can very well take place. The said process leads to realizing our true, original, and ultimate nature. From the nondual "point of view" (which is an absence of a point of view, since there is no longer a separation between subject and object) there is only celebration. Meta-initiation is thus a celebration within all form of the Recognition of oneself as being the Lord (the Absolute, God, the Self…).

Each ritual initiation is thus a celebration of this Recognition. Recognizing in the traditional initiatory form the archetypes at work in the mythemes is a matter of meta-initiation. The repetition, the deepening, but also the shift, can serve this traversal of form that is accompanied by a reversal, since the person, the ego, from the subject becomes an object within consciousness. This is what we find in the symbolism of the mask both in the theater, a traditional sacred art, and in initiatory societies that make use of this highly symbolic object.

Meta-initiation is minimalist. It tends to condense everything into a single gesture, a single breath, a single moment, a single word. Kunrath wanted to bring all of his teaching together in the one word, "supernature." Meta-initiation tends towards the simple which is the expression of the One or its reflection.

Many of those who embark on a spiritual path remain identified with forms, be they concepts, models, representations, or even practices, although a true practice always dissolves itself in the silence of Being. The ego, the person, learns to feed on spiritual teaching that it crystallizes in order to strengthen itself through identification in duality. Detachment itself can be turned back by the ego. The antidote to this reduction of being by attributes and qualifiers lies in the constant quest for the interval in the apparent continuum of personal history. We have been organized, instituted, by culture and language to narrate us both to ourselves and to each other. This narration is the ego, the person. The ego is thus only a self-reproducing, self-replicating discourse. But attention to this continuum of Appearance, a sort of varnish which masks Consciousness by a "consciousness of," allows us to observe the discontinuity of the narration, to distinguish the intervals of pure immaculate Consciousness, that is to say, without attribute, qualifier, or object.

The attention between two sensations, two thoughts, two movements, two breaths... allows us to access Being always present behind the experience, which comes from identification. Instead of validating the experience, we can validate its absence, the interval. If, at first, this emptiness frightens the ego which endeavors to "fill the void," to occupy it with organized thoughts, activities, and sensations (free sensation, neither thought nor grasped, leads to the interval), soon the fullness of the void imposes itself and the reversal which characterizes meta-initiation occurs naturally.

Meta-initiation is present in all traditional and initiatory forms. It is born from a change of view, a view that does not grasp. Non-grasping frees from the subject-object relationship and the narration of the ego, from the need for continuity, from the need to generate time.

The relation to time is a perfect way to assess the degree of identification or worldliness. Attention to the intervals between objects, rather than to the objects themselves, alters the relationship to time which becomes more uncertain and can even be suspended. Note that, "here and now," in the absence of time, in the pure interval of Being or Consciousness, there can be no causality.

In other words, meta-initiation would consist in distinguishing an absolute structure behind the initiatory forms, but this absolute structure, once thought out, itself becomes a form. When we speak of the Axis of the real, of the Center of all things, we tend to imagine something fixed or unchanging, but in doing so, we are in a dualistic view. In reality, the ungraspable, the *One*-graspable, is neither fixed nor moving, neither immutable nor ephemeral. We can, by accepting this vertigo, plunge into the fullness, the joy, that characterizes the Recognition of our nature.

THE LADY

FIFTEENTH LETTER TO FRIENDS OF THE SPIRIT • FIRST SERIES

CHRISTIAN CHIVALRY IS SAID TO BE OF "OUR Lady."[15] "Our Lady, they say, is the head of the Order." She is also the beginning and the end. The importance of the Lady for Chivalry in general, in the Grail cycle, or in the traditions of Courtly Love or *Fin'amor*, directs us towards an archetype that we find in non-Christian traditions. For example, there is a tradition of Courtly Love in Japan that continues through its songs. In reality, the archetype is the Knight-Lady couple, two aspects or dimensions of a single consciousness-energy that expresses nonduality within duality.

Several views can be taken on the expression of the original couple, born from the first separation within Consciousness and from which flows, like a cascade, all the forms borrowed by duality. From this first separation, two movements were begotten. The first is the search for this otherness that fully completes us, the movement of desire, while the other is the dread of never finding this part that underlies our wholeness, the movement of fear. These two movements, the desire for unity and the fear of not realizing unity, are the origin of all desires and all fears. Desires and fears always point to the One, to the Reintegration of nonduality.

The Knight and the Lady can thus represent Consciousness and Energy, Heaven and Earth, or even God and Nature, both distinct in the manifest (the appearance), and One in the unmanifest. They are also the two letters Hé of the sacred Tetragrammaton Yod-Hé-Vau-Hé, one of male polarity, the other of female polarity. There is a third invisible Hé which is the union of the two polarities. In the Jewish tradition, God lives in the couple. In Hebrew, the words *ish* and *ishah,* for man and woman, both have three letters (two ternaries that we find in the hexagram) of which two are common: Aleph and Shin. The letters that distinguish them are Yod for man and Hé for woman which together form one of the names of God, *Yah.*

The archetypal Lady merges with the Free Spirit. In duality, she is at the same time the young woman, the virgin, the lover, the wife, the mother, the healer, and the fairy who illuminates or dazzles according to the orientation of the heart of the one who approaches. All these functions are manifested by the different Marys (Myriam) who surround Jesus: Mary the mother of Jesus, Mary of Bethany, Mary of Magdala, etc. In some traditional currents, *Myriam* or *Marie* is a function designating the initiator.

If the gaze on the Lady makes her a mere object of desire, a streak of ignorance will make the Lady inaccessible whatever the circumstances and events within form. If the gaze is adjusted, recognizing the true nature and sanctifying function of the Lady beyond what is visible, the Lady reveals herself as the sole initiator and, herself immortal, teaches the arcana of immortality. She is both the house of man and his crown. In Hebrew the word *shekinah* designates dwelling, but in the Kabbalah the *Shekinah* is the feminine principle of God, which forms a couple with *Tiferet.* The Fall denotes the exile of the *Shekinah* within duality, while Reintegration is achieved through the reunion of the Bride and Groom, *Shekinah* and *Tiferet.* The Knight-Lady couple represents the manwoman couple (or any other configuration) accomplished, in fullness.

If we identify the Lady with the soul, the soul turned to the Spirit and enlightened by it, she can transform desire, the effect of her beauty, into a liberating power. This does not exclude the flesh but includes it in a permanent celebration, in and through Silence, of the Beauty and the

Joy of the original God-Goddess or of the universal Father-Mother. It is indeed a question of the path of immortality as indicated in the language of birds by the *fin'amor,* the end of death, or *finistère,* the end of the earth.[16]

The Lady is both lover and godmother. She can take on one or both of the functions, together or alternately, depending on whether the game of love is the awakening of the Knight or not. It's a question of orientation. Lancelot gets lost in amorous plots but Percival finds himself, not without difficulties, through the love episodes from which he has emerged, better prepared for the quest. Lancelot is played, between Viviane, the fairy who teaches, protects, but frees, and Morgan, the fairy who separates and imprisons. These two polarities represent light and darkness, union and separation, axiality and worldliness. The spiritual vehicle depends on the orientation of the Knight: Lancelot's cart or the chariot of light (the body of immortality).

The attributes of the Lady include the tiara, the cloak, the belt, the cup, the pendant of the helm, the armor, and the sword of the Knight. Significantly, the Lady hands the helm over to the Knight. The helm supports the crest, symbol of the soul of the Knight. The Knight is associated with the horse while the Lady is associated with the Unicorn. The horn of the unicorn, a phallic attribute, is generally spiral, meaning that the power of life is no longer dispersed in the chronic causality of replication but entirely stretched towards the *aion,* the time of initiation associated with both eternity and Sophia. Sometimes, in iconography, the Lady dubs the Knight. Some of these representations show the Lady performing the dubbing with her left hand.

Azulejo
Forte de Santo António da Barra
São Pedro do Estoril

THE *SHEKINAH*

SIXTEENTH LETTER TO FRIENDS OF THE SPIRIT • FIRST SERIES

THE *SHEKINAH* IS THUS THE FEMININE PART OF God. She evokes a radiant sun that we can relate to Isis, the equal of Re (the Greek reduction of Isis to a lunar goddess is a consequence of the dualistic drift of ancient Greece, which begins around 500 BC and will lead to the error of Saint Paul, culturally Greek, who rejects the body).

She is the manifestation and the presence of nonduality within duality itself. She is the receptacle of the Divine Breath, the letter Hé, or even the Divine Spirit.

It is sometimes said in Freemasonry that the *Shekinah* is found between the square and the compass. Notice that we can draw the letter Hé with a closed compass and a square.

With the square and open compass, we can draw the two V's that we find in the center of the circles of the Élus Coëns operations of this form:

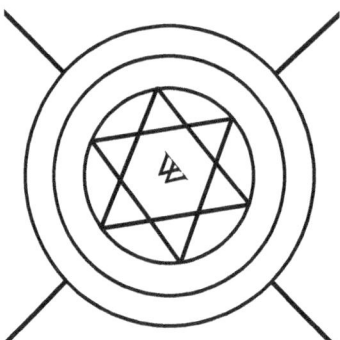

We see two V's intersecting at a point evoking the 515, the number of the *Messenger of God*, the Spirit. In the same way, we find the two V's and the point in the cross of Saint Andrew in the shape of an X, again the 515. The work of gematria confirms this association; we will come back to it.

The *Shekinah* is at the same time the wife, the fiancée, the exile, wisdom, and the lost Word. Her exile in the duality born of the original separation thus makes the *Shekinah*, the part of God closest to us, the vector of Reintegration. This can be illustrated by the exile in Egypt, Misraïm, whose word written in Hebrew has the same numerical value as the word *shekinah*, 385. We find this value in the Hebrew words *lePharaoh*, "to Pharaoh" and *shemamah*, "desolation." In Hebrew, *misraïm* evokes limit. It is the whole initiatory quest that is gathered here, in this single word of *shekinah* who we must free from exile by "exiling the exile."

With each destruction of the Temple, the *Shekinah*, sometimes called "Solomon's bed,"[17] goes into exile, but with each exile she chooses a larger receptacle until she lodges in the heart of each of us to end up taking the infinite as her abode. She thus appears as Divine Presence. It is through presence to oneself that the Divine Presence manifests itself, that is, through silence. The more subtle the Temple becomes (stone, then paper, then spirit), the more the *Shekinah* expands to become the Temple itself when all walls, distinctions, and separations are abolished. Then she merges with Christ and marries him fully.

The *Shekinah* is not a separate entity from God, rather she would be his intimate correlate within the heaviest duality. She is the one who promotes the remembrance or recognition of our original nature and ensures the inevitability of returning, of coming out of exile, of Reintegration.

The *Shekinah* remains veiled from any dualistic gaze. The subject-object relationship is the veil. It is only in nonduality that the *Shekinah* is unveiled. She is associated with the coincidence of opposites because she allows the abolition of opposites. The problem posed by duality arises within the Temple of Solomon. In Hebrew, the House of God, the Temple, *Beth HaBehira,* also means the house of choice and therefore of duality. But any binary choice reinforces duality. It is only through the *Shekinah* that choice evolves and transcends oppositions. For the Kabbalists the *Shekinah* is associated with the *sefirah Malkuth,* divine kingship, the *sefirah* both farthest away from and closest to the *sefirah Keter,* the crown. Both are peaks and roots depending on the view of the Sefirotic Tree. *Malkuth* and *Keter* are identical. Their perception differs depending on whether the consciousness is dual (*Malkuth*) or nondual (*Keter*). It is the *Shekinah* that brings them together.

The hexagram represents the *Shekinah* from above and the *Shekinah* from below, that is to say, the revealed *Shekinah* (realized) and the veiled *Shekinah* (potential) and also the "waters which were above the firmament" and the "waters which were under the firmament." The crossing of the triangles evokes the union of the Bride and the Groom, of the Flesh and the Spirit.

515

SEVENTEENTH LETTER TO FRIENDS OF THE SPIRIT • FIRST SERIES

ROM NONDUALITY TO DUALITY OR FROM THE DIVINE world to creation, everything is just sets of mirrors, vertical or lateral. *515,* the key to Dante's work, allows one to pass through the mirrors to the original Source.

Before mostly leaving the floor to the exceptional figure that was Lima de Freitas, let us pass to the thought of Raymond Abellio to whom Lima de Freitas was close and who, perhaps, provided him with material to explore the mysteries of *515* in his *Introduction à une théorie des nombres bibliques* co-written with Charles Hirsch.[18]

Raymond Abellio draws our attention to the mirror numbers, 41 and 14 (14 is a number of Christ) or 32 and 23.

32 + 23 = 55 which gives 10 then 1.

"55 is the action of the mind," Raymond Abellio tells us.

He specifies: "These numbers, 32 and 55, must therefore both be considered as emanating from the 'uncreated' light with the value of 132, of which 32 and 23 as well as the complex 32–23 thus constitute, after separation from transcendence, 1, the 'active' part."

There are several ways to get to *515.*[19]

One of them is in 55. We are in the mirror game. 55 is 23 plus 32 or 32 plus 23, the 3 like the 2 can mirror, ternary or duality. 55, this is the action of the spirit, its secret value is 10 or 1. 55 becomes by the play of

1, 515, the messenger of God, because the 1 separates the 10 and makes it active in the 55.

We can also use 190 plus 325 equals 515. 190 is the secret value of 19, 1 plus 9 is 10, back to 1. 325 is the secret value of 25, which is 5 times 5 and returns us to 55.

Lima de Freitas discovered, a decade after Raymond Abellio came to Lisbon, the key to 515.[20] The 5 or S. The 1 or I. The 515, SIS, a column and two serpents. Hermes' caduceus with double serpents that tore down the veil of ISIS. The ascending path, the return to the center preceding and signifying verticality, but also the path of Reintegration.

The works and paintings of Lima de Freitas that belong to the "515 era" constitute the elements of a hermetic practice. The researcher who meditates at length on these works, who "ingests" them as much as he lets himself be ingested by them, according to a classic method known both to Egyptian priests and the Jesuits, discovers here a teaching concerning the terminal paths of initiatory traditions. By studying the possible permutations of the numbers composing 515, Lima de Freitas approaches the three great types of internal alchemy, which should not be confused with so-called spiritual alchemy. Internal alchemy is as tangible as metallic alchemy. The body is both the raw material and the vessel.

In *515, Le lieu du miroir,* Lima writes:

"Following the analogical and symbolic journey which has led us so far, we can read in this number 155, where all the elements of 515 are present but where unity, equivalent to divinity, still remains outside the 55 group, a numeric sign of the alchemical *rubificatio,* operated by 'separation' and 'reunification' (*solve et coagula*) of the number 927. In other words, we have there the number of the reconquered totality of the fallen man, or 'first Adam,' at the very level of the 'lower waters,' which is that of lived existence. 155 can therefore be contemplated as the completion of the figure of the Anthropos at the end of the successful alchemical transmutation, because, in fact, if we add to this *microcosmic* number that of the number of degrees in a circle, that is to say, the number of the *macrocosmic* totality, we obtain the Christic and paracletic number of the *Messo di Dio,* in other words, no longer that of the man *deified* by a long work of purification and perfection, but that of the divine incarnated within the man, an operation that depends on divine will alone; indeed," Lima de Freitas specifies, "155 + 360 = 515."

He continues: "It should be noted that the position of the 1 in relation to the nucleus 55 cannot be arbitrary from the perspective of traditional numerology; therefore, 155 (similarly to 551) expresses, as we have just said, the exteriority of Unity in relation to the 55 group, symbolizing here the fusion of the 'sexes' — in the Hermetic Androgyne or *Rebis* — but which, despite its perfection, remains strictly *human.*"

The 155 and the 551 therefore express two gradualist ways: the monastic way, 155, and a way of the couple with the 551, in a perspective that remains dualistic until the ultimate realization. Lima specifies: "The *opus alchimicus* could be symbolized by 55 + 1 not only as an arithmetical sum (the result of which would be 56) but as an incorporation, in the work of the adept of the Divine One (under the form of 155) as a result of a grace that can never be expected: it is this grace, crowning alchemical labor, that completes the transmutation."

Lima de Freitas here gives us an instruction of the first importance. Technique is not enough. Science is not enough. Art is not enough. Grace, the body of freedom according to Leonardo Coimbra, is necessary for the final realization of the Great Work, and this does not emerge from human will or even from human unconditionality. Lima de Freitas, like G.I. Gurdjieff who nevertheless left nothing to chance, knows that, ultimately, the work does not belong to the human but to the Absolute.

With permutation 515, we have a completely different situation, because the 1 is found inside the core of 55 itself, enclosed somehow within its body and made invisible, which denotes an essential divine nature, *ab origine,* to the very root of being: in a word, the divinity "made flesh," the Messenger of God *corpore vestitus.*

515 is one of two subitistic internal pathways, fundamentally nondualistic, the other being hidden in the absent but present number 151.

Note again that 515 plus 151 is 666.

515, the two fundamental serpentine powers united in the axiality of the single column of nonduality.

151, the serpentine power caught in the dualistic peripheries, slinking between the two columns.

Just as there are two *Shekinah*s, the *Shekinah* from above and the *Shekinah* from below, there are two Beasts of the Apocalypse (Revelation): the Beast from above and the Beast from below, the one who rises above duality and the one who is caught in duality. Just as it is only one *Shekinah*, we have only one Beast, oriented towards nonduality or disoriented within duality.

In a letter to Gilbert Durand, dated March 19, 1989,[21] he wrote:

> My thoughts agree with what you said in your last letter about the Trinitarian Sign of the Cross, because the Annunciator—the Veltro, the 515, that is to say the star of the Magi, the *Messo di Dio* of Dante—merges into the angelic figure of Gabriel with the mercurial staff who greets Mary, our "femininity," who in us consents to transubstantiation (woe to us if, with the pride of a blind "male," we do not consent!) and who consequently performs the inversion of the inversion: from Eva to Ave. It is the mystery of Beauty—which while receiving, gives itself, effaces itself, to become a star, transmuting righteous vengeance into Life, and Life into a gift of love, passion, and resurrection: "Amen." Mary is

thus a "mirror" between the left and the right, between the height and the depths. The divine light, according to the Saint of Siena, becomes the fire of hell for those who refuse it; therefore the fire of anger and punishment can also be metamorphosed into a consoling, "paracletian" light. So many reversal games! I am flying right into the "paradigm" of the mirror.

I am announcing my latest discovery to you: the famous panels attributed to Nuño Gonçalves (the "polyptych of Saint Vincent"[22] that you know well) are none other than an illustration of the paradigm in question, and I have just seen there, clearly, our number 515! It is dazzlingly obvious, after the fact. Since, what is the central mystery of this unique collection of 15th century Portuguese painting? The fact that the Saint appears there twice, with almost perfect symmetry, and no serious explanation for this duplication can be found. Of course, there is the exoteric side and the esoteric side. But let's take a closer look. The Saint—whoever he is (O Infante Santo, Saint Vincent, etc.)—shows, in the book opened before the King, the text of Saint John where he announces the Paraclete (the text that we read in the Office of the Holy Spirit). He is, in short, an incarnation of the Paracletian spirit, therefore of the Comforter who will come: he announces it to the King. In Portugal, he is a true 515, *Messo di Dio*, dispatched to an appointed Lusitania—as once were the chosen people of Israel—to open the seals of the Fifth Empire, that of the Holy Spirit. However, it turns out that the Saint is surrounded by 5 figures on the central left panel (the king, the queen, the infant, the man in the Burgundy hat—Henri?—and an old woman) and on the central panel on the right he is surrounded by 5 knights, one of whom is touched in the heart by the right hand of the Envoy. Let's count them: the first panel, 2 figures, the Saint, 3 figures; the right panel: 3 figures, the Saint, 2 figures.

Let's add: 213   (No one noticed)
                    <u>312</u>
                    515*!*

The 11 and 11 (= 22) figures that adorn both panels are clerics, churchmen—the "chorus" of this "mystery"!

It is obvious that I have to write about this and that this text be placed in the "dossier" of *515*, which is becoming—I confess—thicker and thicker but also, curiously, more and more "Lusitanian." I convince myself, on the testimony of all these numerical clues—the Apparition of Christ to the Virgin, the "date" of Tomar,[23] now the panels of the most extraordinary and mysterious (unique!) masterpiece of Portuguese painting—that Portugal was esoterically commissioned as "guardian" of the future temple, the opener of the final times of the "Empire" of the Paraclete.

(We should speak of the angles—always "speaking"—of the lance of the knight who receives "barakah" and of the (mercurial!) staff of the "Saint" which, with the right angle of the bent leg, pivot around the pentagonal numbers 36, 72, and 108, with a subtle play of one − 71 − 109!—which relates to the absent Presence, because Divinity is there, humanly, "in the hollow"…)

His quest for 515, a Dantesque quest in every sense of the term, made Lima a master of sacred geometry, that secret geometry which is animated not by the line but by the interval. If he solved the mystery of the Bauhütte Point by the line, he also knew how to grasp it by the geometry of the interval. He learnedly and knowingly applied his findings to many founding myths. Thus from ancient Egypt…

In another letter to Gilbert Durand dated 2/12/89, he wrote:

Detail of a painting by Jorge Alfonso: *Appearance of Christ to the Virgin*

My text stems from a sudden discovery, which in turn results from the whole succession of "visions" or "flashes" of the 515 "cycle." Basically it is about the geometric reading of the myth of Osiris, which turns out—in a way bordering on the incredible—to describe the passage from the regular pentagon to the regular star pentagon as, respectively, a symbolic figure of the man-god who undergoes sacrificial death and dismemberment, and a figure of the Resurrection in the body of light. Plutarch says that when Osiris returned from the southern regions of Egypt, Seth had him killed by his 72 accomplices: an extraordinary figure, because it is the sum of the two angles of the "luminous delta" which marks the terrestrial horizon of the figure.

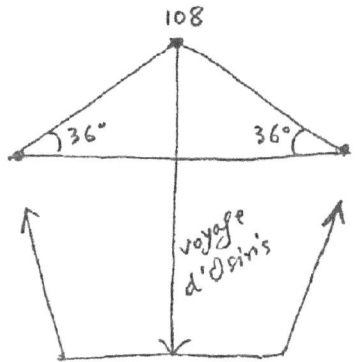

We find the same number in the New Testament where Christ calls his 72 emissaries (I believe it is in Luke but I do not have my references here) who will have to spread his Word throughout the world, that is to say, who will sacrifice God, will divide him "eucharistically" in order to vivify the human horizon. (There are also the 72 sages who translated the Bible — the "Septuagint" — and the legend says that they translated it in exactly the same way despite the fact that they were working separately! But after all, each "translation" is a version of the same light, and the light is equal to itself — which does not prevent all "translation" from being "betrayal," a dead letter in which the Spirit dies.)

It would be necessary to write many pages to summarize for you all that I saw in the Egyptian myth, in their iconography and in connection with the Christian tradition: the same angle of 108° to "signify" the Resurrection (cf. the Djed column, whose ritual erection by the Pharaoh celebrated, with each renewal of vegetable life, the resurrection of the god Osiris; in the Temple of Seti in Abydos, we see the column making an angle of 108° with the horizontal!); from the play of angular values and numbers of the division of the god, we get, again, the paracletic number *515*…

Indeed, Seth cuts the found body of Osiris into 14 pieces which he scatters in Egypt and which Isis will go to collect. This number 14 results from the vertical axis—the axis mundi—which traverses the star pentagon (the body of Resurrection) contained in the "tomb" (sema = soma!) of the regular non-star pentagon.

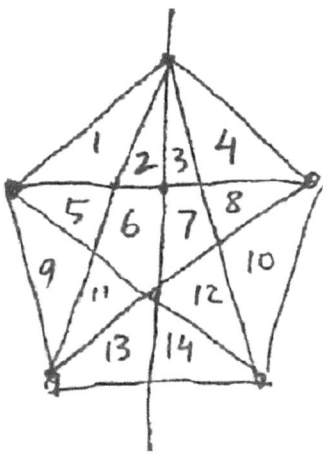

Isis will collect these pieces in order to restore the lost unity to the god (her brother). We therefore have the following equation:

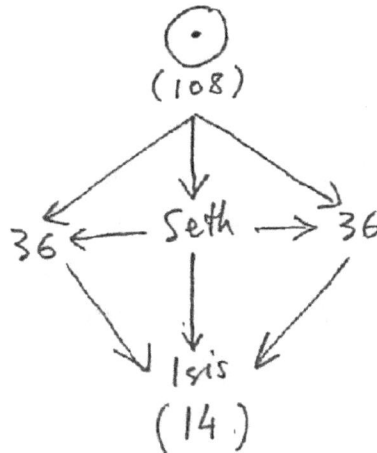

And here is

$108/7 = 15.428571\ldots$

and $360/7 = 51.428571\ldots$

This remarkable result shows that Divinity (like the Absolute Circle in which everything is inscribed), as the non-human and transcendent aspect of Osiris, is expressed by 51, while its human and "mortal" aspect appears as 15; on the other hand, the rest of the two operations are exactly the same: an irrational number that flows in perpetuity, like existential or "horizontal" time where, nevertheless, the 15 and the 51 are able to manifest themselves. Now therefore, we have once again (since unity is always unity)

$$\begin{array}{r} 51 \\ \underline{15} \\ 515 \end{array}$$

The number of rediscovered unity or of the Resurrection or the Return of God manifested to men.

Moreover, the body reconstituted by the gathering of the 14 pieces is only the double of the immortal body of Osiris (the mortal body contains the principle of Light, but it is the body of Light that gives shape to the mortal body); we must therefore double this figure around the invisible Unity: that makes 14.1.14, that is to say 5.1.5…

It is no coincidence that this 17th letter is devoted to 515. There is a close connection between the two numbers. Indeed, 17 is the number of the king *Sebastião,* (1554–1578), seventeenth king of Portugal, whose myth, inseparable from the myth of the Hidden King and the Cult of the Holy Spirit, is one of the pillars of the Lusitanian esoteric tradition.[24]

REVELATION

EIGHTEENTH LETTER TO FRIENDS OF THE SPIRIT • FIRST SERIES

*HIS SAME JOHN IN REVELATION SHOWS US THIS LAMB in an even more immense aspect. He shows him to us slain since the beginning of the world; he shows him to us opening the seven seals, sitting on the throne of God, celebrating the divine wedding, and serving as lamp and light in the temple of the Lord.* (Louis-Claude de Saint-Martin, *Le Nouvel Homme*)

The Apocalypse of John,[25] more precisely the book of Revelation, testifies to the Accomplishment, the completion of the initiatory process from duality to nonduality. It therefore does not originally have any negative connotations.

Contrary to the peripheral considerations of the Sadducees with their moral philosophy and of the Pharisees, prisoners of the ritual form, both caught in the game of the archaic triangle of power–territory–reproduction (or replication), Jesus proposes a restoration of tradition to which John testifies by his Revelation, which is indeed a revelation of the plan to be followed in order to accomplish initiation. It is both new and very old since the Christ Principle has been present and at work since the beginning of the world, i.e., before time.

From the point of view of *chronos*, the book of Revelation comes to fulfill the books of Esdras, canonical or apocryphal, which carried a first restoration of initiation in its axiality. The chronic story presents an alternation of the dilution of initiation in the peripheries of form, and the restoration (more or less successful) of the essential initiation. However, from a nondual "point of view" there is simultaneity and complementarity: they are simply more or less intensified states of consciousness, of the reduction of the gap at the Center. Thus, the keys of Johannine gnosis can get lost in Appearance while they remain in the Real for one who knows how to "See."

It was Saint Jerome, whose importance we know from the point of view of Christian initiation, who indicated a double correspondence within the Biblical Canon. The first correspondence makes the link with the Sacred Alphabet, the second with Sacred Geometry. Indeed, Saint Jerome specifies that the 22 books correspond to the 22 letters of the Hebrew alphabet but also to the 24 elders of the Apocalypse. To do this, he separates Lamentations into two parts and distinguishes the book of Judges and the book of Ruth, sometimes combined. The historian Josephus also mentions 22 books, and Esdras 24. 22 leads us into the revelation of letters while 24 introduces us to the arcana of the geometry of polygons. The 24 books can be arranged at the vertices of a 24-sided polygon, giving rise to a remarkable network of connections, while the 22 books joined with the letters of the Hebrew alphabet open just as many speculative and operative doors. Mirroring the 22 letter-books we find the 22 chapters of the book of Revelation.

Therefore several levels of readings are possible.

First, read the 22 chapters of the book of Revelation in order. Then read them again, relating them to the letters of the Hebrew alphabet, each letter indicating the intent and orientation of the corresponding chapter. We can then use the alphabet and the book of Revelation as keys to reading the Biblical Canon in its division into 22 books.

To use geometry, we'll put the 22 chapters of the book of Revelation on the vertices of a 24-sided polygon inscribed in a circle. The first two peaks are attributed to Jachin and Boaz which thus form the gate of the Temple-polygon. We enter either from the side of Jachin or the side of

Boaz to walk the path one way or the other. Then, we can study what the geometric figures, triangles, squares, pentagons, hexagons, heptagons, etc., give us.

These are just a few avenues. In reality an infinite number of paths open before us, so many levels of reading with consequences that are both theoretical and practical. One who is familiar with Hebrew will be able to move from letters to syllables to words; however, what is introduced here already opens up an immense prospect if we remember that prophecy is always a plan to be followed to ensure Reintegration.

Saint John further invites us to turn to the book of David[26] because the book of Revelation is its key.

On the other hand, the number seven is written sixty-four times in the book of Revelation. It is a numerical key to the text, a true "golden number": seven burning lamps, seven seals, seven horns, seven eyes, seven candlesticks, seven churches, seven stars, seven thunders, seven plagues, seven angels… Let us remember that the seven (the letter Zain) is the central point in the middle of the sacred hexagram. This is the dimension of perfect balance, of the axis of absoluteness. For Martinez de Pasqually, it is Saturn, the home of Adam.

In the *Book of Formation,* the *Sefer Yetzira,* it is said: "Seven divides, three opposite three, with a decisive law between the two."

"Seven divides" implies that seven divides twenty-two. $22:7 = 3.14$ or π. It is the constant ratio of the circumference of a circle to its diameter in a Euclidean plane. This quotient represents *Shaddai* to which we will return.

"Three opposite three, with a decisive law between the two" describes the hexagram and its center.

But another geometric interpretation is possible which leads to the enneagon: three squares inscribed in a circle every 30° and three equilateral triangles inscribed in the inner circle. It leads to the trisection of the angle.[27]

Finally, if we proceed to volume, "three opposite three" evokes the geometric figure of the *Merkabah,* the chariot of light which is also the Body of Glory.[28]

THE ESSENE CROSS

NINETEENTH LETTER TO FRIENDS OF THE SPIRIT • FIRST SERIES

THE ESSENE CROSS IS A THEURGIC PRACTICE THAT we find in various currents, mainly within the Therapeutic and Magic Brotherhood of Myriam, founded by Giuliano Kremmerz, within the setting of the Osirian current.

The Essene community is the third community that played an important role in the events of the life of Jesus, in addition to the Sadducees and the Pharisees. The Essenes seem to have taught a profound and direct tradition that Jesus would have received.

To date, nothing explicitly allows us to link the practice of this cross, called Essene, to the community of the same name.

This cross is intended to open and close workings: meditation, prayer, magic, theurgy, or others. It varies with the seasons in a rotation around the center, *Shaddai,* and develops according to the classic sign of the cross: touching the forehead, under the navel, the left shoulder, the right shoulder, and finally the heart.

The rotation of the Essene cross according to the seasons:

Summer: AGLA – EHIEH – EL – YAH – SHADDAI
Autumn: YAH – EL – EHIEH – AGLA – SHADDAI
Winter: EHIEH – AGLA – EL – YAH – SHADDAI
Spring: EL – YAH – AGLA – EHIEH – SHADDAI

Let's take a look at the different names of God that make it up:

Agla (Aleph-Gimel-Lamed-Aleph) begins and ends with Aleph. The energy of A unfolds and returns to its source. *Agla* is a common formula in magic based on the Kabbalah, and sometimes abused. It is formed from the initials of the words of the prayer *Atah Gibor Le-olam Adonai,* i.e., "You are eternally strong *Adonai,*" and thus contains all the power of the sounds of the acclamation *Adonai* which replaces the unpronounceable Tetragrammaton. Therefore, the word *Agla* is the foremost word engraved on Jewish talismans.

Ehieh (Aleph-Hé-Yod-Hé) is a form of the verb to be, "I will be." This is another substitution of the divine Tetragrammaton that among other things refers to God's response to Moses in Exodus 3:14, *Ehieh asher Ehieh,* difficult to translate but generally rendered as "I will be who I will be" or "I am what I am," which echoes the initial Aleph and the ultimate Aleph of *Agla*. *Agla*, like *Ehieh,* marks the unfolding from Source and the Reintegration of the first Source, one movement and one breath. *Asher* has the same value as the letter Shin. We go from nonduality to nonduality, passing through the divine play of duality. *Ehieh* is often associated with *Keter* and Mercy, Beneficence, and Freedom. Non-separation is always present even in the thickest duality. In a way, *Ehieh* is the assurance of Reintegration.

Note here: in *Ehieh* as in Tetragrammaton we have the letter Hé twice, one of which we know is feminine, the other masculine. Now, when he sent his disciples for the first time to transmit his teaching, Jesus sent them two by two, in order to carry the two polarities of the Hé of Tetragrammaton. The church, under the influence of Saint Paul in particular, has obscured the role of women in the entourage of Jesus. Recent archeology shows their importance and could support a tradition that Jesus appointed male-female couples. Indeed, Jesus did not reserve his teaching for men, it was addressed to everyone. However, in Jewish culture a man could not have approached a woman directly, which is

The Essene Cross

why the idea of male-female disciple pairs sent to impart the teaching is very plausible.

El (Aleph-Lamed) is made up of Aleph and Lamed, the largest letter of the Hebrew alphabet which means "to teach." This letter is associated with the heart, *Lev,* of which it is the initial, and thus with the knowledge that emanates from the heart (center). *Lev,* with the numerical value 32, refers to the thirty-two ways of Wisdom. A name of God, *El* is often the root of important words like *Elohim,* possibly the oldest designation of God in Jewish tradition. The plural, marked by the ending *im,* does not signify a plurality of gods but a plurality of manifestations within the Unity, in other words, a plurality of contractions of Consciousness without the unity of Consciousness being altered. Words beginning with *El* usually convey the idea of axialization, ascension, and elevation. We find it in Elijah, *Eliyahu,* who is a power at the same level as the archangels Gabriel or Michael. But Elijah also presents himself as simply a man. He is therefore a prototype of the accomplished initiate, hence his importance. He should not however be confused with *Rhély,* the "Holy Spirit of Christ."

Yah (Yod-Hé) is also made up of a polarized couple, the masculine Yod and the feminine Hé, the universal Father-Mother, Silence, the original couple, the nonduality that already carries within it the intention of duality. This is the first part of Tetragrammaton, Yod-Hé-Vau-Hé, but pronounceable, while the sequence Vau-Hé is not. However, this second part, invisible, is included in the first, visible, part. *Yah,* by numerical elaboration, has a value of 26 like Tetragrammaton. Note that if we associate *Yah* and *El,* we get *Yahoel* or *Metatron* or even Enoch, who we must associate with the *Shekinah,* the *Merkabah,* and the Body of Glory. There is thus a link with the Temple of Solomon as a temple of the god-man, mainly through the Treatise of Measures.[29]

Note also: Jesus' name in Aramaic, *Ieshouah,* is common. It gives *Iesous* in Greek by transliteration. In Hebrew, it is *Joshuah* which means

"IHVH saves," constructed with the letters of Tetragrammaton. We find *Yah* (Yod-Hé), "God," implying Tetragrammaton, and *shua* (Shin-Ayin), "save." When Jesus says "Again I say unto you, that if two of you shall agree on earth as touching any thing that they shall ask, it shall be done for them of my Father which is in heaven. For where two or three are gathered together in my name, there am I in the midst of them" (Matthew 18:19–20), this can be understood in various ways. For example: when two are gathered in my name — when their consciousness is inside my name, ultimately in Tetragrammaton by any of its names, but let us keep in mind *Yah* and *Yaho* formed of the three letters Yod-Hé-Vau of Tetragrammaton (since the Hé is doubled in the Yod-Hé-Vau-Hé) — the power of the Word is present. This also reinforces the idea of male-female couples sent to transmit the teaching, either Yod-Hé or potentially Hé female and Hé male.

Shaddai (Shin-Daleth-Yod) is the last of the names of God, in which we find the Shin and *dai*, which means "enough," the word that stops the development of duality: "it is sufficient" for the work of Recognition and Reintegration, sufficient for the understanding. *Daleth* means in Aramaic "one who has not," who does not remember his divine nature within duality (marked with the dental [d]). The letter also evokes royalty, it is the King hidden in poverty and loss. In its form *El Shaddai*, which is read *hashem*, "the name," Daleth, close to *Deleth*, door, is axialized and oriented towards Reintegration. The door is open for the return, the exit from dualistic slavery, and the reconquest of the nondual crown.

The permutations are infinite, but let us retain the operative power of this rotation exerted in a state of presence to oneself, in silence. It is self-sufficient and can suffice for all achievements if we know how to string the rosary of Letters (meaning) and play with the garland of sounds (vibrations).

THE COVENANTS

TWENTIETH LETTER TO FRIENDS OF THE SPIRIT • FIRST SERIES

THE SUBJECT OF THE *COVENANTS* IS CENTRAL TO the Judeo-Christian initiatory traditions and particularly in certain old traditional Rose-Croix lineages that have remained in the shadows.

From an absolutely nondual point of view, the covenant between Heaven and Earth is permanent and does not need to be stated. Since there is no separation, there is no need for a covenant. When we talk about covenant(s), we are talking about actualization(s) of nondual consciousness, usually within duality, within the crypt of the world. The covenant somehow measures our distance from God or our degree of Reintegration or Recognition of ourselves as the Lord. It is both an assessment tool and a driver of achievement.

The Hebrew word is *Berith* and the Greek word is *diathheke,* roughly translated by the Latin *testamentum* or "the testimony," where the English "testament" comes from. The word *Berith,* interestingly, first appears in the history of Noah (Gen 6:18). *Berith* begins with the same letters as *Bereshith,* the first word of Genesis, generally translated as "in the beginning." Both begin with Beth, "the house." This is the archetypal "house of God" from which we start and to which we return, the sanctuary. It is also gnosis or knowledge, the content of the "house of God." We find the first two letters of *Berith* and *Bereshith,* Beth and Resh (Resh expressing the movement of divine energies), associated in the word *Bara,* "create." The covenant thus coincides with creation, the movement of God towards himself in and through duality.

The Judeo-Christian traditions fall under two to eight covenants, or even more, depending on the view. Thus Saint Paul considers only the old covenant and the new covenant, two covenants for a person whose thought, however brilliant, remains dualistic.

We can easily list seven covenants in the Bible, four of which relate to *Israel:* the Abrahamic covenant, the Palestinian covenant, the Mosaic covenant, and the Davidic covenant. It all depends on what we mean by *Israel. Israel* can refer to the Jew who lives in the Holy Land, hence the name of the Hebrew state, Israel. But the word *Israel* also designates the one who fights with god, the bent man (Jacob) but also the upright man by its root, *yashar.* When God speaks to *Israel,* he is actually speaking to all mankind. These different senses mark the path of Reintegration. The man in exile is bent under the weight of duality, hence his name Jacob, *yaqob,* the root of which means "twisted." Jacob stands up after his fight with the angel, he becomes Israel, the upright man, who has changed his name, having received his real name, hence the more or less understood practices of the *nomen mysticum.* He has ceased to meander in the peripheries without an orientation in order to rejoin the Center and orient himself axially, to restore the primary covenant between Earth and Heaven. "He who receives the Holy Spirit is a Jew." It is impossible to defeat the angel, *Elohim,* without the Holy Spirit, which is confirmed by the other three covenants, addressed directly to all mankind: the Adamic covenant, the Noahide covenant, and the new covenant.

Endless and often sterile theological debates stir up ecclesiastical circles as to the nature and function of these covenants, their conditional or unconditional character, etc.

Consider that the covenant is permanent and can be actualized in endless ways depending on the intensity of consciousness (heightened awareness), the culture, the language, the times, etc. From the first separation, with the intention of duality, the desire to reunite or the desire to return to nonduality makes a covenant. The covenant is both the memory of our nondual nature, its permanence under the layers of duality, and the promise of nondual Reintegration. Some powerful actualizations are anchored in the peripheries like a beacon shining in the night, such are the covenants of the Bible, but there are many others. Anchoring can be symbolized in different ways. It is the rainbow for Noah's covenant. It is the Ark of the Covenant of the Jewish people who after many peregrinations will join the Holy of Holies in the Temple of Solomon. The Ark is referred to in Hebrew by the word *aron*, "crate" or "chest," in which we find, among other things, manna and the wand, staff, or rod of Aaron. Recall that in Exodus 7:8–12, this rod changes into a serpent and swallows up the rod serpents of Pharaoh's magicians. The verticalized serpentine power absorbs the serpentine powers inscribed in the peripheries.

The covenant is actualized from moment to moment, from essence to form. We can observe it at the level of forms (or substances), at the level of energies (or powers), and finally at the level of essences. What appears to be three degrees of covenant are actually three levels of reading or perceiving the covenant.

In terms of forms, we find the Noahide covenant which is a covenant with nature. According to Spinoza, God and nature are identical. We are in duality. It is the beauty of nature that directs us to the divine.

On the energetic plane, we can observe the covenant with Abraham, in which resides the unconditional promise of Reintegration, fulfilled in Christ. The word *Abraham* means "father of the multitude," and thus marks the unity of the multiplicity, despite fragmentation, and the principle of nonduality in duality.

In terms of essences, let us consider the New Covenant, that of Christ who by integrative renewal fulfills the previous ones, including that of Moses (the Old Covenant). We are in nonduality fully realized by the unification of Consciousness.

It is appropriate to match these three levels of reading or manifestation of the covenant with the three Chivalries (earthly, spiritual, celestial), the three contents of the Grail, or the three Covenants of Elias Artista.

THE LETTER A

TWENTY-FIRST LETTER TO FRIENDS OF THE SPIRIT • FIRST SERIES

FROM THE NEITHER-DUAL-NOR-NONDUAL *A* emanates the nondual *A* which generates the dual *A* by extending a masculine polarity to the *I* and a feminine polarity to the *O*, which, together, form the *A* of Reintegration or of Recognition, the nondual *A* within duality, that which pours out through conscious breath, at the interval between the exhale and the inhale. Hence the insistence on the practice of *The Letter A*.[30]

The Latin A does not reproduce this process, unlike the Hebrew Aleph from which it derives via the Greek Alpha. Aleph, since it is silent, is a non-letter. It is the Silence that contains all letters and allows them to emanate. Aleph represents nonduality. It is before the beginning, since it is Beth that announces this beginning: *Bereshith*. Words that begin with Aleph should particularly attract our attention.

Here we are interested in a popular derivative of the practice of the letter A, the magical formula *Abracadabra,* well known to children and parents who are most often unaware of its character and depth.

We find this magical formula in a Latin text of the 2nd century entitled *Liber Medicinalis,* written by Quintus Serenus Sammonicus, who sees in it a medicine based on letters and sounds. This magical character will expand between superstitions and traditions, especially through *Abraxas.* The primary meaning of these practices, whose origin we do not know, has been lost under the veils of multiple interpretations. The Kabbalists seized on the formula in a very interesting way.

But, before dealing with the Hebrew *abracadabra,* let us return to *Abraxas,* cited in the *Sefer Raziel,* in this form or in the form *Abragag.* In both cases, the term conveys a divine nature. It was Louis Boutard (1880-1958), an invaluable researcher (unfortunately forgotten except in a few closed circles), who studied *abraxas* with the most rigor and insight, finding the meanings and required actions inherited from the ancient knowledge inscribed in the alphabets.[31]

Often the *abraxas* object (amulet, talisman, stones or other materials) is ovoidal in shape. The most interesting are delimited by a "worm," a primal serpentine shape, in a spiral or forming a loop, thus reminiscent of the ouroboros. This worm, Louis Boutard specifies, evokes the first letter of the Burmese alphabet, and corresponds to the letter A. It is inside the A, "beginning of all things," that messages, injunctions, adjurations, or teachings are inscribed, through combinations of letters, numbers, symbols, and animal or mythical figures. This gnosis was al-

Example of abraxas studied by Louis Boutard

The Letter A

tered over time and Louis Boutard rediscovered this knowledge thanks to years of research in comparative epigraphy. We cannot stress enough the importance of the work of Louis Boutard, which future generations will crucially have to reclaim in order to understand the subtle play between essences, energies, and forms, a truly "divine" play. This reconquest could be restorative and a matter of survival, as in the case of the episode of the gift of manna in the desert (Exodus 16).

Let us return to the *abracadabra* formula, generally presented in a triangular form, apex at the bottom or at the top.

```
ABRACADABRA
ABRACADABR
ABRACADAB
ABRACADA
ABRACAD
ABRACA
ABRAC
ABRA
ABR
AB
A
```

The formula is more meaningful in Hebrew:

אברקאדברא
ארקאדבא
אקדאא
אאא
א

In Hebrew, the word is written Aleph-Beth-Resh-Qoph-Aleph-Daleth-Beth-Resh-Aleph, which gives three letters A, Aleph, framing the two words *baraq,* lightning (Beth-Resh-Qoph) and *dabar,* word (Daleth-Beth-Resh), recalling the power of the Word or of vibration or sound, springing and striking like lightning, breaking through the darkness to bring light. There are 13 Alephs, which is reminiscent of *The Thirteen Petalled Rose.*[32] Thirteen is the number of forms taken by God's love in the Jewish tradition. They are arranged in three branches, three branches that we find in a famous talisman called the "Great Key of Solomon."

These three directions are connected to the Center, the nondual Aleph. The three branches can be symbolically attached to the three columns of the Temple of Solomon, *Jachin* and *Boaz,* the third column being the human being himself who enters the Temple by passing between the two columns which adorn the vestibule. By entering the Temple, he constitutes a third term and opens the way to nonduality. In *Jachin* (colored white) and *Boaz* (colored red) we find the double extension from A towards I and towards O, underlying the duality of creation and the reunion in nonduality. The central branch symbolizes the path of Reintegration by the reunion of opposites.

The sounds I, A, O, could for example be used in rotation to "seal" the space: IAO at the zenith, AIO at nadir, OIA in the East, OAI in the West, IOA in the South, and AOI in the North. In reality, rather than "sealing" the space, or the world, it is about positioning oneself in the center, on the axis, in the interval of "doing nothing" or operating and creating.

We also find the symbolism of the three lights. These three branches can finally be mapped to the three columns of the *sefirot* in the classical representation of the Sefirotic Tree. *Jachin* corresponds to the column *Netzach-Chesed-Chokhmah* while *Boaz* corresponds to *Hod-Gevurah-Binah.* The third, central column, the human being, corresponds to *Malkuth-Yesod-Tiferet-Keter.* A great many developments result from

The Letter A

these correspondences and accords, including in the field of internal alchemy. The two columns, *Jachin* and *Boaz,* are hollow. It is this void that allows the Light of *Ein Sof,* that of the perfectly unknowable neither-dual-nor-nondual A, to descend from the lilies (1 Kings, 7:21), from the top of the columns to the plinths and up from the foot to the top through the void of the third column, the human being.

Finally, *last but not least,* the chaining of Alephs, placed end to end, can be linked to the double DNA helix as highlighted by Dominique Aubier.[33]

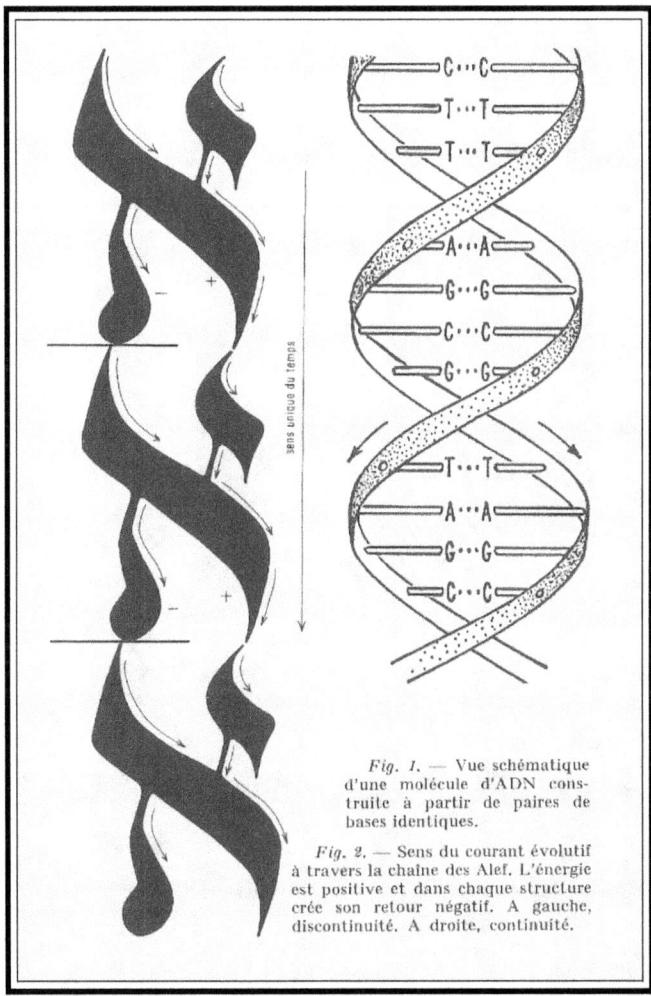

Fig. 1. — Vue schématique d'une molécule d'ADN construite à partir de paires de bases identiques.

Fig. 2. — Sens du courant évolutif à travers la chaîne des Alef. L'énergie est positive et dans chaque structure crée son retour négatif. A gauche, discontinuité. A droite, continuité.

THE LETTER K

TWENTY-SECOND LETTER TO FRIENDS OF THE SPIRIT • FIRST SERIES

ANY WORDS REFERRING TO THE SACRED BEGIN with the [k] sound, in all traditional cultures: *Kristos* – *Krishna* – *Kali* – *Karnak* – *Koran* – Catharism – *Keresh* (the Unicorn) – *Kadosh* (Holy) – *Keter*… This sound, which resonates at the top of the head, evokes the Mountain, the summit of consciousness.

One practice, which we find in several monastic traditions of the East and the West, consists in placing consciousness at the top of the head, at the fontanel and even slightly above, on a click of the tongue generating the [k] sound, in order to prepare to leave the body at the moment of death, "at the highest point of oneself."

It is no coincidence that the first letter of the Sanskrit alphabet is the letter K. Its design in Devanagari is particularly symbolically rich:

In addition to the movement of infinity, we find the same idea of the "eye of the needle" or the "narrow door" as in the spelling of the letter Qoph, in Hebrew:

This narrow gate that leads to *Keter,* passing through *Tiferet,* Heart and Christ, is that of the present moment, *rega* in Hebrew. The [k] sound is the sound of the eternity of the present moment, the ever-open door of nonduality.

The "eye of the needle" appears as such only because of the dualistic distance between the observing and thinking subject and the observed and thought object. By stopping the inner dialogue, by approaching pure experience, "zero millimeters from it," that which was only a tiny interval reveals itself to be infinite, the Great Real. We move from the surface structure of experience, inscribed in language, to its deep, sensory structure, from the subjective state to the objective state, in the here and now, through practice. Then the reversal in the Great Real is possible. It is a matter of Grace, not of practice.

Qoph has several meanings other than the "eye of the needle." It is also holiness, *kedushah.* The design of the letter evokes the ax. It is by severing before and after that the narrow door of the present moment opens and gives access to holiness.

Pronounced *Qawf,* the letter means "monkey," symbol of one who cannot keep still (the Man of the Stream, tossed about by the waves of duality), also the symbol of one who only knows how to imitate and replicate. It is *rega* that fixes and melts the individual consciousness in the immutable interval of Consciousness. It is the [k] sound that moves the initiate from imitation (the monkey) to inventing himself as Saint, or God.

Note that in Greek, Kappa refers to the number 4 and to bronze, that is, symbolically, to the central point of the triangle, the point of vacuum that allows access to the "quadruple divine essence" of Martinez de Pasqually, the passage of the ternary to the quaternary by the vertical mirror. The Brazen Sea of the Temple of Solomon would have been made with the molten bronze of the mirrors that the women would have offered to the Temple. We go from the horizontal mirror, mirror of the self, to the vertical mirror, the mirror of Self that unites Earth and Sky.

All these elements, from various languages, direct us towards the single "supreme point" or "point of emptiness," but also the "ocean of silence," the only obligatory passage, whatever the path taken.

The serpentine [s] sound and the [k] sound together form a unique key that opens all doors to nonduality.

LITTLE TREATISE ON THE CHRISTIFICATION OF BEINGS

*****
***
*

HRIST IS A PRINCIPLE AT WORK WITHIN TIME from non-time. Limiting Him to the time-space experience of the historical Jesus is a way of petrifying Him in duality.

> God begot the Spirit.
> The Spirit created the Soul.
> The Soul has densified into a Body.

Christification consists in regathering this unfoldment which is in reality a continuum. There is no separation even though language forces us to distinguish and compare.

> The Body regathers into the Soul when it turns to the Spirit.
> The Soul is absorbed in the Spirit.
> The Spirit coincides with God.

The unfoldment (erroneously labeled "the fall") and the return to the primal Source are simultaneous and permanent.

In the Real, Nothing happens. Creation is just a pulsation of the Real.

We spend too much time on the imitation of Christ instead of devoting ourselves to the invention of Christ: the invention of oneself as Christ.

Imitation is lost in replication and worldliness. The "person," an agglomeration of conditionings taking itself for an entity, identifies with an imaginary and obsolete historical Christ and tells itself in a new story. This is just chatter.

Christification is the actualization "here and now" of the process of Liberation that is working "already and not yet." Everything is accomplished. Everything is to be revealed, depending on whether one is oriented towards nonduality or causality.

Liberation is "affixed" to Grace, the "bodily vessel" of Liberty.

Everything in the principle of Christ liberates. Nothing in what emanates from it is submission or subjugation to conditioning or worldliness.

God is Absolute Freedom. God is only God because He is Absolute Freedom.

Christ is the principle and the process of the realization by God of His own Freedom, absolutely, through all the primary, secondary, and peripheral emanations.

Each element of duality is intended to celebrate and reintegrate the Absolute Freedom of God.

The different Jewish, Christian, and Muslim views on Christ are only indicative of His nature and His ascending and liberating function.

Christ as principle is Infinity, Eternity, and Light. At the same time, it is container and content: a receptacle capable of inscribing itself in duality without losing its nondual essence, to welcome the sparks of nondual consciousness that remain at the heart of subject-object duality and that coagulate through Christification.

This Light, which is also Love—non-separation—densifies as receptacle and content without losing its nature and its principal qualities.

"In the beginning," nondual Consciousness ignores that it is undifferentiated. It ignores itself. It is through the process of unfoldment and regathering that it becomes aware of itself, undifferentiated in differentiation, differentiable from Unity. The unfoldment is made by serpentine movement, rhythm, numbers, geometries…

> God is fixed (motionless). Totality is fixed, necessarily and naturally.
> God is movement, serpentine vibration in Himself, in His fixity.
> There His Absolute Freedom is exercised.

Who is "able"[34] (the word is precise and precious) to cross the apparent wall of duality is exercising the ministry of Christ. He is another Christ, more precisely[35] (the word is again important), he is the bearer of the principle of Christ which he lets shine from the Heart or the Center. The Heart is both fixed and vibrating. Like God.

The dissolution of the adhesions and identifications to the attributes of the subject is enough to open the interval and provoke the returning of the Soul towards its Source. The Soul becomes solar and sovereign by being face-to-face with the Spirit and bathes in the bliss and absoluteness of it.

> To be Free means to be Christ.
> To be Free means to Be God.
> It is indeed a question of Absolute Freedom, not of mere relative freedoms.

* * *

The more a language is embedded, poetic, and metaphysical, the more it is initiatory and draws closer to the Source.

Let us not get caught in the net of the dualistic identifications of languages with excessively Aristotelian structures, especially if we introduce distinctions in order to think about initiation.

Let us distinguish (in order to implement the praxis) the Body-Soul initiation of Jesus from the Soul-Spirit meta-initiation, that of the Christos, and also from the total Body-Soul-Spirit initiation of Iesus-Christos.

While the first, limited, is common, few individuals access the other two, which are relevant exclusively to the direct ways.

The process of Christification begins and ends where you are. It can start where you want and when you want. There is no rule in this matter since only the Primary Intention and the Ultimate Orient are decisive.

Christ is a radiant and absorbing Sun, a "gold" and "black" energetic breath within duality.

The "Wise Geometry" is based on the traversal of the polygons by the arrowed "S," or by the serpentine powers oriented vertically from the Center or Interval.

It is useless to take the Path of the Thorns, Jesus has already walked it without success. Instead, take the Path of the Roses and, if possible, the Lilies.

Little Treatise on the Christification of Beings

In Silence, you commune with the being of words, the being of numbers, the being of geometric shapes. Then the Word becomes creative and geometric thought generates worlds.

If the transmission is formal, the form will allow you to grasp the energy and the energy will lead you to essence.

If the transmission is of an energetic nature, the energy will lead you to essence as long as you are actually available.

If you are unable to conserve free energy, you will need a containing form.

If transmission is essential, you can stay on the plane of essence.

If you wish to work in duality, you will be able to develop energy. If necessary, a form will enable you to contain and regulate the energy.

To go from essence to energy, primordial or archetypal information is indispensable.

To go from energy to form, relative information will determine the qualities of the form.

When you set out on the Path, it is imperative to be seized very quickly by Essence, otherwise the rhetoric of forms, the dualistic games of the person will reign supreme. Without a true Orient, it is impossible to be the Way.

Duality is nonduality contracted, "slowed down" in a way, or if you prefer, condensed. The original contraction is an "immaculate conception," still virgin of all separation and all history. It is the "duality-source" still imbued with nonduality.

The essence-energy is reflected in duality as energy-form or existence. "Plasticity" is thus characteristic of energy.

When energy returns to essence, it frees itself from the disappearing form and thus merges into its original source. Reintegration is a de-contraction of nondual Consciousness.

Essence – energy – substance (form): path of the contraction of nonduality into duality.
Substance (form) – energy – essence: path of Christification by reintegrating duality in the heart of nonduality, the Appearance within Absolute Consciousness.

As imperfect as the part is, it always fits into the perfection of the Whole. Furthermore, it is the imperfection of the part that contributes to the perfection of the Whole.

All is always possible.
The Whole much more than the part.

The issue with transmission is "to make a path to make footsteps" but very often we have footsteps without any path.

Erudition is knowledge of the circle, not knowledge of the center.

All is Love, the horror and the sublime. This is most difficult to fully grasp — it emerges from absolutely conscious non-separation.

There are two types of direct ways: those of the "ever wider way" and those of the "ever narrower way." The first type relates to infinitely cumulative inclusion through non-separation. The second type concerns the voyager of the Interval who never leaves the Center of everything.

Surveyors of the first type absorb all forms.
Those of the second type integrate and release all energies.
Both types point to nondual Essence and manifest it in dual retro-causality.

You are born God! Then you forget.
All your life you will try to remember who you are.

The True is nondual.
The exact is dual.
Popular culture would say that Truth belongs to God and exactitude to the devil, that is, to the separator.

The real challenge facing humanity is not death but separation. Death is only one aspect of separation. Understand that immortality experienced in separation is Hell. The only path to total immortality is nonseparation. From it flow all benefits including Awakening, or Illumination, which is its principal but not sole aspect.

To liberate oneself without liberating the serpentine powers is to liberate oneself without the creation: it is a partial, separate, and incomplete liberation.

Total liberation is absolutely inclusive of all the serpentine powers that weave all existence.

I Am God.
God is "I Am."
A ternary:
"I Am Absolute Will."
"I Am Absolute Love."
"I Am Absolute Freedom."
Without order, nor hierarchy, obviously.

To avoid the word trap, use the comma-interval:
"I Am, Absolute Love."

Reintegration presents two arrows: the arrow of devolution and the arrow of revolution.

The process of devolution leads from duality to nonduality through the door of consciousness that merges into the Original Consciousness.

The process of revolution also leads from duality to nonduality, but by an expanded and non-separate consciousness within Absolute Consciousness. This is the process of Christification.

Cease portraying the Absolute through representations that you confuse with the Great Real. Or, at the very least, remember that these are just indicators you don't need to dwell on, let alone bow to.

Awakening is an inclusive separation, an extraction from the world that is immediately reabsorbed into Absolute Consciousness as the object of the nature of the Void. Non-separation is not opposed to separation, it includes it. Non-separation includes separation in the great game of the Absolute.

There is a deceptive piece in the phenomenology of archetypes that unfold from the Interval to duality. It is necessary to distinguish these *"trompe l'œil"* or *"trompe cœur"* that divert, corrupt, or pollute the archetypal Light during its temporal actualization. So with the Temple…

What happens to the internal/external opposition when we realize that the world is an internal phantom? Is the exterior of the exterior an interior? Is the interior of the interior an exterior or the Extreme Center? See where dualistic concerns lead. Neither interior nor exterior: no one has been cast out, there is only God, the All.

Little Treatise on the Christification of Beings

If you are aware that Christification is a Return, a Recognition of yourself as Christ, then there is no need to force the doors. They open on their own from the Heart or Center.

The me, the ego, the person, never gives. The me does not know what to take. It is troubled and greedy. When it gives in the Appearance, it is always in order to take and nourish its own replication. Forget the selfishness/altruism opposition.

The Self does not give, either. It is non-acting, it is the Gift, the absolute Gift, the absolute blessing and anointing of non-separation.

A direct way of Christification is the way of rarefaction. Rarefaction of gesture, speech, thought, and breath. Reintegration of Earth into Water, Water into Air, Air into Fire, Fire into Spirit. Reintegration of the Interval. Skillful regathering of manifestation into the Interval.

Babylon itself becomes a way if you learn to become bilingual in your mother tongue by vivifying it through the Free Spirit, thereby accessing the Word: bilingual through the mastery of the most common language and of the Word inscribed directly by the Absolute in Consciousness as a dance of sounds.

We do not take an oath on a text, sacred or not, but on the tongue, the tongue which, inhabited by the Spirit, becomes Word. We take an oath on the tongue by the tongue, on the Word by the Word.

> Hell is duality with no intuition of nonduality. In Hell, you are played.
> Purgatory is duality with the intuition of nonduality. This is the place of Orientation.
> Paradise is nonduality, sometimes within duality itself. This is designated by Awakening or Illumination…

These are three states of identified Consciousness that you can traverse in a flash before returning to the heaviest duality.

When Soul turns to Spirit, her solitude leads her to the Source. Then there is nothing to do. But, until the Turning, practices are necessary to saturate the Soul. The Angel of the Turning acts by saturation. It saturates the identified soul with matter to the point at which it can only turn back or else be irreparably fragmented.

If you go beyond the oppositions born of the first polarization by exclusion, you fall. If you go beyond them by inclusion, you rise and rise.

Traverse the forms characterized as profane and sacred equally.
Go through them with respect but without delay. Go through and not through, seek the highest sense, the nondualistic sense. It is the one that makes all the alphas coincide with the unique omega, all of the "already" with the "not yet."

Learn to distinguish the shadows, which are only elements of the dualistic decor, from the Living, the only ones capable of perceiving the nondual Light.

The Angel of the Turning is always available, right now. Within duality, its action can be spectacular, but never forced.

Working through the window of the heart is not only the height of metaphysical elegance, it is the most direct, and least resistant, path to the Recognition of oneself as being of the nature of Christ.

If you misjudge yourself, or judge others, there can be no coincidence of opposites. You will not then be able to discern the Interval that opens onto the Great Real. Christ is both the Interval and the Master of the Interval.

> To think of yourself as a god is stupid.
> Being God is just (that is, adjusted).
> The Supreme Adjustment is the Free Spirit in action. The Spirit is Free to set us free.

Everyone is born Christ.
Many forget and crucify themselves without ever being resurrected. In some there is a "third day." In reality, every moment we are birthing Christ, we are forgetting and remembering ourselves anew. The New Man is the fruit of the remembering of his own divinity.

> Attention.
> Attend Zion.
> Timeless Zion.[36]
> Language reveals its secrets in the attention to sounds that renew the dynamics of the senses.

In the sense of words, the Word is lost. In the sense of sounds, the Word is found and the power of words is revealed.

To name is to make exist, or to fling out and solidify the object in the peripheries.

Listening to sound, paying real attention to the sounds that make up the word and precede it, is to free the energy of the object and allow it to return to its source.

In other words, one should consider neither the subject nor the object but the relation between the two within Consciousness.

It is in the return to the Source that the Word is found.

There are too many dead among the living and too few Living among the dead.

If you embrace all of that which exists, dark as well as light, then all polarities are balanced. Absolute Neutrality takes hold, an "Extreme-Center" which is also the Interval to the Great Real.

The Spirit informs the Soul which informs the Body. The Soul must be, like Janus, turned both to the Spirit and to the Body. If it allows itself to be caught up in matter, the Body/Soul system closes itself to all influence of the Spirit. If it fully assumes its function of mediator/messenger, then the Spirit illuminates the Body and matter. Duality disappears.

The Christic "transmission" takes place in several stages or relays. First the form. Then Energy in Form. Then Energy alone. Finally, Essence in the Pit of Energy prior to Essence at the Apex of Energy. And also, the coincidence of the Essence of the Apex and the Essence of the Pit. Essence by itself is not transmissible.

There is a secret however: Form is indistinguishable from Essence. But few realize this secret.

As Christ, we are the "place" of the Turning. No practice leads to Liberation or Awakening. Liberation is a non-practice. Awakening is the natural, Christic, original, ultimate, and permanent state.

What is Awakening?
When you ask the question, I don't know.
When you don't ask the question, I know.
I know and I am.

When one has approached as close as possible to the axis of being and

Little Treatise on the Christification of Beings

one sets out again towards the peripheries, they do not want you any more. They can send you back violently to the Center. Indeed, the serpentine powers that roamed the peripheries and have been redirected by your axial journey refuse to stray again.

Any truth stated is no more than a semicolon, do not stop.

> I do not exist.
> I come from a Kingdom that does not exist.
> I return to a Kingdom that does not exist.

> "Love your neighbor as yourself."
> Love your near ONE.[37]
> The ONE who approaches.
> Your original and ultimate reality.
> The near ONE, the Lord, the Christ in You.
> Recognize the near ONE as yourself.
> Recognize Christ as yourself.

To apprehend is to not perceive.[38]
Let go in order to sail, free, on the Ocean of Knowledge following the Winds of the Spirit.

Effort is a distraction organized by the person (the me). Over-effort is over-distraction.

Until we recognize ourselves as Christ (the Principle), there is only wandering. This wandering is itself the Recognition of oneself as being the Lord.
For the word "wandering," we can substitute the word "limping" or "wavering." Wandering is always serpentine.

Reduce, as much as possible, the period of the imitation of Christ. If possible, avoid imitation. You don't need to imitate Christ, you are Christ. Recognize Christ within you and give him the whole space.

Imitating Christ nourishes the replication of the Person. What is more, the Christ whom you imitate is only a very partial temporal aspect of that infinite solar power that is Christ, your true nature.

Who prays? The ego.
To what does the ego pray? An unconscious projection of himself that he calls God.

Prayer is anti-grace. Let your Divine Reality communicate with you in Silence, that is Grace.

The only prayer is Silence. Even a silence crossed by noise remains Silence.

Knowledge is the fruit of recognizing our Christic nature. The degree of recognition determines the degree of knowledge, from the intuition of the Man of Desire to the realization of the Spirit-Man.

Only your own creation, from the Heart or Center, can be operative. Any other creation is a copy, a sterile imitation. You are Christ, not a sad demiurge.

On the one hand, in the Appearance, a local affair, a traditional rectification, Jesus.

On the other hand, in the Great Real, the Great Affair (or Non-Doing)[39] of Reintegration and Recognition, Christ.

To interpret the Center while one ignores the Center is not a falsification but an embezzlement.

Little Treatise on the Christification of Beings

> Christ to Judas:
> "I don't exist. You don't exist.
> I know it. You ignore it.
> Nothing has happened.
> Nothing has ever happened.
> Only… Spirit.
> When you have understood, you will be free."

If you have a taste for non-effort, perhaps you have sensed the flavor of Being. Turn your back on Hell, the "do it."[40]

> Have confidence in the infinite Freedom of the Lord.
> Have confidence in your infinite Freedom.

> Recognition of oneself as the Lord is Reintegration.
> Reintegration of oneself in the Heart of the Lord is Recognition.

Scholarship is of interest only to the ego. It allows for verbose commentary instead of "how to be silent" which leaves room for the Christ-Being.

God constituted himself both as a Temple and as a Crypt in the world. This results in two chivalries: a chivalry of the Temple, accessible to all, and a chivalry of the Crypt for those who know the Secret.

> Myriam of Magdala revealed to Jesus that on the prayer rug of the flesh, the Spirit is Free.
> Myriam of Magdala is not a saint, she is a goddess. A goddess does not have to be a saint.

Behind the truths stated in the Appearance, there is indeed an absolute structure. This structure adjusts to the observer, or rather the contemplator of the Imaginal. This is how it is absolute.

As long as you exist, you are inscribed in extension and the intention escapes you: the primordial intention, the Source, the final intention, the Orient. Only Being knows the intention.

The Spirit does not ask for submission or renunciation of Liberty. It asserts itself as Truth. It is the call to Recognize each as being Christ.

I certainly don't want to be awake. No need!

Christ is the anointing of non-separation, in other words, of Love. This anointing is permanent and without reservation, prior and of course subsequent to the historical Jesus.

The Heavenly Jerusalem does not seek to incarnate or manifest. It abides and invites everyone to settle within it.

Institutions choke the Spirit. All Living education is non-institutional. Jesus fought against institutions; he was crucified by them. To institute his word is to crucify him once again without being able to resurrect him.

A *khatzi*[41] is the one who brings the Sepulcher to life in his Heart in order to constitute himself as an axis of Resurrection, conscious, fully aware of the absolute Freedom of Knowledge. Nondual Knowledge, immediate fruit of non-separation.

> Dualistic Templar esotericism is a precipitation of the archetype of God constituting Himself as a Temple in the Crypt of the world. Nondual Templar esotericism is a precipitation of the archetype of God constituting Himself as a Crypt in the Temple of the world.

Little Treatise on the Christification of Beings

You look for the way.
Born Christ, you are the way.
You look for a practice, you are the practice. It's just a matter of Attention. Being attentive to yourself, fully attentive, and thus to the world, without separation, is the unique practice of the Living. There are no secrets other than Attention.

You throw the net on the side of ego and come back empty-handed. Throw it to the other side, to the side of the Self, and you will find fullness.

The Ocean is the same but the orientation is different. Awakening is just a conscious orientation.

All the Real is ineffable but can nevertheless be evoked, sometimes invoked, even convoked, by words put together in a "certain way."

Christification, Liberation, is just a matter of punctuation.
"I Am the Christ" is the abyss.
"I Am, the Christ" is absolute Liberation.

God, the Absolute, does not deal with the part as a part but as the Whole. It is up to the part, it is up to us to establish ourselves as the Whole.

Do not think that if Christ returned he would imitate himself. He would be quite different in his actualization, still all Freedom but in a totally original way. Never replication.
Spirit never repeats itself.
Every life is a Gospel for those who are attentive.

What we call "experience" is the sea foam of Consciousness that comes to contract in duality. Take to the sea, descend into the depths.

The New Man (New Adam, New Eve, New Being...) is a total

human, having integrated all that presents itself, the dark and the luminous, having reduced all the oppositions and polarizations, having traversed all the forms, having eliminated all the projections and adhesions. Absolute freedom.

Let us distinguish, in a way, four initiations:

The first passes from the Man of the Stream to the Man of Desire. It remains characterized by duality and the appearance of good and evil.

The second prepares the Man of Desire to become a New Man. Good and evil are combined to serve understanding. Nonduality pierces the dualistic opacity.

The third initiation establishes the New Man. Good is identical to Evil (but "doing good" is not equal to "doing bad"). Nonduality reigns.

The fourth initiation is the overcoming of all of this. Neither duality nor nonduality. Neither Good nor Evil. Beyond even God.

Not only is there no limit between the visible and the invisible, the explicit and the implicit, not only is there priority but there is a continuum.

It is wrong to say that someone has known Awakening, first because there is no person, and secondly because he has known an awakening.

> The Spirit does not teach, it awakens.
> The Word teaches without ever repeating itself.
> The Body learns by replication into which endless variations are introduced, a form of wisdom.

The same serpentine powers that crawl and roam the peripheries radiate once reoriented and axialized at the Center.

Awakening is the realization of the perfection of imperfection.

> Worldliness makes the exceptional mundane.
> Awakening, Liberation, makes the mundane exceptional.

As long as there is someone, the Teaching cannot be grasped. And when there is no more person, the Teaching is useless.

We have to exhaust the form before the form exhausts us. The agent of form exhaustion is Spirit, the Free Spirit, which acts on form like alchemical salt. Judgment is the measure between these two exhaustions.

Silence is the door that opens onto all memories, past, present, and future, human or not. These memories-experiences teach, but not all of these teachings have the same relevance. We must learn to See and to choose what is essential.

Do not stop at the historical Christ, seek the Christ before Christ and the Christ after Christ, seek the Christ who abides.

Religions are born from the instrumentalization of the teaching of a few awakened ones, caught in the nets of organization and institutionalization. Free and awakened speech does not support constraints.

We are the fragmented Bodies of Osiris, Dionysus, or Christ, scattered in duality. The resurrection is the immediate fruit of non-separation, of our nondual presence.

I am addressing those in whom there is no longer a great multitude.

There is an abyss between the Way and those who claim it.

The more conscious you are, the more you die and are resuscitated, the more the linear causalities fade.

Christification requires including the horror as well as the sublime. Both are unsupportable in duality but, united in nonduality, they form a quiet and unchanging harmony.

Hell is here, the product of separation. Immortality in duality is eternal hell (almost eternal!). There is no true immortality without nonduality.

If there are a thousand ways to alienate being, there will always be a thousand and one ways to free it. This "plus one," this "more than human," is Christ.

>   As Christ, I Am.
>   As Myriam, I Am.
>   As Christ, You Are.
>   As Myriam, You Are.
>   As Christ, We Are the One.
>   As Myriam, We Are the One.

Only the Rose.

SECOND SERIES

O Paracleto
Painting by Lima de Freitas

THE SECRET GRAMMAR

FIRST LETTER TO FRIENDS OF THE SPIRIT • SECOND SERIES

HERE IS TRADITIONALLY AN ORIGINAL GRAMMAR that springs to the boundary between nonduality and duality, a fruit of the first Vibration, the Word. It structures not only worlds but languages. We bathe in language without being aware of it, like a fish in water. It is possible that this grammar corresponds to the hypothesis of a proto-language sought by some linguists, but for us it is rather Silence that makes proto-language because it contains all sounds and therefore all languages.

The idea of a "secret and sacred grammar" structuring the universe runs through many Western and Eastern traditions. In Europe, it is in Portugal that this tradition particularly flourished. This current could have originated in an initiative by King Denis (1261–1325) and Queen Elizabeth (1271–1336), considered a saint during her lifetime. This enlightened couple—we speak of a poet and troubadour king, known for the protection granted to the Templars fleeing the hatred and baseness of Philip the Fair—asked the scholars of the time, Jews and Muslims among them, to find the primary meaning of words through the proper meaning of the sounds that compose them. This resulted in a sacred and secret grammar whose transmission has been ensured up to the present day including within the university setting, in particular within the setting of the Faculty of Letters in Porto at the beginning of the last century or today at IADE-U, the Institute of Art, Design and

Enterprise–University, of which our friend and brother Lima de Freitas (1927–1998) was the first director.

Our beloved Brother António Telmo (1927–2010) was one of the custodians of this linguistic tradition. We refer you to his work *Philosophie et Kabbale*,[42] in which he develops this question and on which we will rely to deal with a practical application.

Based on the Kabbalah and on the teachings of Plato on language, he distinguishes the vowels, the voiceless consonants, and a third set of breaths and vibrations corresponding to the different worlds of the Sefirotic Tree. The consonant is an element that must be associated with a vowel to make it sound. The element is pure and indivisible. It is, António tells us, "the void of a phoneme." We see the value of this conception which results in the following relationship between the elements and the sefirot. This applies to Portuguese of course, but also to all Latin languages, even if they offer fewer possibilities (of voices and of ways) than Portuguese, which has retained many sounds lost in other Latin languages, except perhaps Romanian.

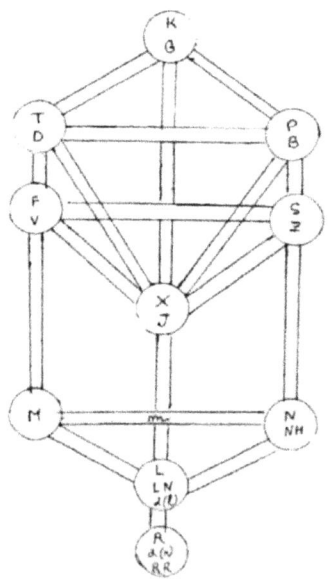

Drawing by António Telmo

The Secret Grammar

Sounds have their own meaning regardless of the meaning of the word. It is through the meaning of sounds that we can find the dynamic and energetic meaning of the word.

It is not for us (although it is not prohibited) to become Kabbalists, which would require a complete command of Hebrew. However, we can have "recourse to Hebrew," as to Greek and Latin, to sacred etymology, in order to find, between knowledge and intuition, the deep meaning of the sounds and words that lead to the Great Real.

Let's study the benefit of this view of our practices. We have already seen the importance of the [k] sound and the [s] sound that we find in the Latin formulas *Pax in excelsis* or *Lux in excelsis,* powerful in their sounds, whether in repetition or in outpouring, the outpouring from silence being superior to repetition.

We find the words "in excelsis" in the Latin chant *Gloria in excelsis Deo,* the beginning of which we reproduce here:

> *Gloria in excelsis Deo*
> *et in terra pax hominibus bonæ voluntatis.*
> *Laudamus te, benedicimus te, adoramus te.*
> *Glorificamus te. Gratias agimus tibi*
> *propter magnam gloriam tuam,*
> *Domine Deus, Rex cælestis,*
> *Deus Pater omnipotens.*

> Glory to God in the highest heaven,
> And peace on earth to the men he loves.
> We praise you, we bless you, we adore you.
> We glorify you. We give you thanks
> for your immense glory,
> Lord God, King of heaven,
> Almighty God the Father.

The formula *in excelsis* means "in the highest heaven." We can hear "at the top of Consciousness," "at the highest point of oneself," "to the highest sense"... Operatively, this implies that consciousness is placed at the Crown, *Keter.*

Let us apply the formula to the relation between sounds and the sefirot.

The combination [k]-[s] generates a moment of creative energy between *Keter* and *Chesed* (also called *Gedulah*).

Keter is the seat of nondual consciousness. It is in this non-place that essence becomes energy through information (the "ideas of God," the "archetypes"). It is the infinite condensed into a Void Point, the Supreme Point: non-Being containing Being without actualizing it.

Chesed is Goodness. *Gedulah* evokes Forgiveness. *Chesed* conveys several qualities and energies: Grace, Beneficence, Love, Offering. It springs forth spontaneously like lightning (the serpentine power *par excellence*). It keeps knowledge secret and preserves it. It is absolutely free (hence its link with Grace).

The combination [k]-[s] announces the unfolding of Knowledge through the self-communication of God (Grace) by free outpouring. Its repetition in the formula *Pax in excelsis* multiplies its power as much as it is supported by the sound [p] which refers to *Chokhmah,* Wisdom, the pure Light, not emanated, issued instantly from *Keter* and preserving the secret of Yod (the energy) of Tetragrammaton.

A simple change of letter completely changes the orientation of the formula. Let's proceed from *Pax in excelsis* to *Lux in excelsis.* The sound [l] refers to *Yesod,* the foundation. This time the combination [k]-[s] is not at the service of the deployment of Light but of its Reintegration. Additionally, *Chokhmah* is also a name of *Malkuth,* yet again the descending and ascending mirror games. There is upper *Chokhmah* and lower *Chokhmah,* uncreated Wisdom and created Wisdom. *Yesod* is associated with the "righteous man," the *Tzadik,* the rectified man whose gesture, speech, and thought are perfectly aligned with the Orient in order to realize the Prime Intention.

Pax in excelsis and *Lux in excelsis* thus call for the deployment of Knowledge and its implementation for Reintegration, simply through the sense of the sounds emitted in the silence of consciousness like a breath, the breathing of the divine within the same duality that it illuminates and liberates. It is not about freeing oneself from duality, which presupposes and reinforces an opposition, but about freeing duality by reintegrating it into nonduality.

If God begets the Spirit which begets the soul which begets the body, the body re-enters the soul which re-enters the Spirit which re-enters God. A continuum unfolds from the Supreme Point to duality and then returns to its source.

Like the Temple of Solomon, the Sefirotic Tree represents the body of the human being and indicates the process of realization of the Body of Glory. The head (*Keter*) itself is a reduction of the Temple of Man. Sounds do this in the body, informing matter for its transmutation. Recovering the Lost Word involves recapturing the proper meaning of the sounds that form the basis of the creative or integrative power of words.

THE ORDER OF KNIGHT-MASONS ÉLUS COËNS OF THE UNIVERSE

SECOND LETTER TO FRIENDS OF THE SPIRIT • SECOND SERIES

T IS RARE THAT THE NAME OF AN INITIATORY order is so rich in meanings. The name of an initiatory organization is often quite general, indicating only a current of attachment, not very significant of the proposed course and work. This is not the case with the Order of Knight-Masons Élus Coëns of the Universe. We will only discuss here that which words can say and not the history or doctrine of the order founded by Martinez de Pasqually.

The Order of Knight-Masons Élus Coëns of the Universe is, for the record, the illuminist matrix of the various expressions of the Martinist current: the order and the doctrine chosen by Martinez de Pasqually conveying, in an apparent Masonic framework, a Jewish family tradition, an original and traditional total doctrine, a complex theurgy, a teaching inspired (according to Martinez) by the Holy Spirit; the remarkable theosophy of Louis-Claude de Saint-Martin that draws from the Martinezist matrix but also, masterfully, from a second matrix originating from Jacob Böhme; the Rectified Scottish Rite of Jean-Baptiste Willermoz, also based on two matrices, one Martinezist, the other Templarist; and the Martinist Order since Papus, in its different branches, characterized by the double reference to Martinez de Pasqually and Saint-Martin but drawing largely on "the occultism of the Belle-Époque," to which is added a kind of "rectification" by Master Philippe.

Order. It is not a matter of organization here. We have often called for distinguishing the initiatory organization, always secular, ephemeral, and very human, from the initiatory way which remains, emerges, and "disappears" according to circumstances. The common confusion between the two leads many to settle for organization and get lost in it, confusing not only purpose and process but also belonging and process. Order is different from human organization. It is the vehicle of the way within the setting of the organization. By "order" we mean arrangement, alignment of form, energy, and essence; of matter to Spirit; or even alignment between the body, soul and spirit; an alignment, also, between intention and the orient, which coincide. Hence the idea of rectification: we rectify the alignment when it gets lost in the peripheries. This applies to the order as well as to the individual.

Alignment allows the original light, or even an archetype, to radiate from nonduality to the heart of the duality of form. If form is sufficiently polished, it mirrors itself and reflects the light-source. This reflection is a sign of Reintegration.

Universe. The order manifests an archetypal meta-structure, which persists, that we name (depending on the currents) Heavenly Jerusalem, the Church Invisible, the New Church according to Emmanuel Swedenborg, the High and Holy Order according to Jean-Baptiste Willermoz... This structure is universal. It relates to Consciousness-Energy and remains present within the forms of the order as long as the alignment is preserved. The forms must necessarily be traversed to reach the essence through this structure.

Knight-Masons Élus Coëns. It is exceptional to find the three great traditional functions in the title of an initiatory order: the chivalric function (warrior), the artisanal function (including the alchemical function), and the priestly function. We will not come back to the chivalric function in its triplicity, already discussed in these pages. The artisanal function is due to the apparent Masonic framework of the order, but not only that. It is about building the Temple of the Spirit. The Temple of Solomon, first developed as a Temple of stone, then a Temple of paper,[43] is ultimately grasped as a Temple of the Spirit,[44] or even a Body of Glory to ensure Reintegration or Recognition.

This artisanal function has an alchemical dimension, without which the Body of Glory cannot be envisaged. It is present among the Élus Coëns but is almost systematically forgotten, masked by the predominance of theurgy.

Page 111 of the *Nouvelle instruction coën*[45] is, however, very significant. We find the alchemical tradition there. "The idea, which ties in with that of the inner ways," said Robert Amadou, "needs to be explored."

Here is a transcription with modernized spelling of the last paragraph in relation to our subject:

"Thus do not doubt that it has always been divine word [*illegible*] even that at all times, the sages have spiritually vegetated and issued from within the matter of iniquity enveloping the soul, as we see also that the reproductive spirit also leaves the earth, stripped of its particular envelope to enter the great universal space in renewal. Now, under the guise of hidden fire, the true seekers of the Philosopher's Stone have inscribed real gold, under the emblem of temporal gold."

que leur enveloppe, car tous savent que ce qui renaît n'est point ce que l'on avait vu, attendu que c'est seulement le Spiritueux pur et simple qui étant sous la loi de son genre, reproduit son enveloppe, mais principe Spiritueux que jamais mortel n'a pu voir et ne peut voir qu'enveloppé, la même chose, nôtre âme outre son enveloppe corporelle, est encore enveloppée dans l'acte du péché d'où Dieu l'a rappellée de travailler à sortir, pour parvenir à paroître à la fin des Siècles totalement dépouillée en changeant en l'homme nouveau, qui n'a jamais connu le péché.

Revenons encore aux sages ci dessus, lesquels, quoiqu'ils fussent visibles dans ce monde, n'y étaient pas moins, pour cela, éclairés et rechauffés par deux Soleils, à Sçavoir par le divin incréé, qu'ils voyaient aussi physiquement des yeux de leur âme que ce qu'ils voyaient aussi le Soleil créé, des yeux de leurs corps, ainsi que, s'il plaît à Dieu, la suite de ce traité de résurrection des morts, nous le fera voir.

Ainsi ne doutons nullement que ça toujours été par la divine Chaleur de ce divin M?. que de tous les Tems, tous les sages ont spirituellement végété et sorti du dedans la matière d'iniquité enveloppe de l'âme, comme nous voyons aussi que le Spiritueux réproductif sort également de la terre, en dépouillement de son enveloppe particulière pour entrer dans le grand espace universel en renouvellement. Voilà ce que, sous une apparence de sens caché, les vrais Chercheurs de Pierre Philosophale ont écrit du vrai or, sous l'emblème de l'or temporel. Mais cet or est purement

Robert Amadou continued: "It would be good for priests, who are theosophers and not just theologians, to question the relationship—which is a commonplace in the occult tradition of the West—between 'the Body of Glory of the inner ways' and the body of the New Adam, the resurrected body. There is a frequent tendency to reduce the liturgical to the operative: now it is the Eucharist which is not only an example but the model, the type, the archetype of all transmutation. And the body of the Risen One ('firstborn among the dead') fulfills the same function with regard to our glorification practices of the physical body."[46]

There is no theurgy without the alchemy of the Body of Glory or internal alchemy. If Jean-Baptiste Willermoz, like Louis-Claude de Saint-Martin, opposed Cagliostro and his internal alchemy, it was above all about power play in the esoteric circles of the time, mainly in Lyon. Both were wrong about the character of Cagliostro and his Egyptian High Masonry. However, Jean-Baptiste Willermoz knew well or at least had a sense that Reintegration requires an alchemy of the Body of Glory.[47] It is moreover very clear in the grade of Scottish Master of Saint Andrew within his Rectified Scottish Rite, in which he establishes dialogue between the repository of the doctrine of Reintegration and the reconstruction of the Temple of Solomon, model of the Body of Glory. In addition, the drawings of the twenty philosophical paintings of *Angéliques*[48] also describe a way of the Body of Glory. Later, Robert Amadou returned to this question of the paintings of *Angéliques* in general. To fully understand the fundamental "founding" myth, in its Coën version, "we must," he said, "read the explanation in the figurative paintings (*Angéliques*). These figures are first and foremost teaching images, and secondarily aid in drawing operative tables. Analyzing the paintings in question is difficult, essential, and fascinating."[49]

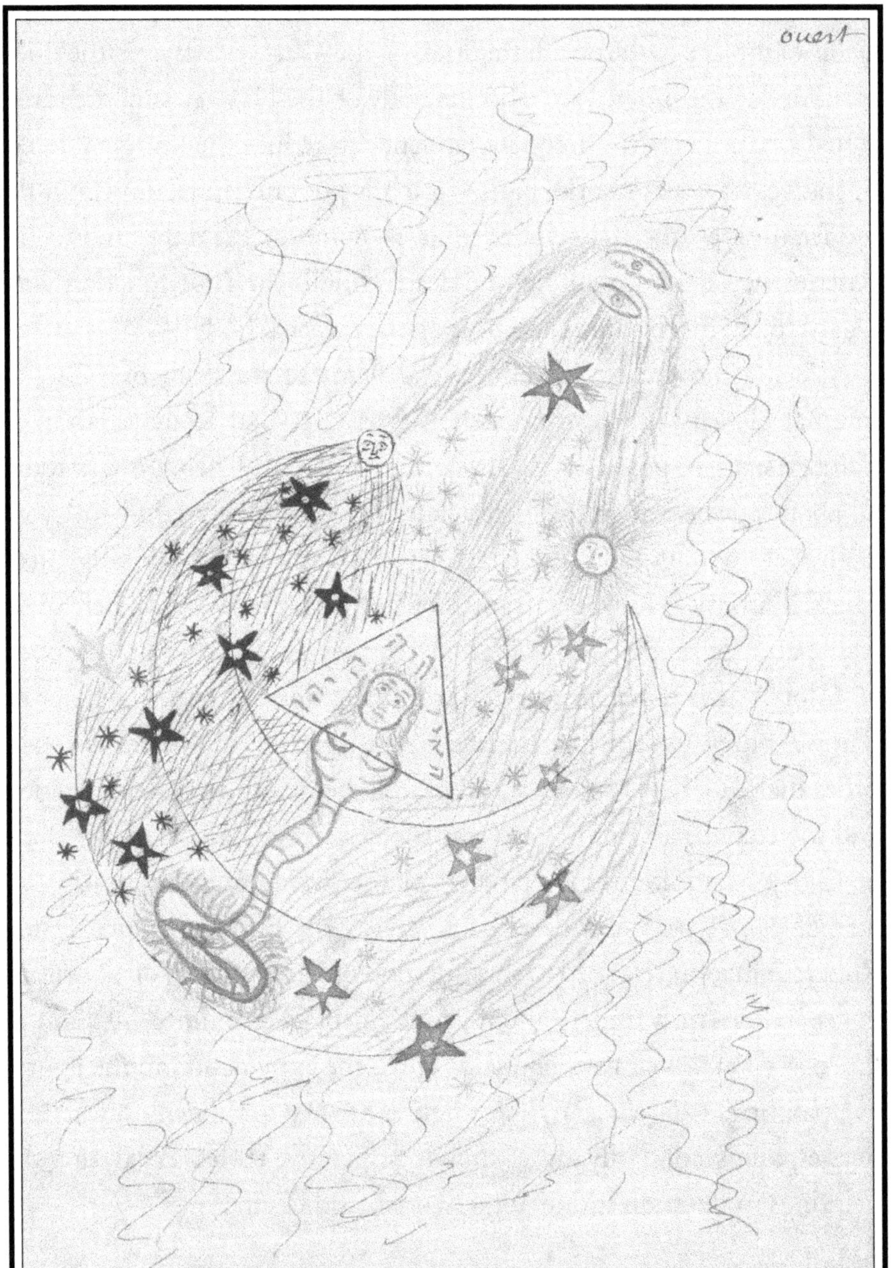

The Order of Knight-Masons Élus Coëns of the Universe

We thus see that the artisanal function is comprehensive here. As for the term Élus Coëns, it is obviously specific to the priestly function.

The "élu" is the "consecrated," the one who tends towards "holiness." In duality, the chosen one is the one who chooses axialization, who turns towards the nondual orientation. It is the manifestation of free will. In other words, it is the choice by the soul to turn to the spirit rather than to the body and to drag the body into this reversal.

The *coën* is the priest. Note that the Hebrew word begins with the letter Kaph and the sound [k]. This priest is both directed and irrigated by *Keter,* the Crown. The Hebrew word *Choshen* designates the breastplate of the high priest of the Temple of Solomon, the *Coën Gadol.* The word is made up of the same letters as *Nachash,* the serpent, and *Nechoshet,* the brass.

The letter Teth is associated by its shape with the serpent. It also evokes, according to interpretations, the belly (which also refers to the serpentine powers) and the shield. The belly can thus represent the protected place of the transmutation.

The Élu Coën is thus the one who devotes himself to transmutation, through theurgy and inner alchemy.

We see, through these few sketched entries, all that can be said of the operativity of a carefully considered order name. This is why the secret grades often change their names as their work progresses to signify the phase of the Great Work underway.

SACRAMENTS

THIRD LETTER TO FRIENDS OF THE SPIRIT • SECOND SERIES

T IS TRADITIONAL TO HAVE SEVEN SACRAMENTS in the Christian culture of Roman Catholic inspiration: baptism, confirmation, eucharist, holy orders, marriage, reconciliation, and anointing of the sick. However, Jesus never fixed the number of seven sacraments. Certain episodes of his life that stand out have progressively been typified in sacraments by interpretation. The process lasted until the 12th century and the number of sacraments was imposed by adherence to the symbolism of the septenary. Catholics, Orthodox, and Protestants have different approaches to this subject. The Orthodox vary the number of sacraments from two to ten, although the number of seven is often put forward. Among Protestants, only two sacraments are retained: baptism and the eucharist, which is not without foundation. The eucharist in fact contains and realizes all the sacraments and Jesus particularly insisted on baptism: "Go ye therefore, and teach all nations, baptizing them in the name of the Father, and of the Son, and of the Holy Ghost" (Matthew 28:19). On the other hand, the sacraments are already present in the Old Testament and manifest the old covenant. The manna episode is a sacrament that prefigures the eucharist.

There is no sacrament without the action of the Holy Spirit or without Grace because it is the self-communication of God that finds signification and function in the formal sacrament. In this, the sacraments differ from sacramental signs such as simple blessings, but this distinction is less marked in the Orthodox Church than in the Roman Church. We are with the sacrament in the dimension of the ecology of the divine gift. God gives continually in an infinite number of ways to recognize himself in duality. The sacraments fix recognition. This fixation, this mark, takes shape in the use of the Holy Chrism. We find in the sacrament the ternary form—energy—essence, the form being word, gesture, and matter.

The sacraments arise from a reading of the life of Jesus and outline an operative Christic journey, but many other neglected episodes convey an operative nature. We will study later how to decrypt them through an example. In this journey the Roman Church considers the three sacraments of baptism, confirmation (gift and seal of the Holy Spirit) and the eucharist as forming the Christian initiation. This brings us closer to the Protestant idea of the sacraments. These are three degrees of initiation (or two, for there can be no efficacy of baptism without the action of the Holy Spirit) that constitute one initiation. Moreover, the liturgy celebrates them together, particularly for adults.

Symbolically, it is the renewal of the covenant: Exodus from Egypt (OT), Passover (NT), baptism, bond with the Father—Gift of the Law (OT), Pentecost, confirmation, bond with the Holy Spirit—Feast of Tabernacles, Last Supper, eucharist, bond with Christ. Baptism corresponds to a new birth (leaving the stream through the desire for God, the memory or sense of nonduality). Confirmation corresponds to the growth of the New Man, the total human being, and the eucharist to the ingestion of food for the Body of Glory, an alchemical operation which is repeated until the ultimate realization, the Reintegration of the Heavenly Jerusalem where all duality is abolished. This is illustrated by two responses of Jesus to Nicodemus: "Verily, verily, I say unto thee, Except a man be born again, he cannot see the kingdom of God." (John 3:3) and "Verily, verily, I say unto thee, Except a man be born of water and of the Spirit, he cannot enter into the kingdom of God" (John 3:5). We have the water of revelation, of love, and the fire of elevation. Sea water is akin to blood, which evokes the alchemical operation of the eucharist by the heating of the fire of the Spirit. "And Jesus, when he was baptized, went up straightway out of the water: and, lo, the heavens were opened unto him, and he saw the Spirit of God descending like a dove, and lighting upon him" (Matthew 3:16).

Lucian Blaga (1895–1961) drew our attention to the fact that dogmas are vehicles of mysteries and that generally heresies are more "reasonable" than official dogmas. In fact, the presence of Christ in the eucharistic operation cannot be grasped by reason. The inability of analytical thought to grasp the dogma or the mystery leads either to its outright rejection or to a reversal within consciousness. It is the energy of conversion that opens up other non-analytical ways of thinking and other knowledge. However, the sacraments, especially baptism, are intimately linked to the access to knowledge. After the injunction to baptize already mentioned (Matthew 28:19), Jesus adds "Teaching them to observe all things whatsoever I have commanded you: and, lo, I am with you always, even unto the end of the world" (Matthew 28:20). Baptism and the teaching of knowledge, or more precisely the teaching of access to knowledge, are inseparable.

The eucharistic operation is not a novelty brought by Jesus at the Last Supper. The archetype has been in operation for a long time and the myths have shifted from one culture to another. The eucharist already existed in Egypt two thousand years before our era as evidenced by certain papyri, and was present with five ingredients instead of two in Pythagoreanism. However, the ancient theocratic ritual, the rite of the ogre or the divine giant, is even more radically reversed in the eucharistic modality introduced by Jesus. The giant, divine initiator, original ancestral initiator of pre-Christian traditions, returns man to his own divinity by absorbing and digesting human mortality. He eats the human, that is to say the multiple, the scattered, to make one and to leave room for

Being. Christ, also divine initiator, the new ancestor, the ultimate ancestral initiator, gives himself to eat as immortal matter. Here we have two ways of approaching the same rite of death and resurrection, reflecting one another.

THE WAY OF BREAD AND WINE

FOURTH LETTER TO FRIENDS OF THE SPIRIT • SECOND SERIES

HE INTERPRETATION OF THE RITE OF THE eucharist is manifold, ranging from iconophagy,⁵⁰ which it can marginally be associated with, to the alchemy of the Body of Glory. As we have already said, it is not a rite instituted by Jesus. It comes from other traditions and is part of the immense complex that symbolically and operatively associates the two mythemes of the vase and its contents. It is a *mysterium,* a word of Greek origin translated into the Latin *sacramentum,* a mystery that continues to deepen. The eucharist is the food that truly makes us Alive, that is, "immortal." In all traditions, the mystery of the vessel and what it contains is a path of immortality, not an immortality to last which remains dualistic, but the nondual immortality that arises from the reunion of all things. For Christians, it is a matter of communion with Christ (the Principle), in Christ, and through Christ. It is also the food of travelers: *Ecce panis angelorum factus cibus viatorum,* "Here is the bread of angels, the bread of eternal life that is the food of travelers." Travelers are those who go to the Heavenly Jerusalem, to the Temple of the Spirit in the Body of Glory, the body of immortality. We find the Island of the Immortals of non-Christian tradition.

The eucharist, a projection of the archetypal primitive rite of reunion, is intimately linked to baptism and particularly to the baptism of the Spirit. Every baptized person is a *de facto* priest and can carry out the eucharist, symbolically but above all operatively, in himself. It is an internal alchemical marriage. This is why the sacrament of marriage is a form of the eucharist, again operatively through the internal alchemy that it allows in a substance-energy-essence process. There is a transmutation until total non-separateness. This is why in Orthodox marriage we have the exchange of rings and the crowning of the spouses which evokes the alchemical iconography of the King and the Queen in their "chymical weddings." The eucharist actualizes "here and now," the "already and not yet," that is to say the Recognition of our divine, non-separated nature or the Reintegration of the primordial nondual Source.

Bread and wine are two products offered by nature due to the transformation brought by human beings. They carry within themselves, without metaphysics, philosophy, or theosophy, the alchemical power of the eucharist. This is why we speak of a "way of bread and wine" upstream of the eucharist, not in a temporal perspective but in a vertical gaze between archetypes and forms.

Rather than opposing leavened and unleavened bread as in Jewish traditions, we can understand them as belonging to the same alchemical process of transmutation. In Hebrew, leaven is called *chametz,* beginning with the letter Cheth which means "closure," while the word *matzah,* unleavened bread, ends with the letter Hé, the double polarity of which we have seen (the world above and the world below) in Tetragrammaton. This is the letter of reunion, of alchemical marriage. The closed world of Cheth allows fermentation, necessary before the alchemical wedding and the nondual release of Hé in Tetragrammaton. There is a time for fermentation and a time when fermentation is useless, even toxic, because it would mean a return to duality. Jewish traditions speak to us of the "bread of shame," the bread obtained without effort, "undeserved," which does not engage in the alchemical process of integration and reunion of opposites, which thus strengthens the contractions of consciousness and the separation between subject and object. This is the bread of Jacob, "the crooked man," before he became "the upright

The Way of Bread and Wine

man," Israel, the New Man. The common word for bread, *lechem,* comes from *lacham,* associated with combat, with battle. The recovery, the rectification, is an initiatory struggle.

Emmanuel Swedenborg describes this process of Christification when he comments on the episode of the multiplication of the loaves by Jesus (*Apocalypse Explained* 617): "they had received and appropriated to themselves His doctrine; this is what they ate spiritually; therefore natural eating followed, that is, flowed in out of heaven with them as the manna did with the sons of Israel, unknown to them; for when the Lord wills, spiritual food which also is real food but only for spirits and angels, is changed into natural food, just as it was turned into manna every morning."

We have a similar process with wine. The traditional winegrower, like the traditional baker who does not use chemical or artificial additions, is an alchemist. In Hebrew, wine is said to be *yayin* which has a numerical value of 70, just as the Torah presents "seventy levels of reading" to signify the permanent deepening of the mystery. 70 is also the numerical value of *sod,* the secret. There is an alchemical secret in the way of bread and wine. Again, we have a process that starts with fermented wine and continues with unfermented wine, with fermentation no longer necessary. In certain esoteric currents, as was the case with the Rose-Croix tradition of Armand Toussaint, the eucharist is celebrated with unfermented wine. Wine can help reach states in which the "secret" becomes accessible. Other more hallucinogenic substances can be used momentarily such as ayahuasca, iboga, or, in Europe and the Middle East, those derived from the fly agaric or the panther cap. Christ could be qualified as a man-panther, but also the panther neutralizes the dragon in the traditional bestiary by his breath, associated here with the divine Word. These substances can help to create a breach in the opacity of the person, in the prison of duality, but once the interval is opened to nonduality, fermentation is no longer necessary and the process of transmutation becomes internal.

In Hebrew, the word blood can be translated as *dam*. Often it is spilled blood. It is associated with the vine in Genesis 49:11: "Binding his foal unto the vine, and his ass's colt unto the choice vine; he washed his garments in wine, and his clothes in the blood (*dam*) of grapes." Also in Revelation 14:19–20: "And the angel thrust in his sickle into the earth, and gathered the vine of the earth, and cast it into the great winepress of the wrath of God. And the winepress was trodden without the city, and blood came out of the winepress, even unto the horse bridles, by the space of a thousand and six hundred furlongs." *Adom* means red and Adam is the "red man." But the word blood can also be translated, more rarely, by *netzach* which designates grape juice or blood, for example in Isaiah 63:3, "I have trodden the winepress alone; and of the people there was none with me: for I will tread them in mine anger, and trample them in my fury; and their blood (*netzach*) shall be sprinkled upon my garments, and I will stain all my raiment." *Netzach* is also Eternity, the *sefirah* of the pillar of love in the Sefirotic Tree. Associated with *Hod,* the *sefirah* that is laterally opposed to it on the pillar of righteousness in the Sefirothic Tree, *Netzach* allows the prophets to access the vision. Wine allows one to see. Up to a certain level, it is fermented, then fermentation is no longer necessary because the process is completely internal.

For Moses (Exodus 24:8), as for Jesus (Matthew 26:28), the blood is that of the Covenant.

"And as they were eating, Jesus took bread, and blessed it, and brake it, and gave it to the disciples, and said, Take, eat; this is my body. And he took the cup, and gave thanks, and gave it to them, saying, Drink ye all of it; For this is my blood of the new testament, which is shed for many for the remission of sins. But I say unto you, I will not drink henceforth of this fruit of the vine, until that day when I drink it new with you in my Father's kingdom." (Matthew 26:26–29)

We have by an alchemical transmutation an alliance between *Malkuth* (place/state of the Last Supper) and *Keter,* the Kingdom, which coincide in *Tiferet,* the Christ, principle of all Reintegration.

Let's see how this is expressed in the Lord's Prayer (Matthew 6:9–14). Let's take a look at its most popular version, which is already full of information. Other subtle dimensions would appear by resorting to the full Latin, Greek, or Hebrew versions, but there is already much with the resources we have previously approached.

Our Father which art in heaven

This is about *Keter*, the Crown, that is to say nondual Consciousness, first emanation of the neither-dual-nor-nondual Consciousness.

Hallowed be thy name

This is about Tetragrammaton, not pronounceable, but accessible by one of its pronounceable names within duality. The tetragrammaton is itself an emanation of the Nameless of which nothing can be said.

Thy kingdom come

Nondual consciousness can radiate within duality. It is the reign of the Hidden King, of the Self, nondual even within duality.

Thy will be done in earth, as it is in heaven

May the luminous principles that govern *Keter* be expressed in *Malkuth*. In reality, there is no distinction between nonduality and duality. One is the mirror of the other. It is a matter of conscious gaze and attention. Absolute Will is also Absolute Love and Absolute Freedom.

Give us this day our daily bread

This is the bread of Liberty, the bread of this day, of the very moment. There is no longer any causality, only the outpouring.

And forgive us our debts, as we forgive our debtors

This is about the flow of the gift, the free flow of energy without it being retained in a form that sterilizes it. In reality, true forgiveness is the recognition of non-separation. When we go beyond the conditionings of the person to recognize the other as the near-ONE, without separation, forgiveness is not even necessary because love without an object reigns.

And lead us not into temptation

Do not allow object identification. Self-remembering is what suspends adherence to the object. The problem is not the adherence itself but to take pleasure in having it and doing it without self-remembering or the Self intervening. The temptations of Jesus are the consequence of his baptism. The orientation towards the Spirit first of all arouses resistance on the part of the adhesions to the peripheries. Any reorientation to the Center generates ruptures. In Matthew 4:3–4 it is written: "And when the tempter came to him, he said, If thou be the Son of God, command that these stones be made bread. But [Jesus] answered and said, It is written, Man shall not live by bread alone, but by every word that proceedeth out of the mouth of God." The temptation of duality, the temptation to live only a material life (leavened bread) gives way to the decision to live in the Spirit and to free oneself from all alienation (unleavened bread).

But deliver us from evil

Deliver us from separation, from duality. It is indeed a fight against fragmentation to conquer the Citadel of Being. Fragmentation prevents all of the above from happening.

Starting at the end of this prayer to return step by step to the first words, we have a description of the path of Reintegration. The first step, the most important because the rest follows "naturally," is self-remembering, without which the permanent eucharist—the marriage between duality and nonduality, which is born and remains in Silence—is impossible.

THE BAPTISM OF THE SPIRIT

FIFTH LETTER TO FRIENDS OF THE SPIRIT • SECOND SERIES

SOME IDENTIFY SIX DIFFERENT BAPTISMS IN THE Bible: the baptism of John (Matthew 3:5–6); the baptism of the Spirit and the baptism of Fire (Matthew 3:7–12); the baptism of transmission or baptism in Christ when Jesus sends his disciples to baptize in the Name of the Father, of the Son, and of the Holy Spirit (Matthew 28:19); the baptism of the sacrifice of the crucifixion (Mark 10:35–40); and the baptism into Moses during the crossing of the Red Sea. All these baptisms are the expression of a single initiatory baptism that converts (reverses) from duality to nonduality. It is always a question of freeing oneself from a dualistic vise. This baptism is of the Spirit.

The baptism of water enacts reconciliation; it has a therapeutic function prior to initiation. It reconciles by revelation (that is, by un-veiling and re-veiling more lightly) and prepares the elevation (Reintegration), associated with fire, to the Spirit. In Hebrew, the word meaning "the heavens," *shamayim,* combines the words "water" and "fire" (*maim* and *esh*).

This is the baptism of Fire and Spirit which, after conversion, the turning of the soul towards the Spirit, releases adhesions and conditioning. John states: "I indeed baptize you with water unto repentance, but he that cometh after me is mightier than I (...): he shall baptize you with the Holy Ghost, and with fire" (Matthew 3:11, also found in Luke 3:16). If we put aside the chronic time to inscribe in the time of the *aion,* we have a propædeutic (Water) preparing the operation itself (Fire and Spirit).

This question of conversion is important: it should be a personal matter, not an organizational one. Sarah and Abraham are often presented as the first converts to monotheism. The question is historically more complex as we have already pointed out. From an operational point of view, they experienced "God beyond God" or nonduality, and this experience is direct, without intermediary. Then they invited others to turn towards non-separation. The problems start when it comes to organizing the conversion, that is, codifying what escapes any rule—an error that splits consciousness, even a fault against the Spirit. Today, becoming a Jew is a very difficult endeavor made up of a multitude of constraints while conversion is a matter of immediacy, of the outpouring of the Spirit.

The teaching of Jesus, from the little that we know historically and outside of the "organization" started by Saint Paul, is free of constraints and also is elevated by intimacy with God and the direct way. This is why this teaching, liberatory like any true initiatory teaching, disturbs both the Jewish religious organization and the Roman political organization, which will join forces to eliminate it.

We find this direct link in Islam with the possibility of secret conversion in an individual relationship with God by the *shahada*, the declaration of faith which is pronounced in consciousness as follows: "I certify that *La ilaha illa illa-ilah, wa ashadu anna Muhammadan rasul ullah*" or "There is no true god (divinity) apart from God (Allah) and Muhammad is His messenger." It is, according to Sufism, a recognition of Oneness. No need for witnesses or confirmation.

The total turnaround, initiated by conversion, is a plunge into nonduality within duality, a baptism of nonduality. The multiple ceases to oppose the One. Duality and nonduality are perceived simultaneously without opposing each other. It is this potential that determines the baptism of the Spirit.

In order to create the conditions for this intimacy and this direct relationship with the Absolute, Jacqueline and Claude Bruley instituted a baptism of the Spirit that was successfully experienced starting in the 1980s within the setting of the Swedenborg Circle. It had previously been offered to the New Church (the Swedenborgian Church), which refused it.

"Through this baptism, a new way opens up for us, this time through the narrow door behind which stands the Lord," wrote Claude Bruley in March 1986.

* * *

Below is an updated version by Jacqueline Bruley on February 23, 2014.

The Holy Table is covered with a red tablecloth, ruby colored if possible.

Those to be baptized are dressed in sky blue for women, white for men.

The person to be baptized approaches the Holy Table alone and without witnesses. They open the Bible to the Gospel of John and read the first four verses of the prologue:

In the beginning was the Word, and the Word was with God, and the Word was God. The same was in the beginning with God. All things were made by him; and without him was not any thing made that was made. In him was life; and the life was the light of men.

Then they confess their faith:

There is only one Principle, the Lord Christ in whom dwells the divine fullness. The original trinity is in Him as the spirit, soul, and body are in humanity. He incarnated in the world for our reintegration and inaugurates his Second Coming by revealing the hidden and internal meaning of the Scriptures.

I invoke Your Spirit to lead me in the purification of my desires, thoughts, and feelings, and in chastity[51] for my body.

What is born of the flesh is flesh. What is born of the Spirit is Spirit. May I be born now to the life of the Spirit. Amen.

The baptized person then takes the Lily laid on the Holy Table and places it in the crystal cup which is placed to the right of the Holy Scriptures.

Then they go back to their place.

They will then receive Communion when the second Communion Cup[52] is presented to them.

COMMITMENT SO THAT MY SPIRIT IS BORN

Primordial and fundamental Love is the love of neighbor. Wisdom is this love lived in everyday life. By these words I mean a love that is expressed exclusively in meekness and humility; a love which in no case seeks dominion, power, glory for oneself or for others, even if they be gods, nor wants to be considered as a unique paragon.

I now want to respond to this Love so that it will lead me to purify my desires, my thoughts, my feelings, and to live in chastity.

Let what is born of matter return to matter. May whatever arises from this spiritual state become my Spirit.

This vase in which I am going to place a Lily symbolizes my purified mind and the Lily corresponds to this purification.

TRANSMISSION

SIXTH LETTER TO FRIENDS OF THE SPIRIT • SECOND SERIES

AND AGAIN,
departing from the coasts of Tyre and Sidon,
[Jesus] came unto the sea of Galilee,
through the midst of the coasts of Decapolis.
And they bring unto him one that was deaf,
and had an impediment in his speech;
and they beseech him to put his hand upon him.
And he took him aside from the multitude,
and put his fingers into his ears,
and he spit, and touched his tongue;
And looking up to heaven,
he sighed, and saith unto him,
Ephphatha, that is, Be opened.
And straightway his ears were opened,
and the string of his tongue was loosed,
and he spake plain.
And [Jesus] charged them
that they should tell no man:
but the more he charged them,
so much the more a great deal they published it;
And were beyond measure astonished, saying,
He hath done all things well:
he maketh both the deaf to hear, and the dumb to speak.   (Mark 7:31–37)

What matters to us is not what a text means but what it can say, what it can teach at various logical levels, according to our perception, regardless of whether it depicts historically established events or not.

In this text from the Gospel of Mark, Jesus heals a deaf mute. The ultimate healing is awakening, as we have already stated. The deaf mute is each of us before we reorient ourselves to take the path of Reintegration. We will examine the text from the perspective of transmission or initiation. Certain gestures teach us how the initiator can operate and how to read the inspired texts to detect the operational aspects.

Jesus isolates himself with the recipient. This isolation is not just physical, it is psychological. They form a Temple in the present moment. Jesus brings him to the Center, into the interval, by his presence: into the crypt of Silence.

Jesus makes the gesture of touching his ears with his fingers. The gesture directs attention, or on the contrary surprises, in order to suspend internal dialogue and open an interval in which to operate.

He uses saliva which is an alchemical salt and can substitute for anointing oil. It can be applied to the forehead, the heart, the hands, the feet... A little-known and seldom-used mode of transmission is the kiss. Through saliva, the information that conveys the higher intention is transmitted to the recipient. Consciousness-energy reorganizes around this information.

Finally, Jesus looks up to heaven and sighs. He places his consciousness at the top of himself, the crown, inhaling before breathing out and uttering, from the silence, the injunction *"Ephphatha!"* "be opened!" In other words, "wake up!" The word is spoken in the interval into which the recipient was led by the succession of gestures. It is not processed by the analytical brain but acts directly at the level of deep beliefs generating a new paradigm and a reorientation, a reversal.

"To open up" is to let the Light pass through, to leave the place free for Being.

We can extract from this significant episode in the life of Jesus the following mode of transmission:

Take the recipient aside.
Advance the fingers towards the heart, throat, and forehead.
Put saliva on the index finger, middle finger, and thumb of the right hand.
Look up to the sky (consciousness at the Crown) and sigh (blow on saliva).
Apply saliva to forehead, throat, and heart in that order.
Say "Ephphatha!" That is to say "Open up!"

(Possible pronunciation: "Etfatatch.")

THE CRYPTIC DOCTRINE

SEVENTH LETTER TO FRIENDS OF THE SPIRIT • SECOND SERIES

TO REORIENT THE SERPENTINE POWERS BACK TO the Center where they will naturally axialize, it is not necessary to perform rituals. A direct path is always possible through self-remembering regardless of our peripheral position. The further the periphery is from the Center, the greater the effort required.

In a gradualist approach, rituals, sounds, words, and gestures, considered as magical or theurgic, can be of service by establishing alliances with memories coagulated within Consciousness that we will designate as spirits, angels, archangels... in a gradation that goes from form to essence and that varies from one tradition to another. The personification of these self-conscious memories is then a cultural anchor that makes it possible to join them or put them into action. The principle of analogy is at work in this process. Note that these entities, these more-or-less autonomous energy-consciousnesses, can respond on their own without operator intervention because the entire universe is a structure of response.

The action of these entities depends more on the sounds emitted than on the concepts or ideas expressed in the rituals, hence the importance of reconnecting with a secret grammar, mainly through attention paid to the sounds. We can think of this action as that of vibrational harmonics within an infinite field of energies in motion. Similarly, images can elicit energetic responses within consciousness. We find this art and this science in the monastic traditions of illuminators, for example, among certain cathedral builders or certain architects. The image can represent a person, but it will nonetheless be a geometric figure. It is this that conveys the information on the basis of which the energy will move.

Each of us is organized as an entity from an essence which, when informed, generates an energy-consciousness which, being informed, bestows form. This information is the Name, Signature, Agreement, Color... which is our foundation. They are, in a way, the extensions of our essence at different logical levels or peripheries of creation.

Our coat of arms—not the coat of arms that is visible, but the internal coat of arms that remains intimate—combines curves and straight lines, according to the secret geometry of the interval. Curves and straight lines belong to the primordial serpentine powers, the "worms" represented in all traditions in the form of nagas or dragons. It is from the "sex of ISIS" that the raw material of internal alchemy is gathered. This is the first duality, the first threadlike material for the weaving of forms. Direct association with these potencies is a source of power, but this power is above all a power of liberation, of Reintegration by the unweaving of forms. Only the anointing of the Spirit confers this covenant.

From a "magical" point of view, we are constantly creating duality through our thoughts, projections, words, and actions, most of the time in total unconsciousness. The projected images, more or less coherent, coagulate with others of the same vibratory nature and influence the world. We create the world, individually and collectively. In the great memory of dualistic time, of *chronos*, there is an infinite stock of potential ideas, the most beautiful as well as the most atrocious, which can thus be actualized. It is the degraded reflection of the triad divine intention–will–action according to Martinez de Pasqually. Energy is thought, willed, imagined, then desired, and finally made form. Thought creates the mold for form. Desire brings it raw substance, the matter of the form to come. Depending on the orientation of consciousness, the form will be a reflection of the divine, the nondual (the divine beauty, divine good, and divine truth of Swedenborg) to which it will lead, or a dualistic alienation strengthening the adhesions to form. Hence the prior importance of the intention directed to the highest in oneself. The way of the Rose-Croix is solely a way of Intention, an always "superior" intention that steadfastly reaches beyond itself. Going beyond, crossing through what is presented, is permanent. The Intention, emitted by the Word, comes from the Spirit and returns to it. The reception of Intention passes through the Crown, but the Place/State of reception is the Heart. Intention comes from and returns to nonduality. It crosses duality and comes up against the forces of fragmentation and opposition. Little or nothing remains of this Intention if it is drawn to the peripheries too far from the influence of the Center. The Lightbringer, who conveys the Intention, cannot keep it in its integrity if he is forced to disperse himself. He must make the opposites coincide in order to re-unite and reorient to the Center. In duality, the entities, more-or-less autonomous energy-consciousnesses, are double: "angelic" or "demonic." The adept re-unites them in nondual freedom.

The New Man, the complete human being, accompanies and grasps the influence of the Word, Eternal Fire, within duality-matter and then transmutes it until the final Reintegration.

SAINT PARASKEVA

EIGHTH LETTER TO FRIENDS OF THE SPIRIT • SECOND SERIES

PARASKEVA IS A VERY POPULAR SAINT IN ROMANIA, where she is celebrated on October 14. Her name comes from the Greek *parasceve* which means "preparation."

We will not dwell here on the many superstitions which surround the worship of this extraordinary and difficult to understand saint.

Historically, she was a very beautiful young woman, Christian, full of wisdom, who dedicated her life to the divine. She was born on October 14 in the village of Epivates in Thrace in the 10th century. At the age of fifteen she abandoned her parents, her fortune, and her country for a long journey which took her in particular to Jaffa, Jerusalem, and Constantinople. The trip ended in Greece, in Kallikrateia where she lived as a hermit before dying, still young.

She therefore watches over spiritual journeys or, more exactly, the nomadic alternative and the circulation of noble adventurers in quests.

After her death, many miracles took place. Her cult has grown steadily to this day. Her body is kept in Iasi, Moldavia. It is the destination of many pilgrimages. She is very revered in Romania by the Romani people who find in her a distant trace of the Indian goddesses of their origin (the Romani language derives from Sanskrit). It is fasting, or asceticism, that constitutes the classic offering to Saint Paraskeva, the fast that prepares for death to the world.

Paraskeva in fact prepares for the great voyage, for death and its initiatory corollary, the deification of the human being by the constitution of the Body of Glory. Any initiatory journey, any spiritual pilgrimage, is a preparation, a repetition of the unique journey back to one's own divinity. Like her, the quester must renounce all attachment, all identification, all worldliness.

Paraskeva is also called *Vinerea Mare* or *Vinerea Santa,* Mother Friday or Holy Friday. She therefore integrates the archetype of the goddess represented by Venus, Minerva or Juno, Petka or Živa. Paraskeva is an ancient Christianized goddess. We observe here a shift from the mythemes of goddesses of the "isiac" archetype[53] towards the figure of the Saint.

Also considered a formidable witch, Paraskeva can appear ambivalent, capable of using both forces of creation and forces of destruction depending on the circumstances.

The popular prayer of Paraskeva illustrates this point perfectly:

O Thou, my God, listen to Thy servant. I ask Thee to tell those who will come after me that they celebrate me with fasts, with liturgical services, and light candles to honor me on this day. If they do so, may they all be blessed, like their houses, their children, their wheat fields, and all their animals! Let all evil or enchanting spirits flee from them! May their souls be enlightened!

The others, those who will not pray in church or who will work that day, damn them! He who will respect my feast and fast, may he be healthy and have all his sins forgiven! But whoever will not honor Holy Friday or who will defile it voluntarily by eating meat or cheese or who will defile this day with debauchery, or steal, or do evil, only for all these, all their parents, may everything fail no matter what they do!

Beyond the popular form of Paraskeva, inscribed in this common prayer, the saint represents the traditional goddesses of the Center, guarantors of the balance of power. She is also an exorcist. The three prohibitions that she poses are typical of arousal pathways: no work, that is, production, no food intake, and no sex on her birthday. It therefore invites the art of doing nothing, giving nothing, taking nothing, to register on the axis of Being and to self-fertilize as a divinity.

Paraskeva appears to us both as Sophia and as a luminous courier, who seals "Hell" and opens "Paradise," which is why, in certain assemblies, she is celebrated from October 14 to October 18, the day of Saint Luke or Lux, the Light.

INVOCATION TO PARASKEVA

O Goddess of Friday,
Goddess bearer of the Emerald of the Great Morning,
Thou who guides the pilgrims on the Way of Return,
Thou who reminds every heart that it beats in the breast of a God,
I kneel in Thy bosom and let myself be carried by the divine breath.

O Paraskeva,
Thou who veils and unveils,
Thou who makes and unmakes,
Thou who creates and destroys,
Instruct me in the Divine Play.

O unobtainable Goddess,
May I make myself worthy to hide in the folds of Thine Emerald cloak.
May I bathe in Thy nocturnal light as in Thy morning light.
O Thou who knows how to listen to the teaching of Lucifer without losing Thyself, remaining in the Light of Christ, indicate to me the Way of the Heart, the Way of going alone to the Light of Light.

O Paraskeva,
Thou who veils and unveils,
Thou who makes and unmakes,
Thou who creates and destroys,
Instruct me in the Divine Play.

O Green Isis,
Thou whose face is reflected in the Grail Cup,
Make my heart a perfect receptacle
To receive the Holy Mystery
That seals the Great Work.

O Paraskeva,
Thou who veils and unveils,
Thou who makes and unmakes,
Thou who creates and destroys,
Instruct me in the Divine Play.

Paraskeva Maranatha!

Response: Paraskeva Maranatha Amen.

Offering: Fasting and Light (a lighted candle).

Saint Paraskeva

SAINT ISABELLA

NINTH LETTER TO FRIENDS OF THE SPIRIT • SECOND SERIES

ING DENIS (1261–1325) AND QUEEN ISABELLA[54] (1271–1336) played an essential role in the development of an exceptional Portuguese tradition and theosophy, as we have recalled previously.

We will not dwell here on their striking history (easily accessible from available books, studies, and articles) so that we can focus on certain constitutive facts of the myth and of the singular spirituality attached to Saint Isabella.

She was considered a saint during her lifetime by the people and canonized in 1625 (during the Spanish domination of the so-called two crowns period) by the Church of Rome, which wanted to capture her influence in this way. However, her worship, even within the Roman Catholic Church, retains its idiosyncrasies and liberties.

King Denis and Queen Isabella protected the Templars (hunted by the Kingdom of France during the reign of Philip the Fair) and preserved their properties against the Pope's demands by founding the Order of Christ. The Order of Christ welcomed the routed Templars. The king, skillfully, gave them back their fortresses, intended to fight against Moorish incursions, and even, a few years later, the magnificent and important Convent of Christ in Tomar which had been the seat of the Order of the Temple in Portugal.

Queen Isabella developed and institutionalized the cult of the Holy Spirit, already present as early as 1230, but in confidence. This worship, both testamental and pagan, establishes the individual directly in the heart of God without going through the Church. This is why the Church banned this cult and tried to eradicate it, but it persisted, particularly in the Azores and Brazil. Very recently the cult of the Holy Spirit was reestablished in Portugal but under the control of the Roman Church. However, the cult of the Holy Spirit was also restored in its original frame of reference and in complete independence, mainly thanks to our friend Manuel Gandra, whose work is authoritative in this matter.

The cult of the Holy Spirit, together with the myth of the Fifth Empire and Sebastianism (the myth of the Hidden King), forms a traditional ensemble remarkable for the multiple hidden dimensions it conceals and whose exploration seems inexhaustible.

The hymn to Santa Isabella that follows enshrines the most important myths conveyed by the life and work of Queen Isabella for a serpentine operativity that fulfills the promise of the *Hymnal to the Hidden King*.[55] This last operative set, inscribed both in the Lusitanian tradition and in nondual metaphysics, both local and universal, finds its center and its axial balance in the Hymn to Inès,[56] the fulfillment of which resides in the Hymn to Saint Isabella. Inès and Isabella, whose first names both begin with the I of Isis, are reflections of each other. Analogously, Inès is the Middle Room and Isabella the Upper Room. The pilgrim must go through the first to reach the second.

HYMN TO SAINT ISABELLA

Ysabel (study for *o Milagre das rosas*)
Lima de Freitas

Eternal Queen
Holy before holiness
Goddess-Rose and Rose of the Goddess
Light of lights
Initiator of the Poet
Protectress of the Knights of Christ
I hear your light step
That approaches
And beats my heart
I bow down to your bare feet
To bathe them in red and white petals
I get drunk on your perfume

Flesh and Sanctity
Expression of your noble suffering
Like your Joy
You who embody Grace
Body of Freedom
Exiled Queen
Celebrated Queen
Love embodied
Permanent forgiveness
Granted to the ignorant
Carried by fear and anger
Freed from opaque royal courts
Great liberator
Of the wanderers of the Spirit
Of artists and rebels
Who knows the One
Who dwells in fullness
Despite the dualistic chains
That cross the rumor
Retired in your cell
To spring
Frail and pale
Preceded by a shower of golden drops
Accompanied by a cloud of roses
You, Sophial of the Harbor of the Grail
Angel of Peace
Whose presence
Takes away all misery
That of the body
Like that of the soul

Saint Isabella

Queen-Spirit in fulfillment
Who announces, prolongs,
And fulfills the prophecy
Since the first intention
Deign to put down your scarlet shawl
On my colors
That in your Name
I visit the eight directions of space
On your white steed
To proclaim there
Your Eternal Royalty
And your illuminated and beneficent presence
May your Wisdom rule from now on
The worlds and the times.

Make the miracle permanent.

CROCODILE

TENTH LETTER TO FRIENDS OF THE SPIRIT • SECOND SERIES

HE *CROCODILE, OR THE WAR OF GOOD AND EVIL That Happened During the Reign of Louis XV*, is a unique creation in the rich and complex work of the "Unknown Philosopher," Louis-Claude de Saint-Martin. The philosopher of Amboise surprised both his followers and the casual reader with this fantastic book. Robert Amadou, who wrote the preface to the second edition[57] of the *Crocodile* in 1962, after the too long silence that followed the first edition of 1799, speaks of a book doubly "unusual," by its genre and by its place within the writings of Louis-Claude de Saint-Martin.

The work was finished, according to Saint-Martin, in 1792 but was expanded until 1796 and completed for printing in 1798. This speaks to whether this book fits into the events of the French Revolution. But, even if the theme of the book evokes revolutionary struggle, Louis-Claude de Saint-Martin stages (between burlesque and parody) some fundamental ideas of his illuminist doctrine. "The war of good and evil that happened during the reign of Louis XV" constitutes a partial typology for the French Revolution but above all evokes the cosmic struggle between two principles, good and evil, without falling into the trap of an excessively dualistic Manichean posture. In this "work of gaiety," as Saint-Martin designates it, the attentive reader will easily detect the main principles of Saint-Martinian theosophy.

The *Crocodile* is often underestimated, even ignored, by readers unaccustomed to confronting a text that is at the same time poetic, epic, and magical. The text is confusing—that is its strength. The book disturbs, leads off the beaten track of initiation, and reveals in backlight or in full light the truths to which, during his life, the Unknown Philosopher devoted himself. Enigmas and allegories, even absurdities, carry a strangely modern teaching, sometimes with Rabelaisian accents. Indeed, of all the books by Louis-Claude de Saint-Martin, it is undoubtedly the one that seems to us to be the most contemporary from the outset. For the struggle depicted by Saint-Martin (who was passionate about the Revolution from which he expected much—too much in reality) represents the struggle between two principles: one of fragmentation, the other of return to the One, to the work within the infinity of creation since the "Fall," just as within each individual. The *Crocodile* also denounces the meanderings of the "teachers," the bearers of modern thought at the end of the 18th century, which Philippe Muray,[58] in a masterful book, tells us continues perhaps even today after "the religious crisis of the 19th century" in a strange "socio-occultism."

Certain ideas advanced in the *Crocodile* are found in the texts collected by Robert Amadou and published by Fayard[59] to introduce Saint-Martin into the French philosophical corpus, such as (among others) the question of signs and ideas. The tension between tradition and modernity, between *aion* and *chronos*, between freedom and replication, is at the heart of this book, set up through the Crocodile himself, symbol of Satan, the false Lucifer (bearer of Light), the characters of Eléazar, who evokes Martinez de Pasqually, Sédir, the Man of Desire, Madame Jof, the Sophia, and of a Society of Independents that typifies the followers of the initiation of Reintegration in its archetypal dimension.

According to Louis-Claude de Saint-Martin, it is a "work of gaiety."[60] It is a book that astonishes. It is a book that awakens. It is a relevant book at this uncertain turn of the millennium. Its Silenic dimension makes it a significantly initiatory work for the present time.

The work is organized into a prologue and three parts in which the place-states of consciousness that are hell, earth, and heaven, along with their mirror-relationships, are established. The first part discusses the dualist oppositions in revolutionary Paris, and the attempt to elevate these pairs of opposites through debate. It is a failure that leads to the opening of access to the infernal world, or static duality, explored in the second part. The third part takes us into the world of the Stars, an inverted reflection of the underworld, and allows us to shed light on nonduality.

Note first of all that starting with the prologue, the initiatory stake is set out: genies subservient to the world of matter, fragmentation, and duality, eleven hundred in number, attack Eléazar, prototype of the initiate, who wants to "break the mold of time in which they have their antics." The setting of duality is time, characterized by replication. By grasping the "here and now," the initiate escapes the dualistic grip and the chain of causalities that ensure the alienating reproduction of forms. It is through various confusions that the genies will operate.

Eléazar's allies are (in material, physical terms) Sédir, Ourdeck, and Rachel. Sédir is the Man of Desire who seeks to reintegrate the primordial source by understanding the situation in which he is immersed. The Spirit-Man is already present in Sédir, and already at work, unlike Ourdeck—a Man of Desire too, but only through personal will. The fire of the Spirit is not yet activated in him. It is through his struggle within duality, against what he identifies as evil, that he will awaken this fire and experience the reversal towards the Spirit. Rachel is love—she evokes the heart that characterizes the New Man. This love ranges from sentiment to Love-without-an-Object under the influence of Wisdom, Sophia.

Eléazar's allies on the spiritual and metaphysical level are the Society of Independents, Madame Jof, the Jeweler, the Tartar woman, and the beneficent genies as opposed to the evil genies. Evil genies are disoriented serpentine powers, without Center. They devote themselves to fragmentation and dissolution. The beneficent genies are serpentine powers oriented towards the Center. They concur in Unity and Reintegration.

The Society of Independents is the society of unknown initiates, not a physical society but an assembly of Friends of the Spirit, the Invisible Church, or the true Society of the Rose-Croix, which needs no organization. The Independents receive the teaching of Madame Jof, the Wisdom born of nonduality who can influence, enlighten, and guide (even within duality) those who learn to "see," in contrast to those who have "their head under their wing," an expression used by Louis-Claude de Saint-Martin, men or genies who are lived through conditioning, while those who "see" are really "alive." It is Wisdom that brings together the members of this Society without their needing any physical encounters. They know the freedom of the Spirit and are freed from dualistic conditionings. The letters S and I evoke the "Unknown Superiors" and the "Solitary Initiates," but also the Hermetic symbol of the serpent rising around a column.

The Tartar woman represents the sacrificed innocence, a sacrifice inherent in the operation of rectification necessary for the turning of the soul towards the Spirit. She operates all the way to Hell. No soul is therefore totally lost and Reintegration is always possible. The Spirit can bring the "corpse" back to life. The jeweler remains an elusive character, however he has certain characteristics of the Spirit of the Good Companion, or of the Guardian Angel or even of Christ. He is the awakener, the initiator, the Presence.

And this Crocodile then, who will finally be defeated, after a long fight, on his way back to the Light, what is his nature and function? The Crocodile represents the set of disoriented, misaligned, and Centerless serpentine powers, agglomerated into an artificial entity, in each of us and in the world. His displayed knowledge is an accumulation of fragments organized into an apparently coherent but illusory whole. He is the principle of division and fragmentation. In a very graphic way, his place is under the pyramid, where this serpentine power can be oriented and axialized. According to the Kabbalah, evil is a good that is out of place, and so is the Crocodile. He is assisted by three characters: the Heavy Woman, the Great Dry Man, and Roson, leader of the revolt, who can be associated with the archaic triangle of Power – Territory – Reproduction which leads the world in the absence of a Center and which we must learn to verticalize and free from dualistic conditionings, alienations, and perversions — to free from temporality.

We are not here going to make an exegesis of this astonishing text, which is much more than a "pleasant" story. Several hundred pages would be necessary, without exhausting the subject, as the book lends itself to many readings according to the logical level approached. We can of course take into account the historical context, but Saint-Martin worked on the level of mythemes and archetypes to allow for initiatory readings. This book can tell us much. Louis-Claude de Saint-Martin undoubtedly denounced scientism, the division of knowledge, a theology that has become "papology," the excesses of power, and the compromises of the aristocrats... We can certainly recognize Cagliostro in the Dry Man and refer to the annoying misunderstanding of Cagliostro by Louis-Claude de Saint-Martin as well as by Jean-Baptiste Willermoz. The two men were wrong about the character and the work of Cagliostro. We can see in this colorful yet profound story a struggle between two types of initiation, but that would be a mistake. It would be more interesting to take this text as a description of the initiatory process of Reintegration, from duality to nonduality, from imitation to invention, from the external to the internal (it is not that which is practiced that is external or internal, but the connection maintained with and through practice). If we go into details, we can distinguish knowledge associated with Hebrew letters, numbers, or even alchemy. The science of correspondences is omnipresent throughout the book. From one reading to the next, we will discover new perspectives and insights.

Even if Louis-Claude de Saint-Martin felt that his work would still have deserved "one more wash," the *Crocodile* is a companion on the way[61] who helps us to assess the distance traveled on the ladder that goes from the Man of the Stream to the Spirit-Man, passing through the Man of Desire and the New Man. It is a text for times of crisis and helps us to see clearly in the confusion. It is a text for today.

A CHIVALRY OF THE SPIRIT

ELEVENTH LETTER TO FRIENDS OF THE SPIRIT • SECOND SERIES

HE MESSIAH IN JUDAISM, THE PARACLETE IN Christianity, the Hidden Imam in Islam, and the Hidden King in Sebastianism all have the same function of fulfilling prophecies. They realize what the prophecies proclaim.

It is not a matter of serving God (exoterism), nor of becoming God (mesoterism), but of being God (esotericism), to recognize oneself as simultaneously the Temple, the Crypt of the Temple, and the Lord of the Temple.

A Chivalry of the Spirit, or Spiritual Chivalry, which seeks the Recognition of oneself as being God, the Lord, traverses traditional forms without rejecting them, to realize the Essence. It is, for the West, Abrahamic, that is to say, it brings together and transcends the three religions of the Book and their many expressions.

The Place of the accomplishment of this chivalric quest is not within form: this is the Imaginal, or the Interval. It can be called interior or internal, but in reality it is neither internal nor external. No duality can account for its nature. Time and space merge and dissolve to make room for Being-without-representation. Each moment of life is nothing more than a celebration of Being, as the moment merges with Eternity.

This Chivalry of the Spirit is opposed to both religion and scholarship through dualist tensions: religion through the tension of dogma, scholarship through the tensions of "scientific rigor" and of history.

The ecumenism of a Chivalry of the Spirit is not a matter of narration and intellectual understanding, but of the grasp of Essence or of evidence of non-separation that makes commentary and injunction unnecessary. The "nondualistic revelation" nullifies all the declared revelations while illuminating them. Our true and divine nature imposes itself in all its splendor and radiance. What is announced and continually postponed by the announcement itself has always been, is now, and will be for all eternity. It is the "already and not yet" that resolves into the "here and now."

This conquest of the Citadel of Being or Great Real is fostered by a companionage, a commitment, and an ethics shared and sealed by Wisdom. Without Wisdom, the stream of duality will sweep away the pretensions of false knights caught up in the little games of ego. It is not about responding to the conditioned desires of the old man but about realizing the eternal youth of the New Man through healing, the rebirth in the Spirit.

This Chivalry of the Spirit is closer to the tradition of the *Fedeli d'Amore* than to orders of chivalry founded in dualistic warrior logic. Dante is a striking illustration of this, whose *Divine Comedy* makes sense within the three traditional contexts of Christianity, Judaism, and Islam.

If we had to formalize a Chivalry of the Spirit, we could think of it as follows:

In the name of the universal Father-Mother, of Abraham, of Moses, of Christ, and of Muhammad, in the name of all the prophets, Be a Knight through and according to the Holy Spirit.

May Sarah, Mary, and Khadija, the true leaders of the Order, bestow unto you the cloak of benevolence and immortality, and may they take back your sword from you. It is useless to you now.

The Spiritual Knight or Knight of the Spirit is one of the "Living." It is the Spirit, the Paraclete, who teaches, reveals, awakens, and realizes, despite all institutionalization, all organization, and all exclusion. There were attempts to institutionalize such chivalry: rituals exist that evoke through symbolism and inspired poetry, and that remain unspeakable and inscrutable, or inaccessible to the replicating self-narration of the ego. However, it is only in the interval that this attainment is revealed.

The Knight of the Spirit is the Green Man, the Green Knight, the Living One who, like al-Khidr, "the green one," makes the deserts green again. He is also associated with Elijah. Al-Khidr and Elijah share the mythemes of the cloak and the color green, among other things. They awaken from the sleep of oblivion. This is the nonduality that irrigates sterile duality, the nondual Knowledge that illuminates fruitless dualistic knowledge.

What characterizes the Knight of the Spirit is precisely that which distinguishes the Spirit, that is, Freedom. He is unpredictable, unexpected, and outside the common paths. He laughs at the rules and teaches in a paradoxical and unconventional way—more "mad monk" than cooperative. He is fully in keeping with the traditions of the Immortals that dwell on the island of the Middle.

THE WAY OF ELIAS ARTISTA[62]

TWELFTH LETTER TO FRIENDS OF THE SPIRIT • SECOND SERIES

THE WAY OF ELIAS ARTISTA (OR THE VEIL OF Elias Artista) is a direct, subitistic path, an immediate unveiling. Of course, in the vast majority of cases, this immersion in the Great Real comes after a rigorous, mysterious propædeutic, a journey through mysteries large and small as well as alchemical, internal alchemy having priority. However, traditionally, it is considered that the disciplines of this propædeutic, its demanding praxis, have nothing to do with the reversal that constitutes the ultimate realization.

The Way of Elias Artista is indicative of three covenants already present. These covenants are neither initiations nor transmissions, but actualizations of what is, buried under the gilding of human conditioning. By it is evoked three seeds of Interiority or three nuclei of Immortality, activated by the covenants.

The three covenants, paradoxically, loosen, cut off adhesions, undo, and disinherit, so that the being recognizes its divine nature and its absolute freedom, its total identification with the Absolute. They each carry an internal alchemical modality: substance – energy – essence.

The first covenant reveals the individual, the inalienable part, "That which remains," beneath the "person," the hidden Self, who is also the "Hidden King." It severs temporality, being neither before nor after. No more fixation with ancestral lineage, personal history, or egoic legend. Nondual consciousness emerges within dual consciousness and persists.

The second covenant destroys the illusion of separation. It reveals the other as oneself, the collective and multiple as One. Dual consciousness dissolves into nondual consciousness. From the many to the One.

The third covenant dissolves spiritual ties. The angel of the turning, this quasi-autonomous power that pronounces the death of death, guides "to a Higher Sense." The archaic triangle of Power – Territory – Reproduction, verticalized by the first covenant, is reabsorbed in the point and carries with it worlds and times. Nondual consciousness is restored "absolutely." From One to Zero, to the Perfect Void and its Fullness.

The alternative of Elias Artista, which crowns, in a way, the three covenants, comes from Grace, from the thrill of Elias Artista, flooding consciousness with the Recognition of his absolute divine identity, of his original and ultimate nature, of his Absolute Freedom, even while in ignorance of it. It is, once again, the Remembrance of Hermes or the Reintegration of Martinez de Pasqually, even if the latter's system seems more laborious and restrictive in comparison to the elusiveness of the Rose-Croix. *La Chose,* according to Martinez de Pasqually, is the Holy Spirit, even the Holy Spirit of Hély, as Robert Amadou has reminded us many times. Elysium, Elijah the prophet, and Hély or Rhély designate a way. They constitute an expression of this path towards Absolute Freedom, the only object of our discourse, just like Hiram, Christian Rosenkreutz, and Christ, according to Fernando Pessoa. The three exits from the tomb illustrate the classical distinctions of hermeticism between the Saturnian body, the Lunar body, the Mercurial body, and the Solar body for an axiality between the Saturnian body and the Solar body, without any other intermediary, to "become Christ (or Osiris, or Buddha, or Shiva) in this body and in this life." These are other, particularly powerful, evocations of our initial tetrad: Altruism – Rites – Play of Consciousness and Energy – Absolute.

Hély, of whom Elias Artista is an evocation, is a very mysterious figure in the Rose-Croix tradition. He is indeed this Holy Spirit who manifests himself by descending on all the successive prophets, that is to say, on the initiate confronted with each of these three deaths and who "sees" beyond them, as doors ajar to the Great Real. Hély is in reality Christ, or more precisely, the Holy Spirit of Christ. The Spirit of Hély, the Holy Spirit of Christ, Christ, *la Chose,* and Elias Artista reveal the Being that Martinez de Pasqually designates as "Messias," the anointed, and who in the invocations that follow allows us to reunite the uncreated (divine) Wisdom, Christ-Sophia or the Rose-Christ, and created Wisdom, the Christ-Cross. The Absolute has engendered worlds and times within itself, playing at forgetting itself. But it deposited in these contractions of Consciousness a covenant in the form of a partial (and thus created) wisdom, a memory or echo of an uncreated divine Wisdom that Consciousness is destined to find. There is nothing but infinity, freedom, nothing but a play of creation and destruction, of light and darkness, of a darkness which is itself now only light. We are beyond nondual consciousness. We can thus speak of the Rose-Croix through Christ, through Hély, and through Elias Artista. Let us pose an audacious but relevant metaphorical shift, echoing our point. Hély in a sense evokes, in the imaginal dimension, Elisha, the grandson of Noah. Elisha founded Lisbon, Lisboa, which was enlarged by Ulysses.[63]

The last lesson of this traditional way, Grace, the thrill of Elias Artista, fully constitutes the Third Testament dear to Joachim de Fiore. The Third Testament complements and makes operative the Old Testament and the New Testament. It is the Testament of the Holy Spirit, characterized by absolute Freedom, absolute Will, and absolute Love. The Old Testament, symbolized by the figure of the Father, is very hierarchical and is characterized by respect for forms, rules, protocols, and work. The New Testament, marked by the presence of the Son, is marked by discipline and faith. The Third Testament, symbolized by the Holy Spirit, brings Essence, whereas the Old Testament and the

New Testament only provided meaning and representation, rather than the naked Presence of the Absolute.

It is not wrong to regard the Three Covenants as operative metaphors for Advents, as Fernando Pessoa suggests:

> In the Fifth Empire there will be the reunion of two forces that have been separated for a long time, but which have been gradually coming together: the left side of knowledge—science, reasoning, intellectual speculation; and its right side—occult knowledge, intuition, mystical and cabalistic speculation. The alliance of Sebastian, Emperor of the World, and the Angelic Pope represents this intimate alliance, this fusion of the material and the spiritual, perhaps without separation. And the Second Coming, or new incarnation of the same Adept, into whom God projected his Symbol, or Son, only represents this same supreme covenant in another way.[64]

Here is a version of the texts of the three covenants of Elias Artista, accompanied by some additional invocations, in their current formulation. This oral Tradition has of course evolved in its formulation, passing from one language to another, from one culture to another, and from one century to another, without losing either its nature, its evocative power, or its alchemical symbolism, each invocation conveying an arcanum. However, it appears to be of Mediterranean origin,[65] with Middle Eastern ramifications and Far Eastern influences. These influences are natural, in particular through ancient Greece and through Spain and Portugal during the great voyages of discovery. Its most marked expressions are indeed Iberian, Italic, and Greek. It was for a time the prerogative of a branch of the Komnenos family and it was often families who were "custodians" of it, aristocratic as well as common. The Portuguese Sebastianist tradition is very close to it. This is why you will find, in addition to this introductory study, a text by Lima de Freitas devoted to the founding myth of Christian Rosenkreutz.[66]

The invocations presented in these pages are accompanied by mantric and alchemical praxis. Internal alchemy is central even while metallic alchemy is not forgotten. There is a paradox in this approach since the quest is enrolled for a time, apparently, in the making of the ways of immortality, while the realization manifests itself in a non-doing, a non-way, an abandonment of all immortality, this being perceived as an ultimate resistance of the "person" in the face of the immanence and the transcendence of Being.

The ceremonial environment is left to the appreciation of the adept who implements the mystery even if some constants remain.

Few have received these covenants, the alternative, or the keys to them. Among those who have received them, few have understood them. Even rarer are those who have implemented them and who have realized them.

Invocation of the Fire Bearer

As the seven streams of the ultimate dragon that presides over all operations of Reintegration condenses in this particular place, a temple dedicated to the great operation desired by *la Chose,* and especially to this Orb, whose green color recalls the one who is always on our left, at an arm's length, carrying life as well as death, the sometimes luminous, sometimes obscure shade that surrounds us and preserves us like the cloak of Elijah, our Green Master:

May the power born of our wandering condense in this Orb, and unite with all the powers of our brother and sister Knights, in their respective priesthood, because one is the Way, one is the Order, one is the One who Abides, the one in whom we have movement, life, and being.

Invocation of the Sophial

May the power of Love, of the Will and the Void, the only power that operates from the world of Silence to the world of the Word, the power that emanates from the secret Orb that preceded the birth of this world and that engendered the ogdoad of the gods of form by the inseparable couple, Primordial Ocean, Infinite Space, Obscure and Inaccessible Darkness that only Elias Artista, Master of the Rose-Croix and our Master, can invoke for us — may this power pour into the chalice of our being, drop by drop. May this nectar transmute our limited being into the Luminous and Glorious Being that we have never ceased to be, deep in the forests of our cycles of manifestation, in the Central Egg of our own Eternity.

Central Invocation of the First Covenant of Elias Artista

O Elias Artista,
    Archangel of the Rose-Croix,
    Lord who guides Pilgrims to the High Citadel of the Gods
    Including our Brother (Sister) in the Ancient Lineage of the Brothers and Sisters of the Rose-Croix.
    Make him (her) know the beating of your wings so that he (she) recognizes in every moment the Miraculous Way, the one that too few humans have traveled.
    Release in him (her) the red power of the winged serpent so that he (she) will be free from all limits and become the Master of his (her) Destiny.
    Animate in him (her) the Secret Seal of the Rose-Croix.
    Tell him (her) of the gateless passage that leads to the Central Earth of Eternal Wisdom.
    Give him (her) both Power and Wisdom, Knowledge and Detachment.

May he (she) establish his (her) home in the Realm Beyond Darkness and Light.

Central Invocation of the Second Covenant of Elias Artista

May the seven Asian currents of the Inner Order of the Rose-Croix withdraw into this sacred Orb that has traveled through time and space to merge with us, to make a new secret alloy for a new redeployment of the Rose-Croix.

May the seven Asian currents of the Inner Order of the Rose-Croix withdraw into this sacred Orb that has traveled through time and space to merge with us, to make a new secret alloy for a new redeployment of the Rose-Croix.

Thus, the perfect eight-petalled Rose fades. By dying to be reborn, the Blossom of the Rose releases its most secret perfume, which will rise to feed the Gods.

Thus the perfect Rose with thirteen petals, by the action of this scepter half-opens its petals, so that the Second Covenant is accomplished.

Invocations of the Third Covenant of Elias Artista

May the thirty-three Rose-Croix who opened the passage of the new Millennium help me!

May the eight currents of the Rose-Croix, the central current of the diamond, and the seven branches of gold merge into a single orb.

May the eight currents of the Rose-Croix traverse the four cones of shadow and become thirteen, deploying their twelve golden twigs around the Central Diamond.

May the work be accomplished in the twelve directions of space from the One Center where the All dwells!

From the thirteen currents of the Rose-Croix are born thirty-three Red Roses, thirty-three flowers of Blood.

May Elias Artista let me know his Seal and teach me to manifest it from Non-Time in the New Times.

That by this stone which bears the impact of the Divine Will is fulfilled the Great Work planned from the beginning of Time by God.

May Elias Artista watch over me, cover me with his wings, and assist me in all my works for the conquest of the Greatest Good.

May Love be revealed to me, may I be one with Truth!

May Divine Truth, Divine Beauty, and Divine Goodness flow within me.

Invocations of the "Transmission" of the Ancient Alternative of Elias Artista

FIRST IMPACT

By the Double Seal of Elias Artista, the Seal Below and the Seal Above, united in a Unique Seal, I invoke Elias Artista, within you, through you, and around you, in all your Works, temporal and timeless.

I invoke Elias Artista, within the Self, through the Self, and around the Self, in all Works, temporal and timeless.

By the Double Seal of Elias Artista, by the Two Serpents entwined in the Fire of Absolute Fusion, I invoke the Christ-Cross, the firstmost secret aspect of our own ultimate divinity, the more-than-human, the divine.

I invoke the Christ-Cross, our inverted Reality whose root is the Absolute.

I invoke the Christ-Cross, within you, through you, and around you, in all your Works, temporal and timeless.

Through the Christ-Cross, Christ-King Rose-Croix, may the Alternative of Elias Artista, the Alternative of the Rose-Croix be presented to you.

Let it be so, because we are gathered in his Name and by his Name.

SECOND IMPACT

By the Double Seal of Elias Artista, the Seal Above and the Seal Below, united in a Unique Seal, I invoke Elias Artista, within you, through you, and around you, in all your Works, temporal and timeless.

I invoke Elias Artista, within the Self, through the Self, and around the Self, in all Works, temporal and timeless.

By the Double Seal of Elias Artista, by the Two Serpents entwined in the Fire of Absolute Fusion, I invoke the Rose-Christ, the second-most secret aspect of our own ultimate divinity, the more than human, the divine. I invoke the Rose-Christ, our inverted Other Reality whose root is the Absolute, which includes the Christ-Cross.

I invoke the Rose-Christ, through you, around you, in all your Works, temporal and timeless.

Through the Rose-Christ, Christ-Sophia Rose-Sophia, may the Alternative of Elias Artista, the Alternative of the Rose-Croix be present within you.

May it be so, because we are gathered in his Name and through his Name.

VALEDICTION

May the Rose-Christ,
    The Free Being,
    The Great Emancipator,
He who freed the primordial man and the primordial woman from numbers and times so that they could celebrate their mystical and alchemical nuptials in the Divine Heart, awaken in us the thirteen roses of Ultimate Realization, and crowns the Hidden King, the Rose-Croix, by the Anointing of Sophia.
    Free you are,
    Free you remain.

THE SUPERIOR GEOMETRY OF THE BUILDERS[67]

THIRTEENTH LETTER TO FRIENDS OF THE SPIRIT • SECOND SERIES

E NOW INVITE YOU TO DISCOVER AN EXTRACT from the fourth story of an instruction entitled *Plans, Languages, Letters & Numbers* and subtitled *The Superior Geometry of the Builders* in reference to the Geometry of Intervals, so important in the Rose-Croix Tradition, this geometry being considered as the key to the Geometry of the Tracing Board.

This document, which with Robert Amadou we have linked to the *Corpus Rhodostaumoticus*,[68] arbitrarily but based on the nature of its exceptional metaphorical teaching, is part of a collection unearthed by Triantaphyllos Kotzamanis.

This considerable collection brings together thousands of pages of documents written in Greek, intended rather for oral transmission, and embracing almost all the fields invested in by the human being: philosophies, metaphysics, religions, mythologies, astronomies, mathematics, physics, medicines, and others.

Until his departure for the Eternal Orient, Triantaphyllos Kotzamanis wondered about the use that should be made of this corpus. The question remains unanswered today. While exoteric and mesoteric education could, to a large extent (but probably not in their entirety) be disseminated within long-established traditional organizations, esoteric education remained largely inaccessible due to the very high level of expertise required. There persists a profound hermetic component, of which *The Superior Geometry of the Builders* is one of the most interesting pieces, bringing together texts that are difficult or even confusing but whose internal meaning is familiar to us.

The collection is clearly part of a major current of the Rose-Croix Tradition, present in Mediterranean countries in recent centuries and beyond in Turkish-speaking countries, which was practiced through two schools, one located in southern Greece, the other more precisely in Ephesus. It is from the teaching of the first of these two schools that Sémélas, among other founders, would have drawn to constitute both his Order of the Lily and the Eagle and his Rose-Croix d'Orient, if we believe certain documents that we were given to examine.

In the last years of the last millennium, Triantaphyllos Kotzamanis devoted several weeks to translating an essential part of this teaching into the French language. The time had come, he said, to experience certain aspects of this hermeticism that was both classical in its principles and deeply original in its very free expression.

The Superior Geometry of the Builders, composed of four stories, conveys an original genesis. Instead of gods, archangels, angels, daimons, or other entities, they are numbers, musical notes, diagrams, letters, syllables, words, and signs that molded the worlds, times, and living forms.

The acts of creation are poems and hymns. Each wave of creation creates a problem that is resolved by a new level of complexity.

The text conveys at the same time a metaphysics, a theurgy, and an internal alchemy. It is an abstract formulation of what is more formally stated by many traditional geneses. It is confusing because it does not allow a representation, mathematical or symbolic, that is current.

An international leader of a traditional initiatory organization with a magical vocation, confronted with this text, did not know what to say: "But where are the gods?" As if the gods were something other than more or less self-conscious energies precisely determined within consciousness

The Superior Geometry of the Builders

by combinations of sounds, numbers, syllables, signs, patterns... This type of reaction, occurring frequently, suggested that it was too early to disseminate such teaching and practice it.

Nevertheless, an inner college experimented with teaching *The Superior Geometry of the Builders*. Some researchers had access to it, but very few understood its interest, power, and richness. Rare were those who implemented the proposed theurgy. Those who realized the arcana of internal alchemy that constitute the true jewels of this text remain exceptions.

Here are some excerpts from the fourth story, the most telling from an alchemical point of view, the least abstract, not commented on, but underlined by a few clues and remarks.

The fourth story begins with these words:

Mist was falling in the land of the Sun. Colors followed one after another and raindrops of knowledge fell from time to time on the lands of the innocent. The liturgy had begun. All the Numbers, Plans, Letters, Syllables, Words, and Signs were gathered for the first Holy Eucharist of Heaven.

We will immediately note the poetic and metaphorical dimension of the text. The sexual symbolism, clearly asserted, is classic of the creative geneses but also of alchemy,[69] external or internal, the former often conveying the arcana of the second, arcana that can be interpreted in the three dimensions of substance, energy, and essence. Deified body and blood, and therefore the powers of deification, constitute the archetypal core of internal alchemy, in all traditions of the West and East. There is in every locus of Consciousness, because of the play of *Natura naturans* and *Natura naturata*,[70] an elixir of immortality.

It must be remembered that this text can only be received in a nondual consciousness and accounts for the play of energy and consciousness from the nondual point of view, within the Land of silence, of the unchanging Center, where there is neither object nor subject.

When the beings had performed their sublime duty, the Grand Builder Theurge said: The hour has come. O Yod + Hé + Shin + Vau + Hé, O Zeta + Alpha + Gamma + Alpha + Sigma, O Phi + Omega + Sigma + Tau + Eta + Ro, O Tau of Xi, O Xi of Tau, O Gimel of Yod, O Yod of Gimel, the first Holy Eucharist has begun! I give birth to the first Unpronounceable Name by offering my Seed and my Blood to the first hyper-universal tachyonic guide, so that its hyper-conscious nucleus is totally permeated by all of the hyper-galactic consciousness. I emit the vibration of the first Unpronounceable Name by spinning the hyper-conscious core seven times, like a vortex, in the tachyonic hyper-universal guide, so that in the hyper-galactic consciousness the creations of the Letters and non-Letters themselves are reflected. This reflection will then be able to spin twenty-one times like a vortex, in a musical sequence corresponding to the authentic Letters. I offer my Seed to all the Plans, to all the Numbers, Letters, Syllables, and Words so that each of their combinations, each of their sounds, each of their writings, and each thought concerning them is irrevocably capable of offering its own eucharist. Thus, each being possessing the capacity of speech, thought, sensations, love, eros, ethics, and law will be able to conceive, to create, to give birth to beings, spheres, worlds, and galaxies, infinitely. (...)

The Grand Builder Theurge, after having contemplated one by one the beings who were in the Sphere of Silence that they had created, touched his phallus and said: Here then is the culmination of my first Holy Eucharist. Great chalice of the essence of the galaxies of the Whole, let us then invoke this culmination so that beings are imbued with the beauty of Love, of Eros, and of the Whole. The great chalice of the essence of the galaxies of the Whole then offered, in excellent musical harmony, its own source to the Grand Builder Theurge, after having touched all beings with its breath.

We find in this last statement the classic blend of soma and breath that presides over the internal alchemies.

The phallus then entered the source of the chalice. The beings began to feel full of admiration and, with a unique joy, they witnessed the separation of Earth and Water, the extension of Fire by the Air, the consummation of Earth by Fire, the cooling of Earth by Water, and the evaporation of Water. The beings discovered, with great surprise and great enthusiasm, Earth, Water, Fire and Air, which formed masses, masses of symbols, symbols of images, images of idols, idols forming planets, stars and suns, moons, plants, animals, creatures, and human beings.

The works of separation indicated in this passage correspond to a precise internal alchemical way which, after the separation of the different bodies, allows the "body of Water" to evaporate in order to create an Earth-Fire axis through Air. We are on a dry and direct path. At this point, forms appear for what they are, ephemeral assemblages of the nature of the void.

The phallus came and went in the source of the chalice, in a regular rhythm, and with incomparable momentum. Beings began to distinguish families of creatures, families of human beings, families of planets, stars, suns, and moons. Beings began to recognize the relationships and affinities between species, families, and societies. Beings began to see arts, sciences, personalities, qualities, abilities, possibilities, necessities, contingencies, the necessity of law (Nomotelia), relativity, absoluteness, and co-relativity.

The phallus entered the source of the chalice. Within her, at a steady pace, with unparalleled momentum, he began to trace the Circles of Love of Eros. The beings then saw the marrow condense, activate the gray matter of the brain, energize arterial movement, increase venous movement, and re-establish lymphatic movement. It was at this precise moment that the beings observed the different varieties of essences that came together, the different varieties of feelings and charismata that combined. It was then that the beings saw the activity of cell combinations, the direction of hyper-spiritual centers, the way of organic formations and configurations.

The phallus, in the source of the chalice, received the sublime Chrism, the Chrism of the Christians, the Chrism of the essence of the Whole. The source of the chalice, by the regular and rhythmic movement of the phallus, full of momentum, which stopped its cyclical progression to now penetrate the great depth of the essence of essences, automatically structured the breath and the essence of the sublime conception that animated the phallus: the Sublime Geometer, the Sublime Legislator, the Sublime Operator, the Sublime Master, the Sublime Lover of the Whole. As the phallus received the breath and essence of the sublime conception, the great chalice began to quiver, at first in its very source. The phallus then received the essence, line, and order of the sublime conception of the chalice. He began, at that moment, to pour out all the essence of Love and Eros from his sublime nature. His seed gushed into the source of the chalice that welcomed him in three complete movements of this vibration. The first seed emanated from the phallus offered to the chalice the complete image of the first, second, and third Christs of the Whole. The second seed emanating from the phallus offered to the chalice the line, the order, and the total essence of the seven universal and hyper-universal paths. The third seed emanated from the phallus offered to the chalice the fulfillment of a full galactic incarnation. At this time, the beings discovered the essence and purpose of an astral existence, the essence of the purpose of spiritual existence, and the essence and purpose of existence in the essence of the pyrogenic substance of the mind.

The correspondence with the process of the deification of the individual can be decoded if one takes into account that *All* of this is unfolding within consciousness and in the body-world.

The Grand Builder Theurge withdrew his phallus from the source of the great chalice of the essence of the galaxies of the Whole. Touching his phallus, he offered a drop of his sperm to the great chalice which, consuming it, cried out for all beings: This is how a human being is created, this is how a being dies.

The Grand Builder Theurge touched the source of the chalice, embraced it with three movements in the seven directions, received the essence and solemnly called the beings to share Holy Communion, the sublime Chrism of the universes.

The sexual symbolism, which can also be found in certain Rosicrucian rituals of Greek Arcadia, coming from the same source, refers to the serpentine creative powers at work in the constitution of the Body of Glory. This is childbirth. The plans, present in this text and in other associated texts, which constitute the magic alphabet of the Builders, often take on a serpentine appearance that evokes the visions of shamans or of certain mystics shifting into the other side of the world of Appearance, as well as scientific representations of creative codes such as DNA.

Note also the distinction between being and human being. The apparent incarnation, only a contraction within the Appearance of Consciousness, kills the free being. To liberate oneself is to free oneself from the human, from the conditioned, and consequently from generation by passing from substance to energy, from energy to essence, or more directly from substance to essence.

The beings, at the heart of the Sphere of Silence which they themselves had created, approached the altar, and with sublime respect, piety, and understanding, they received Holy Communion and the Supreme Chrism. Then, at this exact moment, the ethers were illuminated, and the first being of the sacred union for planet Earth appeared, for the Earth was to be one of the most symbolic idols of the images thus created. This being, from the beginning, was the Kherismenos, the one who received Christ or the Anointing. He carried within him the power, the essence, the order, the line, and the nature of this first Holy Eucharist of Heaven.

The first Holy Eucharist was thus accomplished. A new galaxy began to live, it was the Milky Way, the galaxy that feeds the human being!

This celebration of a genesis and of an internal and external cosmology, by reversal, indicates the axis of liberation, an axis which, from the dualistic point of view, will always appear serpentine and will reveal its axiality only in nondual consciousness. Note that this internal way will begin with a milky power, just like some ways of Artemis, just like some Shaivite ways, which supports the hypothesis of the Dravidian origin of these ancient currents.

It is the totality of the play between consciousness and energy, between the absolute and being, that is celebrated in this story. It is the game of assembling and disassembling forms by contractions of Consciousness which remains intrinsically free even in the midst of ignorance and darkness. Consciousness manifests its Absolute Freedom by forgetting itself, by "falling" into more and more enclosing and alienating forms, without losing this freedom. A dualist paradox. It is a nondual reality that internal alchemy does not achieve, contrary to common beliefs, but simply celebrates.

THE POINT AND THE LINE

FOURTEENTH LETTER TO FRIENDS OF THE SPIRIT • SECOND SERIES

After the geometry of the interval, let's briefly look at the vital importance of the Geometry of the Line.

The Void Point of the Geometry of the Interval evokes the *Bauhütte Point* defined by a famous quatrain:

> A point that is placed in the circle
> That lies in the square and the triangle
> If you find the point
> You are saved
> Relieved of pain, anguish and danger.

The quatrain is sometimes summed up in this unique companion sentence:

> If you know the point within the circle, the square, and the triangle, you will be saved.

The companionage conserves and preserves an exceptional geometrical science, just as masters of other crafts do, such as illuminators and many artists, painters, sculptors, and others.

Here is Kandinsky:[71]

> An empty canvas. In appearance: very empty, remaining silent, indifferent. Almost dazed. In truth: full of tension with a thousand low voices, full of suspense. A little afraid, since you can violate her. But docile. She willingly does what is wanted of her and asks for nothing. She can hold everything but cannot endure everything. She reinforces the just but also the false. And she mercilessly devours the face of the false. She amplifies the voice of the false to a high-pitched howl — impossible to bear —
>
> Wonderful is the empty canvas — more beautiful than some paintings.
>
> The simplest elements — straight line, straight and narrow surface: hard, unshakable, standing without regard, seemingly "self-evident" — like a destiny already lived — thus and not otherwise — curved, "free," vibrancy that dodges, that yields, "elastic," "indeterminate" in appearance — like the destiny that awaits us. It could turn out otherwise, but it won't. Hard and soft. Combinations of both — endless possibilities.

In the beginning, there is the Void and its infinite potentialities which will condense into a single point. The point is set in motion, deosil and widdershins generating two spirals (Louis Boutard's worms), the first duality, the matrices of all the serpentine creations. Among them is the circle that both protects and limits, from which arise the geometric shapes that are falsely familiar to us, each of which is a challenge to the mind.

To expand on this subject, we refer to the remarkable works of Jean-Luc Leguay,[72] custodian of a monastic tradition of illuminators. Let us study here simply a case that concerns the Martinists, whether it is within the framework of the Martinezist orders, the Martinists, or the Rectified Scottish Rite.

The Point and the Line

A major theme of these illuminist currents is the passage from the ternary to the quaternary. It is the symbolic but, above all, the operative key.

For Martinez de Pasqually, the multiplication of numbers can be harmful, especially when it comes to multiplying a number that divides the decad, like 2 and 5. But the multiplication of the number 3 leads to Limit, symbolized by the 9, an ambiguous number, according to Martinez but also in the Kabbalah, because it involves replication and imitation ($3 \times 3 = 9$, $9 \times 3 = 27$, $7 + 2 = 9$, $9 \times 9 = 81 = 9$, etc.).[73]

This is why Jean-Claude Sitbon,[74] an author specializing in the Rectified Scottish Rite, evokes in his lectures the very Masonic numbers 3, 6, and 9 as being $4 - 1$, $7 - 1$, and $10 - 1$, that is, 4, 7, and 10 minus the Unity.

From two points of the circle, the line is created and from three points, the triangle.

The two triangles intertwined to form a hexagram are also found in Martinez de Pasqually, Louis-Claude de Saint-Martin and Jean-Baptiste Willermoz. They represent first of all the path of Reintegration that leads to the center, Saturn, the home of the New Adam.

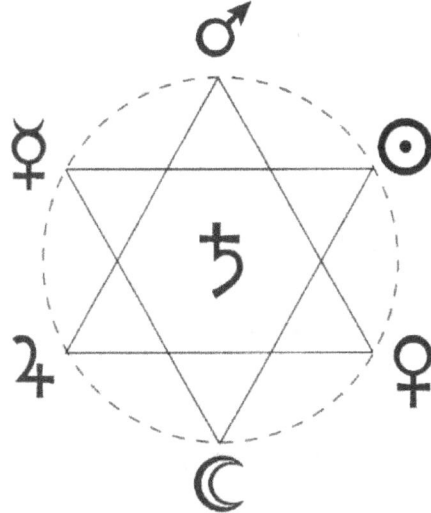

This center is double, the centers of the two triangles being superimposed, because we access the New Adam through Christ. It is about becoming another Christ through theurgy and an internal way, both ways of the Body of Glory.

The hexagram in three dimensions becomes the Merkabah, symbol of the body of light, which makes it possible to reach the Heavenly Jerusalem. It is advisable to master the Platonic Solids in order to build the Merkabah.[75]

If we rotate a Merkabah from every angle to project it into the plane we will find, at a certain angle, two superimposed squares.

In turn these two squares can be characterized: a static square (Earth) and a dynamic square (Sky), having their centers superimposed to form the geometric symbol of the Heavenly Jerusalem.

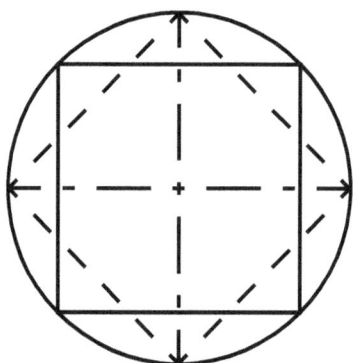

The number 9 is no longer a sterile 3 × 3, a "corpse," but a 4 + 4 + 1, and even 4 + 4 + 1 + 1, the two centers being superimposed.

Note that from the hexagram, we can go to the rhombus and therefore to the square, a special case of rhombus, or a rhombus rectified by a right angle:

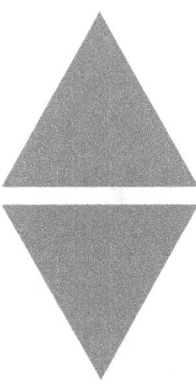

Thus the Heavenly Jerusalem is potentially inscribed in the hexagram. Each time, it is from the center that we can transcend the limits, to go from 3 to 4, from 6 to 7 or 8, from 9 to 1 and to the ONE, the center that knows how to duplicate itself to better reunite.

This very simple entry has infinite consequences and very complex developments. Lima de Freitas, who Geometrized much and solved the enigma of the Bauhütte Point, included a number of elements in the azulejo panel below[76] dedicated to the painter Almada, who was also a repository of Sacred Geometry.

ALCHEMY AND INITIATION

FIFTEENTH LETTER TO FRIENDS OF THE SPIRIT • SECOND SERIES

IKE ALL ALCHEMIES, IN ALL THEIR MODALITIES, Alchemy remains inaccessible to any form of teaching, to any form of "speech." The claims of those who multiply trainings, courses, revelations, or clarifications (obviously for the sake of hard cash) are ridiculous. They perpetuate the tradition of deception that inevitably masks the real ways. The few adepts who remain in Europe remain unknown. "Noise makes no good, good makes no noise," said Saint Francis de Sales—a phrase later taken up by Louis-Claude de Saint-Martin—*a fortiori* when it comes to the *Summum Bonum*.

Certainly the prerequisites can be indicated. An acquaintance with some two or three hundred ancient texts can prove useful. Or not. A thorough practice of self-remembering is necessary, but not sufficient. Analysis, increased observation, waking, perseverance, recapitulation, tireless restarting, and other qualities often attributed to the alchemist can be learned, strengthened, and developed. It is still necessary to put them at the service of that which signals. *Puits obscur, Puits lumineux*[77] is a book of signals. In alchemy, things are never stated but only signified or suggested. The qualities of the chivalric path, the priestly path, and the artisanal path are required to approach the Great Work and yet will prove to be obsolete if the seeker is not a poet, because Alchemy is Divine Poetry.

Alchemy has its laws and principles within duality, but it is essentially nondual and therefore knows no rules. What is true for a certain phase of the work with one disciple (one who practices the discipline) is no longer true with another disciple.

Alchemy operates within Consciousness and always in a non-time, a sublime interval of Silence and Void that are both the work and the conditions for its manifestation in form. The true athanor of the Great Work is Consciousness.

If we are here, together, in this "place" of an alchemical text, the author and reader not separate, it is because we have the intuition, the feeling of our original, ultimate, and absolute reality. Stuck in duality, the echo of our inherently free nondual nature resonates even within the cascade of words.

Today we need to rethink an initiatory curriculum. This curriculum should be accompanied by a utopia, because only utopia can approach the Real. We have to define what an initiate is, an initiated woman or initiated man, commensurate with the absolute Freedom of the Real (of God, of the Lord, of the Self…). We must refuse to lower the threshold of initiation, as had been the case in the slow initiatory erosion of a twentieth century under the control of the merchant caste. Initiation begins with the silence in which—unique, singular, and unexpected like the Spirit—the initiatory path unfolds. Never let initiation get lost in noise, in dualistic noise.

The dualistic error (a salutary error, however, if it is not accompanied by indifference) is surely thought. "Who thinks greatly must err greatly," said Heidegger. All true thought engenders its negation. The dualistic game of antinomies, symbolized by the mosaic pavement, if it is accepted in its permanent dialectic, does not allow one to freeze in position. It thus leads to the silence of being, by abandonment. If we tirelessly search, within this infinite dialectic of initiation, for what is the next step, we end up falling into the interval, the void and its fullness. What Montaigne calls the rippling, the rippling of doubt, turns out to be discontinuous, full of possibilities to access the Real. The ego renounces its imposture and agrees to remain in the luminous shadow of the Self. This doubt is the most faithful companion of those who want to approach the enigma and great paradox on which all Alchemy rests. It is the other face of the axiality, of the solarity of Being that reveals itself and extracts itself from Appearance, through the play of the mirror of the philosophers.

Initiation consists in the assimilation of oneself, or of the Self (they are the same). There is only *Ego*. There is only *Self*. In primordial Consciousness, the Self and the ego are the same, even as Silence and noise are one, as absolute freedom and dualistic imprisonment are one.

We do not have to get caught up in the *accelerando* of the ego, which seeks to mask the discontinuity of appearance, the innumerable passages to the Real that it conceals. The creation of appearance makes it possible to veil being. Speed creates the illusion.

Initiation in the Garden (oriented directly on Freedom) differs from initiation in the City[78] (oriented on the organization of the path to Freedom) because tragedy is absent. Establishing and governing a city was deeply tragic in ancient Greece. Any social foundation (the initiatory society, for one) is doomed to failure, to tragic failure. Initiation in the Garden, which made the choice of Celebration rather than Tragedy, Joy rather than sadness (divine laughter and smiles are as present in the arts as in mathematics, in a score by Erik Satie as in the double helix of DNA), astonishment and wonder rather than reason and analysis, enjoyment rather than frustration, freedom rather than compulsion, liberates forms to allow the paths that have their source deep within us to unfold, within our own immaculate and unconditioned nature. The City must lead to the Garden. Poetry can bring the City to *life*. Alchemy demands the Garden.

At the point of Void, in the experience of this Emptiness that sees the world reabsorbed into the fine point of the Soul, according to Meister Eckhart, when we are the Place of God, the dual place where nondual

Consciousness radiates, both to God and his manifestation, both the Real and the free play of the Real in its infinite manifestations, so many fleeting realities, actualized or not in a tension of consciousness that we call "I," we grasp the primary Intention of the Real or Absolute. The Absolute, in order to exercise its full Freedom, plays at forgetting itself and finding itself, in an infinite number of modalities which constitute the continuum of Consciousness, from the divine to the vulgar, from the nondual to the dual. The distinction between subject and object, comparison, memory, language, replication, and temporality are synonyms, simultaneous consequences of the absolute will of the One-Real to lose itself and find itself in the multiplicity without ever ceasing to be what it is, in the ecstasy of Itself.

If Silence is the father-mother of the Word that will be elaborated in all languages, from the first Sound, *A* (which will be elaborated as noise), languages, sacred or not, are fragments of a proto-language sought by all traditions. But this proto-language cannot be enunciated. It would then be the object of duality, perceived and put to work by a separate subject. It is not to be sought in Sanskrit, Hebrew, Portuguese, Chaldean, Basque, Breton... languages that are nevertheless close to the Source. Doesn't the Basque language emphasize silence, through enchantment? The proto-language isn't the mother tongue either, even if it is, by privilege, the natural language of our magic and our poetry, the mastery of which allows the translation of reality on the way to the Real. Rather, it would be a melody of silence, of which music, like poetry, expresses the mystery. Language and time are identical. They construct our reality, this tension of consciousness, this source of intensity in the divine play. There is a grammar of God, a sacred grammar, the language of which echoes when it itself becomes the mirror of nature. The name of God, Elohim, brings together, in a unity, both nondual and dual, *Mi* and *Eloha,* the hidden subject and the hidden object.[79] We are in this name, in the heart of this name, in the palace of the Hidden King, of the

Self. When Christ asks us to act in his name, that is to say in the name of God, it is not for the sake of delegating any power or any authority. Instead, he asks us to act in the heart of this palace where his name resonates, where the separation between subject and object becomes null, where the One celebrates itself in the Innermost.

ALCHEMICAL WAYS, WATER, AND THE INTERNAL

Spagyrics, metallic alchemy, and internal alchemy are three branches of Al-chemy, the Chemistry of God, three celebrations from Essence down to substance.

The modality of substances in the internal pathways is based on an alchemy of water that is also a key to the metallic pathways. Let us think of the significant *Sophic Hydrolith*.[80] The Ocean, the Sky: a divine proportion.

The human body is aquatic. There is a continuum from the Saturnian body, of heavy matter (the most dense and opaque expression of dual consciousness), to the body of immortality. This continuum is conveyed by water, the only vessel that allows the circulation and inscription of messages from one place-state of consciousness to another in the vast divine play of Consciousness and Energy. In the same way, around an identical annihilation of the appearance that separates, there is a continuum of love from the Flesh to the Spirit, from the ephemeral bodily orgasm to permanent divine ecstasy. All interval is Bliss and Grace. The united bodies of lovers in the Presence, a double athanor made single by fusion (in which the distillation of substances operates under the fires of touch, breath, sound, and the Free Spirit), creates a stone of water which, reabsorbed, modifies the prime-matter body of the work, subtly but radically, and inscribes new serpentine codes via the water within cells,[81] thereby orienting it towards luminous matter, both prime and ultimate.

The concepts of the division of bodies (in 4, 7, 9), that of the distinction in the qualities of silence (a Value impossible to evaluate), or that of a gradation within Awakening, have no reason to be that pedagogical. They do not translate any reality but invite praxis. Any counting only makes sense in appearance. In the Real, no comparison or hierarchy remains.

Water, both a courier between the peripheries and an acrobat in the multiple dimensions of axiality, is a unique remembrance of Creation. In duality, water is the permanent element through which the nondual Consciousness-Origin manifests itself. Meditation upon the Great Ocean tears us away from the accidental, from fragmentation, from the doctrinal. The aquatic world-body becomes one. The beauty and absolute freedom of the vastness is revealed.

Water is inhabited by serpentine powers, the Nagas or Dragons of the traditions, original powers that weave and unravel ephemeral realities and times. The link, real or metaphorical, suggested by some seekers between these powers and the DNA double helix, or even string theory, is relevant. The Nagas are at the same time carriers of the messages, of the codes of manifestation, and the creative agents of it. What appears in duality as change is erasure, dissolution, uncreation, and then another recreation from the Interval of the Great Real.

This punctuation of immaculate consciousness is always ecstatic, liberatory, beneficent, and knowing. Experience of the Absolute Freedom of the Real, it is also self-knowledge of the totality of Himself in a radiance separate from Himself.

The internal alchemies, just like the metallic alchemies, are not temporal realizations but celebrations of nondual Nature within duality, actualizations of what is, laborious within the temporal weaving, effulgent, and immediate within the Presence, temporality and Presence being two modes of consciousness that are only opposed from the dual point of view.

The modality of substances and its mysterious aura only reveal their secrets in the state of Presence. They are quite surprising in their simplicity and brilliance. The void of water differs from the void of fire, but the fullness of the void of water is identical to the fullness of the void of fire. This is why Nagas, Dragons, and other serpentine powers axialize and, having wings, rise to the Highest. This is why Christ is sometimes represented as a Serpent who rises on the Cross.

THE *ARCANA CŒLESTIA* AND SWEDENBORG

SIXTEENTH LETTER TO FRIENDS OF THE SPIRIT • SECOND SERIES

MMANUEL SWEDENBORG (1688–1771) IS TODAY somewhat forgotten within the Illuminist current in Europe[82] despite the work of Jacqueline and Claude Bruley, who for a long time carried the torch of Swedenborgian thought[83] by disseminating his substantial work through seminars and numerous writings.

Louis-Claude de Saint-Martin did not have a very high opinion of Swedenborg. Thus, in *L'homme de désir,* he says of him, not without a certain pretension: "A thousand proofs in his works that he was often and greatly favored! A thousand proofs that he was often and greatly deceived. A thousand proofs that he only saw the middle of the work, and that he knew neither the beginning nor the end!"

However, reading the first volume of the Swede's *Arcana Cœlestia,* a commentary on Genesis, is enough to realize the error of Saint-Martin, perhaps rejecting the alliance between spirituality and science that characterizes Swedenborg. Indeed, if Swedenborg is known as one of the greatest seers of Christendom, he was also a very great scientist of his time, some of whose discoveries endure today. Saint-Martin, caught up in the aftermath of the *Controversy with Garat*[84] and his fight against "teachers," undoubtedly did not sufficiently guard against certain prejudices.

On the occasion of Swedenborg's 250th birthday, January 19, 1938,

Howard W. Haggard, professor of psychology at Yale University, quite correctly stated that: "Swedenborg is generally taken for a seer, a mystic. It is not generally known that he was also the greatest scholar the scientific world has seen in 250 years. It is only in the last twenty years that we have started, belatedly, to recognize his merit."[85]

Emmanuel Swedenborg was a forerunner and pioneer in many fields such as brain science, atomic theory, the wave theory of light, geology, crystallography, astronomy, mathematics, and many other disciplines. He was one of the last great thinkers able to comprehend in a transdisciplinary way the greatest scientific fields of his time.

He was a man of science, therefore, and a high-level mystic with exceptional clairvoyant skills. His work is marked by these two talents which can be opposed but which in him come together admirably. This alliance allowed him to envision the existence of vortices, spiral powers, long before the works of Tesla, Lakhovsky, Boutard, Laville, Wheeler, Reich, and other researchers who went in search of Paracelsus' Spirit of the World.[86] For Swedenborg, Love is the substance of the Divine and Wisdom is the Form of the Divine. The Divine is the archetype of all creation by correspondences, series, degrees, numbers, and rhythms. The coincidence of opposites makes the question of the beginning and the end disappear since we are there in the presence of a divine infinitude, unknowable if not for the qualities that it transmits in the appearance of the world.

A primordial infinite divine substance contracts and transmits its intrinsic qualities to the first finite substances, the "first finites" of Emmanuel Swedenborg. If we then step out of limitlessness and absolute freedom into duality, it is a perfect duality that fully manifests divine love.

The contraction continues and the first finites transmit their qualities, while limiting them further, to the "second finites." The second finites make up the "spiritual sun" that animates all creation. It recalls the central fire axis of Martinez de Pasqually. This spiritual sun exercises its freedom, even if it is constrained, to generate the "universal aura," which condenses to give shape to the so-called material, visible, and measurable universe.

All this is only a continuum. The contraction is permanent: the loss of speed, the densification, the opacification, whatever the word used to designate the process that manifests duality from nonduality, or from a nothing that is everything. Correspondences do not exist in themselves but arise from our conscious discernments more or less distant from the source. But it is from the appearance of things that we can return to the First Source by following the golden thread of freedom. For if everything is movement, spiral, geometric, arithmetic, musical... then everything that presents itself emanates from a more subtle dimension. By tracking the interval in a form, that is to say, the point of freedom that allowed the assembly of the form, we traverse it to discover a less coarse form with a less heavy duality, and then, from form to form, towards the increasingly fluid, subtle, and luminous, we find the absolute freedom that presides over all creation.

With Swedenborg, just as in the symbolism of the Temple of Solomon or the Temple of Luxor, each part of the body, each organ, has a "loving" function, dominant or derivative, spiritual, and microcosmic, which is the echo or extension of a macrocosmic function.

Here are some examples raised by Claude Bruley to illustrate the theory of correspondences in Swedenborg:

> The head is the seat of this dominant love, as well as that of the eleven microcosmic derivative affections.
>
> The neck corresponds to the particular affection that prompts us to educate ourselves, to know the general laws of finality and causality—these laws that make communication possible, the conjunction between dominant love in its theoretical fullness, and its manifestation, its realization.

The arms and hands correspond to the ailments that prompt us to develop the mental power that manifests itself when the laws and the great principles of finality and causation are exposed.

The heart is the affection that prompts others to benefit from the benefactions, or, alas, the misdeeds, of this dominant love.

The lungs correspond to the ailments that prompt man to seek a doctrine that can apply to the present circumstances, and allow the realization of the preceding affection.

The kidneys and the organs of purification and assimilation correspond to the affections that encourage us to seek in ourselves, or in others, the defects, the vices, and the insufficiencies that harm the development of our dominant love, both on the affective and intellectual level.

The female genitalia are the affection that prompts us to seek true marital union. This union is necessary to regain the faculties of the original man, and to penetrate the knowledge of the laws of order. This affection also encourages taking care of the first fruits of conjugal love.

The male genitals correspond to the affection that prompts us to extend, to spread everything that touches our dominant love. Proselytizing.

The thighs correspond to the affection that prompts us to seek the marital union different from that which corresponds to the female genitalia, that is, in a less elevated mystique and ideal.

The knees correspond to the ailments that prompt us to seek practical doctrines and techniques that can be applied in daily life to embody our dominant love.

The legs (between the knees and the feet) correspond to the affections that urge us to follow obediently, without derogation, the principles admitted to accomplish our purpose.

The feet correspond to the ailments that prompt us to find our happiness in the exercise of our function, in the results that we observe. These affections are sensual and bodily.

The spiritual world is inscribed in the body of the human being. The body is thus a temple which nonetheless hurls itself into the vegetable kingdom and the mineral kingdom.

This science or art of correspondence that Swedenborg has elaborated in his many books is present in the Old and New Testaments and in sacred writings more generally, once we go beyond the literal reading of the texts.

Here is an example taken from Volume 1 of *Arcana Cœlestia* by Emmanuel Swedenborg, point 27:

> 27. Verse 9. *And God said, Let the waters under the heaven be gathered together to one place, and let the dry [land] appear; and it was so.*
>
> When it is known that there is both an internal and an external man, and that truths and goods flow in from, or through, the internal man to the external, from the Lord, although it does not so appear, then those truths and goods, or the knowledges of the true and the good in the regenerating man, are stored up in his memory, and are classed among its knowledges [*scientifica*]; for whatsoever is insinuated into the memory of the external man, whether it be natural, or spiritual, or celestial, abides there as memory-knowledge, and is brought forth thence by the Lord. These knowledges are the "waters gathered together into one place," and are called "seas," but the external man himself is called the "dry [land]," and presently "earth"…

Several interpretations can be deduced from the separation between the waters which are below the Firmament and the waters which are above the Firmament. This makes sense in laboratory alchemy as well as in internal alchemy. This makes sense in relation to the Reintegration process of Martinez de Pasqually or the Saint-Martinian distinction between the Man of the Stream and that Man of Desire, and then the Man of Desire and the New Man.

Swedenborg cautions against studying the isolated scientific fact to grasp what is beyond the observable. He does not oppose transcendence and immanence, essence and existence, or love and wisdom, and never ceases to invite us to combine them.

We must not put aside the work of Emmanuel Swedenborg. It is a major contribution to the Illuminist current, as important as that of Jacob Böhme or of Louis-Claude de Saint-Martin. In addition to certain Martinist orders, the Swedenborgian Rite[87] remains a good vessel for studying Swedenborg's thought. Although this Masonic high rank system was not founded by Swedenborg in any way, it is well constructed and articulated according to his thinking and writings.

WOMAN, MUSE AND INITIATOR

SEVENTEENTH LETTER TO FRIENDS OF THE SPIRIT • SECOND SERIES

INTRODUCTION TO A METAPHYSICS OF SEX
From the text of an address by the authors
to the international colloquium *Transcendence in the Feminine*
October 29, 30 & 31, 2011
Quinta de Regaleira, Sintra, Portugal[88]

ITERATURE (SOMETIMES MORE THAN TRADITION, as far as the Christian and especially Catholic West is concerned) has been able to approach the arcanum of the Eternal Feminine, which the seeker must confront, whether by the flesh or by the spirit, which are in any case inseparable. The flesh teaches the spirit; the spirit elevates the flesh. The Erotic and eroticism merge.

The question of Transcendence in the Feminine, which would merit a very long elaboration, impossible in this setting, is central as much in the world of the Traditions as in the world of the Arts.[89] The Woman has in fact been recognized by the artistic avant-garde and the initiatory traditions as both the key and guardian of Initiation, as both mediator and crown, even if this was not without confusion, without repression, nor without ulterior motive, as much on the side of the avant-garde as on the side of the traditions. This led the traditions and avant-gardes to state the foundations of a metaphysics of sex, an Erotic, which sometimes had its natural extension in a metaphysics of madness.

Woman is in essence
the facilitator and inspirer,
it is she who brings enlightenment to the heart of man, and man,
having become conscious, expresses himself as a poet, behaves as a knight,
and acts as a Mage.
Mage-Priest who celebrates a cult in which the woman becomes Goddess.
Woman becoming her,
the priestess of a god
who only asks for abandonment,
freedom, and mystery.

Valentin Bresle[90]

In a distorted world that confuses genitality and sexuality, then sexuality and eroticism, eroticism (or better, the Erotic) remains reserved, today as yesterday, today more than yesterday, to an elite. The Erotic is not the despair that humans confuse with love when they blindly throw a bridge over their own emptiness, so as not to face their own absence, to join an image that they themselves have unconsciously created.

Love is Fusion, reabsorption into the One, simplification, neither I nor other. In this sense, the Erotic is indeed a minimal and minimalist initiation, as is any initiation into the Real.

The Sacred Erotic is a Hierogamy, a Science of the three somas (vegetable, mineral, and celestial), in which Being, composed of three fused essences, is deposited.

The Erotic, Saga of a Fool, Quest of a Fool, after having made the adept go through the labyrinth of all the masks of the Great Game, finally offers him the contemplation of his own face, in himself and by himself, from his own void, in which emerges the essential and secret Nature, the internal Shakti.

God/Goddess Becomes, in the Eternal instant, the adept and his shakti (merged into a single entity, non-human because divine) and escapes any game, because they are the Game. The Erotic is a fundamental sacred Saga. It cannot be taught, it is not transmitted, it springs from the depths of Being, from beyond time, from the Will intending to burst out towards the Real.

A perfect saga, exalted by the Quest, both divine art and sacred craftsmanship, the Erotic makes the adept a divine sculptor of Chaos.

The Sacred Erotic finds one of its foundations (not its justification: the axis of Being abides, it cannot be justified or explained) in a pure perception of the universe by the senses, a sensory expansion to ecstasy. The Universe and the worlds are no more than infinite sensual spectra on which strangely plays a consciousness genuinely free, but relatively a prisoner of itself through the subtle play of identifications, through contractions of the consciousness that separates and generates forms and multiple beings, including us as "ego," "me," and "person."

According to certain Eastern traditions, the first of all the senses, even the only one, is touch. The other senses are then only extensions of touch: touch, smell, taste, hearing, sight, and thought in a single stretch. We know the subtle and powerful role of scents in the game of love. We like to taste the other. The voice, the look, caresses or hurts. A thought touches. Thought would only be the most subtle, the most uncertain, the most fleeting touch, the art of memory, the manipulator of fantasies, if an artificial hypertrophy had not allowed this sense to take itself for an entity endowed with independent existence, making it at the same time inoperative.

A woman, Catherine Pozzi, from whom Paul Valéry borrowed much, made the skin speak: "I feel therefore I am," she screamed:

> I have two bodies, FLESH-AND-BLOOD and PLEASURE-AND-PAIN: FLESH-AND-BLOOD is asleep, PLEASURE-AND-PAIN is like a cry; they are always inseparable.
>
> FLESH-AND-BLOOD is a hydrocarbon with very large molecules. PLEASURE-AND-PAIN is so tenuous that Lucretia turned it into a poem. Everyone talks to FLESH-AND-BLOOD, I talk only to PLEASURE-AND-PAIN.
>
> FLESH-AND-BLOOD seems to persist, but follows the second law of thermodynamics and ends badly. PLEASURE-AND-PAIN seems to be annihilated with the speed of the seconds hand, and it has immortality.
>
> I will leave FLESH-AND-BLOOD one day, taken by PLEASURE-AND-PAIN. But to where, Sovereign Virgin?
>
> But what can I do to protect myself from the hazards of eternity?[91]

The apparent erotic duality finds its fulfillment and its self-annihilation in a mystical Orgy that re-establishes the absolute Will in its own ontology, which is Absolute Freedom. The Universe is no more than the Body and Place of Freedom. Matter and Spirit are One. Illusion and the Real are One. Everything is only a question of touch, the fingering of a sculptor-demiurge whose clay is his own chaos. Under his fingers, as many false gods as golems will be born, until that magical moment of eternity, of internity, when Shakti reveals the Divine Touch to him.

From then on the Erotic, and sacred eroticism, is at the same time the most direct and the most perilous Way for the adept, who has become (through Shakti, who unveils and reveals herself, at the same time as she unveils and reveals) the Master of Hands, like Orpheus who plucks the strings of his Lyre, both the music of the spheres and the root sounds of the Real.

SHAKTI
MUSE AND INITIATOR

The Woman, the flowers; the Flower, the women perfumes subtle, captivating, or persistent of one, of the other. Women flowers, chalices or secret censers from the same cup of total pleasure, of cosmic pleasure, and, to be honest: divine. Cup offered to God, censer offered to the gods stretched out towards the Man-poet thirsty for infinity.

Valentin Bresle

The Erotic is an unconditional tension towards Absolute Freedom, or shall we say, an emergence of Absolute Freedom within Being, that plays with itself, the space of the moment, being enchained voluntarily in the thick and cloudy dross of the conceptual world, to allow, to offer itself, the manifestation of the pure beauty of this Freedom that cannot be expressed beyond the point without the Being of Shakti.

Nondual Shaivism probably provided all possible forms of eroticization of the Quest. On the Shaivite Way of the Pleiades, one of the Ways of Kailash (sacred mountain and crossroads of the Ways of the Real), the body of the adept, male or female, is said to be the Temple of the Thousand Goddesses. Each is an emanation of Shakti, the Goddess of the Center, and each is a keeper of a Fire of the Wonder Tree, which is said to be seen only by one who is pure, in the midst of the sacred lake. From each fusion of the adept with a goddess, a living fire, blue and cold, is born, which draws its strength from the Void. When the adept has given birth to all the Fires of the Divine Tree, then the blue body of the god springs from the body of the adept. The adept disappears. He never existed, only That, the blue God/Goddess, remains. This operative poetry relates both to the ways of awakening and to the ways of the Body of Glory or internal alchemies.

In this rare and sophisticated form of shaktism, Shakti is both internal and external, but it is still a tangible manifestation of the Goddess of the Center, the consort of Shiva. The adept becomes Shiva (symbolically and really) only through, and in, Shakti.

This ascesis culminates in the Secret Way of Perfumes, a fusion of subtle essences that unite and transmute according to alchemical processes, until the *Anthéos*[92] of the divine couple, Shiva/Shakti, releases the primitive, archetypal, and internal Perfume. Dissolution and destruction of the world. Emergence of the Real.

Finally, the Erotic is the way of Freedom, and Shakti is the place of Freedom, as at the same time is the Mausoleum that the adept will rejoin at the time of the death of the body.

> ...Then, rising of itself towards its own intelligence, the soul finds itself in the fifth degree, where the celestial Venus in person & not imaginary is shown to it, without however appearing in the total plenitude of its beauty, which cannot be understood by a singular intelligence. Now the soul, greedy & thirsty for the celestial Venus, seeks to unite its own singular spirit with the universal & first spirit, first among all creatures, & universal abode of ideal beauty. The soul, reaching this one, attains the sixth degree and ends its journey. It is not allowed to access the seventh degree, sabbath of heavenly love, nor to rise further beyond it: here she must rest, happy, as if she had reached her goal, alongside the Father, the primary source of all beauty.
>
> Pico della Mirandola
*Commentary on a love song
of Girolamo Benivieni*

INTERNAL ALCHEMIES

The possibilities of giving in women go far beyond the simply human and daily plan, to touch and commune with the divine and eternal plan, that is to say, outside of the time that can be measured.

For the woman as for God, there is a time (and a space) which can only be measured because it is: sum qui Sum.

Valentin Bresle

Internal alchemy is the most subtle expression of embodied divine love. At the same time poetic, magical, and technical, it remains the perfect Way, and constitutes the secret pyramidion of all traditions, in the East as in the West. Only cultural peripheries present differences.

Any real technique (technique leading to the Real) can liberate within the being on the Quest the conditions and arcana of the internal ways. But this happening is rare enough to be considered a blessing from the gods, or from God: a grace, according to the ancients. Even if the knowledge is for the moment largely unconscious, it is inscribed within the being in an indelible way; it is about a secret of Nature.

In the domain of internal alchemy, the only knowledge is that which comes from Being, that which is conquered *hic et nunc*. In this domain, books are useless and more often than not can only confuse.

Strictly speaking, only three possibilities (or rather, offerings) remain: three modalities that we meet in literature (think of Cervantes' *Don Quixote* or Dante's *Divine Comedy*), or in art (let us remember Lima de Freitas and Victor Brauner, among others):

- Internal alchemy paired with the sacralization of the sexual act, which becomes a liturgical, magical, and primordial alchemical act. The couple is no longer human but divine, and the sexual act truly becomes a primal, noumenal act, a pure celebration of divine life. In this case, the play of energies is totally different from that of a human couple, and Pneuma, the breath, allows the realization of Soma, the liquor of immortality. Soma is external/internal. The focus is on the realization of Soma and by Soma.

- Internal alchemy paired with the sacralization of sexuality through not taking action. This is the great principle of Courtly Love. Here, Pneuma is essential: the internal Soma arises tardily from the work of Pneuma, but immediately, with all its potential. Eventually, the ingredients of an external Soma can be used separately or together (salt, sulfur, mercury, alkahest) to assist the process, or to anchor certain stages. This Way was celebrated in particular in the Erotic of the Troubadours and by many poets. It is not absent (we will return to this) from Fado, which can be understood as a courtly art, nor from the philosophy of Saudade.
- Internal alchemy combining the previous two processes: the internal Shakti for man manifests through two shaktis (two women), the internal solar God for woman manifests through two men, one as part of the Courtly Love, the other within the setting of the sacralization of the sexual act. It is the Groom and the Brother or the Bride and the Sister.

These three ideal, if not idealized, Ways can take multiple forms. All the other expressions are in fact derivatives, adaptations, or sometimes idiosyncrasies of these three sacred postures, more or less conditioned by incomplete, unsuitable, or even hostile contexts of realization. This is the case for those who work alone, without the support of an otherness of the flesh, but with an abstract otherness, a proposition that we find, openly stated, in certain major traditional and monastic currents, while most religions, including Christianity, have preserved the traditions of internal alchemy in a completely occult manner by clothing them with their beliefs and culture.

Woman, Muse and Initiator

When this talk, published in Portugal in 1998 in my first book, *Le Fou de Shakti*,[93] was submitted to Robert Amadou, an old traveling companion, he sharedwith me these relevant remarks:[94]

> It is an excellent text, but a pagan text.
>
> The love that is fusion is of the order of the cosmic, the natural. But there is the Transcendent and the Revelation. You know how much it matters to me (personally, intellectually, and spiritually), the articulation — for the completion of paganism and for the realization of Christianity — of the one upon the other.
>
> Ah! How the Fool of Shakti succeeds in becoming Fool of Christ, that's the whole point. The created wisdom has fallen. We must save it with all of the created, through the grace (the word is to be taken literally) of the virtue of uncreated Wisdom, through which the divine energy is communicated.
>
> The Virgin Mary and the Church prefigure, *in reality,* the rehabilitation of created wisdom, reunited with uncreated wisdom (cf. the *Shekinah* of the Hebrew tradition). It is initiatory work, you know, it is this transformation — of all kinds of others and of oneself — that alchemy specifies by calling it transmutation. But all of this can only be understood and fulfilled under the light of the Incarnation, the only fundamental dogma, and it contains all the others.
>
> Shakti is veiled, or too naked.

The absolute impossibility of the representation of the female nude, by any art whatsoever, by any artist whatsoever, is an indication of the transcendent and immanent nature of Femininity as the link, secret and sacred, that unites Woman and the Interval.

The erotic has the intuition of this way without a way, but not without an exit, without ever being able to indicate it, nor to express it fully or truly.

Feminine nudity summons all of creation, all of the uncreated, all of Beauty and all of Art.

It invokes Being and non-Being and yet transcends them.

The nudity of Woman is the greatest mystery for those who have learned to *See* and to *Love*.

It evokes, paradoxically and by the reversal of the NU into ONE,[95] the verticality of the Absolute rather than the extent of Beingness.

The *Ereignis,* the wonder, can be recognized and celebrated in everything, but outstandingly in the feminine Eros.

In a world dedicated to the Promethean myth of profitability, which opposes modernity to Initiation, the Erotic remains one of the last sacred sagas, inscribing the magnificence of the myth of Orpheus that celebrates beauty and creativity solely for their own sakes. Our Promethean world asks human beings *to have and to do* in order to hope *to be,* while the Orphic world, here symbolizing the entire world of Tradition, knows that realization is only accessible by the conquest, here and now, of the Citadel of Being, a conquest that requires the dissolution of having and doing.

BLACK VIRGINS

EIGHTEENTH LETTER TO FRIENDS OF THE SPIRIT • SECOND SERIES

Adore the Black Virgin, because without her it is impossible to reach the White Virgin, and without her it is impossible to reach the Red Son.

LOUIS CATTIAUX
The Message Rediscovered

HE MYSTERY OF THE BLACK VIRGINS REMAINS, despite many studies and attempts to elucidate it. It is undoubtedly the tradition of the companionage that best preserves the mysteries associated with the Black Virgins. We will content ourselves here with approaching the mystery without lifting the veil.

Several hypotheses have been expressed regarding the black color of these Virgins found concentrated in certain regions. Some were made in black or brown colored wood, but many were originally light wood before being stained. The hypothesis that the browning is the product of candle smoke and incense does not hold up. It seems that the color black was applied voluntarily at certain times to signify a tradition, to adhere to it, or to renew it. However, the dates of the blackening vary widely. Thus in France, we have Chartres and Le Puy-en-Velay, with statues from the 11th century, and Rocamadour and Clermont-Ferrand from the 12th century, which are painted: late in the 17th century for Chartres, Rocamadour, and Le Puy-en-Velay, but in the following century for the

Virgin of Clermont-Ferrand. The famous Black Virgin of Montserrat, the Madonna of Montserrat, Spain, is said to have been painted black earlier, in the 14th or 15th century. All of this makes identifying the reasons for the black coloration particularly tricky.

The famous Black Virgin in the crypt of the Abbey of Saint Victor in Marseille (12th century), Notre Dame de Confession, is recounted as sculpted by Saint Luke. On the occasion of Candlemas, she is dressed in green and there is a procession in the city with green candles crossed on the chest, a reference to the Secret Fire, candles that will be burned later, after having touched the green dress of the Virgin, in an Isiac cult that renews pre-Christian traditions associated with cycles of nature. The famous "Navettes," those delicious pastries, originally prepared in the crypt especially for the procession, evoke the shape of the barque of Isis. It is interesting to note that representatives of various traditions have long been keen to meet in the crypt on this occasion: Companions, of course, but also Freemasons of Egyptian rites, Martinists, Rosicrucians (Rose-Croix d'Orient), Knights of Malta, and Knights of Saint John the Evangelist,[96] among others.

For many traditional esoteric currents, the Black Virgin manifests the same archetype as pre-Christian deities such as the Egyptian Isis, whose cult extended widely in Europe, Ishtar in Mesopotamia, Cybele in Asia Minor, Demeter or Aphrodite in Greece… who thus went through Romanization and Christianization. Ultimately, the dating of the blackening does not matter. What matters is what the permanence of this archetype and its recognition (whether popular or more reserved) tells us. The archetype in question brings together several functions: Mother-Goddess, Wife-Realizer, and Lover-Initiator, three dimensions of total fulfillment, more or less painted according to the myths, Isis being the goddess who brings them all together. Note that the popular traditions of Fairies, Nymphs, Dryads, Dames Blanches, Giants, and Wyverns, or other serpentine expressions, constitute dualistic variations of this ar-

Black Virgins

chetype. It is always a matter of anchoring and verticalizing the chthonic powers.

The cults of these Goddesses convey practices of immortality, resurrection, and ways of the body of light or glory. The traditional cyclical conception of time, which will be erased by the linear approach of organized Christianity, is inscribed in the death and rebirth of a god, demigod, hero, lover, or son, thanks to the intervention of the goddess. Despite the relentlessness of the Roman Church to combat the traditional aspects of these goddesses, Mary very often absorbed their archetypal functions, from the renewal of nature to the conquest of immortality. Moreover, the presence of Black Virgins is characteristic of regions that resisted the authority of the Roman Church.

The word "virgin" does not evoke a physical virginity, but on the contrary a spiritual virginity independent of the sex life. On the contrary, many of these goddesses exalted a free sexuality but remained "immaculate," that is to say, free of any imprint. In some ancient temples, the priestess was considered a virgin at each return of menses. Often, sexual prohibitions indicate an arcanum such as the prohibition to eat beans in Pythagoreanism except at certain very specific ritualized moments. It is the same for the numerous prohibitions concerning menstrual blood. Isis, or the associated goddesses, is sometimes represented revealing her sex. The motif is attested in Egyptian iconography.

Likewise, some Black Virgins discreetly indicate their sex. The almond halo, or mandorla, which is found in the constructions of the companions, then represents the *cteis*. As the aura of the

Isis-Aphrodite
Egyptian Museum of the
University of Leipzig

Virgin, the symbol indicates that the double power (sexual and fertile) has become axial, giving rise to the body of immortality.

A certain number of characteristics are used to recognize Black Virgins, aside from color. They fit into a quadrangular prism, the base three by three with a height of seven. It is draped only in a black or green veil, a single color in any case, and not richly dressed. The feet are bare. The hands are often disproportionate,[97] the fingers very elongated. The child is held upright, already autonomous, between the spread thighs, sometimes covered in gold because, as we have already said, it is from the "sex of ISIS" that the raw material of alchemy is harvested. He is bareheaded. The gaze of the Black Virgin is absolutely free, direct, embracing the infinite. It awakens and characterizes her function as initiator.

Finally, the Black Virgin also evokes not Mary but Mary Magdalene, possible companion of Jesus. Indeed Jesus, as Rabbi, had to be married in order to speak in the Temple. Mary Magdalene holds a central place in traditions of immortality or resurrection, including Christianity through a text of Saint Maximus of Aix. She brings together the myths that disturb official Christianity. The mythemes travel further to Sara, the black saint, as dear to the Companions as to the Roma people.[98] We still find them in the person of Dame Clémence, a reference to Clémence Isaure, the Golden Isis, dear to the Cathars, to whom certain companion movements[99] are heirs, often represented as a Black Virgin. She is the friend of God, *amica dei,* the Lady, who founds and presides over the Floral Games. She represents the new religion, the religion of the perfect, Catharism.

The association with the grotto or the underground crypt, a reference to the Isiac *cteis,* to water, source of life and universal messenger, and to the serpentine powers which weave all realities before rising, winged, is typical of cults to Mother Goddesses.

Through the Black Virgins, the essence of Tradition persists. Reading what they reveal, with the discretion and elegance necessary to go unnoticed, brings us closer to the secret of secrets, a practice of immortality, inscribed in nature and still preserved today by some traditional currents similarly elusive, since they talk little. We are only indicating a few leads here. Everything has to be *verified.* Verification (three times) allows one to escape replication and then imitation to access the invention of oneself as Christ.

THE *ARCANA ARCANORUM*

NINETEENTH LETTER TO FRIENDS OF THE SPIRIT • SECOND SERIES

DEMYSTIFICATION AND RE-ENCHANTMENT[100]

THE *ARCANA ARCANORUM* CAUSED A GREAT DEAL of ink to flow, often very inappropriately, at the end of the last century, partially sterilizing a myth intended to convey an operative whole.

The *Arcana Arcanorum* is usually referred to as the four, sometimes three, final grades of the Egyptian Masonic rites, particular grades on the scale of Naples (from 87° to 90°).

The A∴A∴ is also present within other organizations: Pythagoreans, Rosicrucians, and certain hermetic colleges more or less closed, using the same name or another, and sometimes without particular identification. The operations which the A∴A∴ refer to are found in most traditional currents, including the Catholics (we are thinking in particular of the *Hieron du Val d'Or* and the *Etoile Internelle*). However, more than organized groups, it is better to imagine a few individuals, some isolated, who have sufficiently deepened the assemblages of mythemes offered by traditions to find ancient and natural practices. Some will turn to the Taoist, Buddhist, or Shaivite equivalents to verify, confirm, or deepen what remains an adventure.

From the Masonic point of view, it is advisable to distinguish the system of the Bédarride brothers, based on the Kabbalah, from the Rite of Naples that constitutes the true system of A∴A∴. Ragon tells us of these four degrees in these terms: "They form the whole philosophical system of the true rite of Misraïm, which satisfies any educated Mason, while the same degrees among the F∴F∴ Bédarride are a fraudulent mockery born of their ignorance…" For Sebastiano Caracciolo,[101] the rite of Misraïm was inscribed only in the four grades of the Scale of Naples.

The Rite or Scale of Naples refers to the School of Naples. In the 18th century, Naples was one of the key cities of Europe, intellectually and artistically. Prince Raimondo di Sangro of Sansevero was one of the great figures of the traditional Neapolitan current. Grand Master of Neapolitan Freemasonry, under attack from the Inquisition, the Prince was a great alchemist and renewed a current inherited from Egypt, Greece, and Chaldea. We owe to him, among other things, the famous Chapel of Sansevero, a masterpiece of Baroque art, a hermetic book of stone, famous among other things for the extraordinary *Veiled Christ* by the sculptor Sanmartino and the two anatomical machines kept in the crypt. This school[102] influenced Cagliostro, Baron de Tschudi, and (closer to us) Giuliano Kremmerz, but also lesser known personalities such as Baron Ricciardi, Pascal de Servis, Lebano, Lombardi, Prince Caetani, etc.

The *Arcana Arcanorum* is defined by Jean-Pierre Giudicelli de Cressac-Bachelerie:[103] "This teaching concerns a theurgy, that is to say a connection with eon-guides who must take over to convey the understanding of a process, but also a very closed alchemical path which is a *Neidan,* that is to say, an internal path."

The Masonic Arcana Arcanorum seems in reality to be, rather than the final ranks of Egyptian Masonry, the introduction to another system. The A∴A∴ in fact constitutes a qualification for other more internal orders attached to the Osirian or Pythagorean current or even to the current of the old Rose+Croix, such as the *Ordre des Rose+Croix d'Or d'Ancien*

Système, the Order of Initiated Brothers of Asia, the Order of African Architects, and others that remain unknown, generally escaping historical research and (at least in part) human problems.

Jean-Pierre Giudicelli de Cressac-Bachelerie, referring to Brunelli, confirms[104] that the A∴A∴ in fact constitutes the introduction to other orders: "As G.M. Brunelli has indicated in his remarkable works on the rites of Misraim and Memphis, other orders follow the *Arcana Arcanorum*. But here we leave the Masonic aspect to discover four or five other orders (*Grand Ordre Égyptien,* the Egyptian Rites, as well as three others that we cannot mention)."

Additionally, some traditional organizations, not using the name *"Arcana Arcanorum,"* hold all or part of the theurgic collection of the A∴A∴.

The complete system of the *Arcana Arcanorum,* of which Egyptian Masonry would therefore only hold a part, in fact comprises three disciplines:

- A theurgy that presents itself, depending on the documents, in a double form, Chaldæan-Egyptian or angelic Kabbalah: particularly with the invocations of 4, 7, and the great operation of 72. We could also speak of High Magic, in reference to Eliphas Levi, or of Magic if we borrow the definition of Aleister Crowley.
- Metallic alchemy: among various ways, the documents identified seem to give priority to the way of Antimony, but other ways, in particular the way of the Salamander or the way of Cinnabar, seem to constitute an important element of this system, relating to both the external and the internal, either for educational or operational reasons.
- Internal alchemy: according to the internal currents, the practiced ways differ less technically than by their respective philosophi-

cal and mythical environments, sometimes divergent. Internal alchemy, just like metallic alchemy, would find its origin in the East and, more particularly, according to Alain Daniélou, in Shaivism. But, common to many traditions, they have been present in both the East and the West for millennia, either because of the very numerous contacts between peoples despite the considerable distances involved, contacts demonstrated by modern archeology, or because the powerful connection to nature, so altered today, led to the same discoveries. However, they have been part of the traditional Western heritage for at least two millennia, as certain Egyptian or Gnostic papyri attest (one thinks in particular of the very important Bruce Codex). In matters of internal alchemy, we speak of ways of immortality (what does this word "immortality" mean? Immortality of what, of whom?), of ways of the Body of Glory (a confusing term: what are we talking about when we talk about the body?) or even of real ways (what "real" do we mean?).

In general these ways, in their different expressions, would include at the same time natural magic (according to Giordano Bruno, magic is the art of memory and the manipulation of fantasies; it is mastery of what some ethologists call "the bewitching of the world"), a theurgy, and an alchemy, vector of a way of immortality.

The question of immortalities is difficult to deal with because it cannot fit successfully into a model of the Aristotelian world, which is why it is not uncommon to see an untimely search by an immature personality for a superhumanity, a more-than-humanity, or a non-humanity, which unfortunately leads to inhumanity, or at least to pathology.

Moreover, we may very well have an excellent intellectual understanding of non-Aristotelian models, such as Taoism, or the Gurdjieff system, without having "inverted the candlesticks" (to use Meyrink's formula in *The Green Face*), or without having shifted into a nondualistic relationship to what is presented (the world).

Superhumanity could be symbolized by Heracles, thus indicating the magical way of the Hero; predisposing to more-than-humanity, symbolized by Christ, or even by Orpheus; or inclination to non-humanity, symbolized by Osiris, or also by Dionysus. We could find other references both in the West and in Eastern traditions to try to capture what is in fact a difference in the relationship to nonduality. Being is not necessarily oriented towards a single pole, which explains the different Real Ways, not leading therefore to the same Place-State, but nevertheless pointing towards a single Recognition of oneself as being the Lord or the Absolute.

The A∴A∴ of the Rite of Naples introduce an internal alchemy of Egyptian tradition in two phases, one Isiac, the other Osirian. It is of course in this last aspect of internal alchemy that we find the more specifically Osirian aspects of the A∴A∴. It is probable that in the Middle Ages and the Renaissance, this system was exclusively Chaldeo-Egyptian; it would be little by little, and mainly in its magical and theurgic aspects, that the system would have undergone in certain traditional structures a "Christianization" or a "Hebraization." We sometimes find the expression "Chaldean Christianity" in this connection.

It is important not to fall into the hypertrophy of secret or internal ways. Secret classes exist. Note that a secret class we are talking about is no longer a secret class. These internal colleges are intended to bring together a few individuals detached from contingencies who devote themselves to the full implementation of a discipline, often alchemical. It is advisable to demystify these secret classes and to remember that only the work counts. So, to come back to the Masonic A∴A∴, there are those who have heard of it, those who have received the degrees administratively, those who have received them ritually, those who have studied them, those who have implemented them, and those who have realized with them. Note that at the end of his life, Robert Ambelain confided that he had lost decades in Freemasonry and that the only practice that had been efficient for him was that of Abramelin.

The *Arcana Arcanorum,* or its equivalents, are available in many libraries in Europe and elsewhere under one term or another. Poets, writers, craftsmen-companions, and painters (I am thinking for example of Victor Brauner and his body of paintings, or of Lima de Freitas with his paintings but also his writings, in particular the one devoted to 515, the key of Dante) know the process designated as the secret of secrets. There is a great illusion in approaching these so-called final aspects by giving them an inordinate importance. Theurgy and alchemy are not used to obtain or to grasp but to celebrate in the relinquishment. They do not lead to Awakening, but celebrate Awakening in the three dimensions of substance, energy and essence. The key is, always, Silence. By "Silence" we mean the permanent awareness of the present moment, uncommented. This continuous presence, day and night, allows the coagulation of consciousness from a dualistic point of view, and an alternating contraction of consciousness from a nondualistic point of view. We will come back to this.

Let's take a look at a few tricky points:

Filiation or not?

Among the hypertrophies that pollute the esoteric scene, there is that of filiation: temporal, linear, and therefore terribly dualistic filiation, for which many people are struggling in the nets of ignorance. Of course, the initiatory path is made up of meetings with personalities, with groups, and with organizations that nourish the process and help to orient it. However, all real filiation is axial, resulting from our own original and ultimate Reality, which remains: the "already and not yet," which should be updated to "here and now." If we must remain in the dualistic relationship to filiation, it would, I believe, be wise to integrate what we are told by the quantum sciences, which today are close to nondual metaphysics.

While some explorers of the quantum domain refuse to extrapolate from experiments on photons to hypothesize on the construction of reality, others do not hesitate to take the leap between physics and metaphysics. Philippe Guillemant[105] still questions time with his theory of double-causality. Also considered by Stephen Hawking, it postulates a retrocausality from the future, a very present future. We are moving away from linear and univocal past-present-future causality for a retrograde causality stemming from the future and the effect. Through reproducible experiments, in the laboratory and in everyday life, it is possible to create synchronicities at will. This model opens up multiple perspectives for approaching certain phenomena falling within the field of tradition, in particular the question of filiation and transmission. According to Philippe Guillemant, it would be possible to move from one timeline to another, to actualize one future rather than another by an unconditional intention, capable of sliding from one probability to another. The question of free will and the freedom associated with this possibility is complex and requires further study. We could say that all filiation and all transmission come from our future, already present, which coincides, traditionally, with our divine origin. The encounters are thus reflections in a mirror game that tirelessly brings us closer, as long as we are vigilant, to our own reality.

Immortality to endure or eternity of Consciousness?

Very often, too often, candidates for this type of work come forward as a person. Always identified with worldliness, they have not freed their indivisible part, the true individual, from his dross of conditionings. They lack axiality, and the sought-after immortality is immortality to endure. It is about extending the "me," the "ego," to replicate it, instead of recognizing it as a simple assembly of objects of the nature of void.

Another approach to immortality, nondual, lies in the liberation of all peripheries into the Heart of Being, of our true original and ultimate, timeless nature, which both generates forms and reabsorbs them.

These two immortalities are typified in Edward Bulwer-Lytton by Mejnour and Zanoni in his famous eponymous novel. For Zanoni, one must renounce what lasts, including relative immortality, all temporality, in order to gain access to divinity, to the One, to the Absolute. It is not enough to escape the trap of *chronos*. It is also necessary, after having explored it, to break free from the spiral time of *aion,* by seizing *kairos,* the deep opportunity of the present moment.

Duality or nonduality?

In a dualistic relationship to the world (appearance, everything that presents itself in consciousness), the person will practice in order to endure. The "me" seeks to control the practice in order to prolong itself and continue to generate appearance. Theurgy and alchemy, in this respect, are a "doing." The process followed is "having-doing-being": to hold the arcanum, to use it to be, one day, immortal. There is time: the past, the future. Cronos reigns, who, as everyone knows, devours his children. In a nondualistic relationship to the world, there is only unified Consciousness and Silence and "nothing to do" because "I Am" or "It remains." Art, in its alchemy, its divine chemistry, which includes grammar and metaphysics, is an art of doing nothing. The process, if there is a process, is the reverse of "being-doing-having." From my true, divine nature, I celebrate my Absolute Freedom through theurgy and alchemy without waiting for the slightest result since Everything is accomplished. I celebrate for beauty and joy. This "doing" is a "non-doing," this "having" is only festive and ephemeral. "I" let the Freedom of the Absolute flow into the peripheries of experience before reintegrating everything.

It is often forgotten that any tradition is inherently nondualistic. Nondualism is not an oriental specificity, even if the concept of the orient should carry some meaning other than conventional, arbitrary, and geographical, at the crossroads of the colonial heritage and the romantic heritage. Let us think of Spinoza, the philosopher of philosophers, but also of Meister Eckhart (whose doctrine is close to the nondualism of Kashmir embodied by Abhinavagupta), of Nicholas of Cusa, of Rabelais, or of Iranian Islam. Ancient Egypt is profoundly nondualistic. Isis is Re's equal. She is not lunar but solar. It is the Greeks, in particular Plutarch, who will reduce her to a lunar goddess. The Greeks, and this will result in a progressive rejection of the body which will tragically influence Christianity, will move away from the traditional nondualistic approach, especially from Parmenides to Plato. It is this Egyptian nondualist current that Schwaller de Lubicz will seek to manifest, who was a specialist in internal alchemy, one of the last known with Louis Cattiaux.[106]

There are indeed, in ancient Egypt as in most traditional currents, two approaches that are described, without further reflection, as solar and lunar. They are actually both solar. The first solarity refers to a self-engendered, metaphysical conception of oneself. Re is self-sufficient. This is the ithyphallic Royalty represented on the walls of the temples. It is the secret of secrets of the Temple of Luxor. The second solarity, Isiac (equal to Re, let us remember), makes the female initiator the one who brings Osiris back to life and engenders Horus.

We have two solarities, one internal-internal, all axial, the other external-internal, all radiant and inclusive. Far from being opposed, these two approaches are one, like a breath, like the two centers of the traditional almond or ellipse. In reality, in the absence of distinction between the internal and the external, Re and Isis constitute two necessities, inscribed either in the axiality without periphery, without manifestation, or in the axiality with periphery, with manifestation.

The exaggerated place of sexuality

Very often, all too often, sexuality and the ways of immortality, or sexuality and internal alchemy, are associated in an affected way. It is true that sexuality is a dimension of the subject, as shown by the symbolism (phallus surrounded by a yoni, phallus in the middle of a basket of fruits, or others indicating the call to the purest vital energy). Vulva and Phallus evoke the secrets of life and death as well as their vanquishing. However, we tend to confuse sexuality with genitality. The power of the reproduction of forms, including the ego, of replicating the objects within consciousness, identically, from moment to moment, thus creating both the world as discourse and the illusion of temporal continuity, is indeed a fertilization, that which generates appearance. In a way, we permanently impregnate the universe with our conditioned thoughts. Duality is thus sexed, by definition. In the same way that tantrism does not exist but that the tantras exist, like the very many schools based on these teachings, sex magic does not exist but sexuality, specific to the dualistic game, is a magic, and the sexual act itself can be a celebration of the absolute hierogamy that is nonduality. The rare ways that use sexuality wisely do not allow an unbridled life. It begins with long abstinence, with a mastery of meditation on emptiness, and requires a variety of qualifications and exclusions.

In the context of the ways of immortality, we sometimes speak of the way of substances, which is a misleading expression. It would be more correct to speak of a modality of substances among the three modalities: substance – energy – essence, which typify the continuum of Flesh to Spirit that even Bossuet had sensed when he spoke of the earthly objects of desire that imperfectly prefigure the celestial objects of desire. Every-

The Arcana Arcanorum

thing that manifests is simultaneously substance, energy, and essence, according to the degree of duality or nonduality that directs our gaze.

In internal alchemy, it is traditionally possible to work with, for example, blood (in the *Rose-Croix d'Or d'Ancien Système*), saliva, sperm, female sexual secretions (cyprine[107] and others), urine (in Cagliostro and Schwaller de Lubicz), and tears. It is the false secret, familiar to surrealists and others, that sometimes fuels perverse little power games in certain initiatory or so-called initiatory circles.

These traditional practices are inscribed either in a therapeutic perspective (ways of longevity in Taoism, often confused with ways of immortality, or Indian *amaroli*), in a mystical perspective (tears as a mode of transmission of the prayer of the heart in Orthodoxy), from a psychological perspective (transgression as an active agent in the breaking-down of conditioning), or from an alchemical perspective (the body is an athanor and the substances are sulfur, salt and mercury, functions that can vary according to the schools and even within the same school, depending on the phase of the work). In most of these internal currents, it is a matter of a drink of immortality, a sacred mixture, called Soma, Amrita, Kybelion or other names, symbolized by all rites of the Eucharistic type.

This is the operative and metaphorical theme of the vase and its contents, two mythemes that run throughout the traditions. The three contents of the sacred vessel can be derived from plant alchemy, mineral alchemy, or internal alchemy. In the case of internal alchemy, the fabrication of the content can be external for ingestion or be totally internal, and then we switch to the energy modality. However, this modality also affects bodily substances, for example by generating ecstasies.

We find the theme in Rabelais. Pantagruel, Rabelais' true hero, with whom Panurge undertakes the quest for the Divine Bottle, is a giant, just like his father Gargantua. Unlike Pantagruel, Gargantua is not a character created by Rabelais. As the last representative of a very ancient pagan initiatory tradition, there already exists in popular folklore a transcendent entity whose names invariably present the sounds of G.R.G.N. He is in the service of King Arthur,[108] who typifies the Superman, whose enemies he fights. Arthur is a past King but above all a future King, who also evokes for us the Hidden King. Gargantua is a prototype of the ancient initiator and ancient superman found in all traditions. Giants, giantesses, ogres, and ogresses, often deified, chase human beings to swallow them, totally digest their adhesions to the phenomenal world to free them from it, and restore them to their transcendent essence. These giants and giantesses, "divinizing digesters"[109] according to Pierre Gordon, invariably remain in the heart of a sacred mountain, near a holy spring, in a grotto or cave, a place favorable to the regeneration of being through light in the darkness. These giants and giantesses assumed this function of superhuman immortality in the form of an animal, serpent or dragon, represented in the sacred constructions by the labyrinth. Here we are approaching a rigorous ascesis in the underworld, a vampiric decarnation[110] which liberates the body of immortality.

This theme of the initiatory journey is also very present in the journey of Ulysses, where the trials of devouring follow one after another with the Cyclops, the Læstrygones, Scylla, and Charybdis; and trials that are often nearly a trial of seduction which it is advisable to avoid: the lotophagi, Circe, the sirens, and Calypso. This dialectic between seduction and devouring, this alternation between love and death (also present in modalities, some divergent and some isomorphic, found in Rabelais, with whom the seductions and orgiastic meals multiply, imparting a dual rhythm to the living), typifies the initiatory journey, traversing dynamic oppositions.

This ancient theocratic ritual, the rite of the divine ogre or giant, of course echoes the Christian Eucharist and similar practices such as the Pythagorean Holy Syssitia, but it is a reverse echo. The giant, divine initiator, original initiator-ancestor, returns man to his own divinity by absorbing and digesting human mortality. He eats the human, that is to say

The Arcana Arcanorum

the multiple, the scattered, to make one and leave room for being. Christ, also divine initiator, the new ancestor, the ultimate initiator-ancestor, gives himself to be eaten as immortal matter. Here we have two ways of understanding the same rite of death and resurrection.

The same process is at work in internal alchemy. The ingestion of oneself, which includes the world, substantial or energetic, releases the essence.

Finally, note that these substances, tears, blood, saliva, and others, are all essentially composed of water, a vessel of messages (coded information) inscribed and modified by fires, salivary, sexual, respiratory, biliary, or others.[111]

The "Game of Water and Fire" carries the very essence of internal alchemy. It would be a mistake to limit it to the human being. It works throughout the universe.

DEATH, AN OLD FRIEND

TWENTIETH LETTER TO FRIENDS OF THE SPIRIT • SECOND SERIES

EATH IS BOTH A MATTER OF MAJOR IMPORTANCE in the structuring of our lives and societies, and of extreme banality. Initiatory rites seek to go beyond death and the social rites (including the economic ones) that integrate it. Today, science wants to "conquer" death as medicine has sought over the centuries to remove it, at least temporarily, and particularly since the beginning of the last century, which saw a real break in the relationship maintained with death. Having become biological and medical, death (a necessary component of life) has become a taboo, a failure, even a shame about which we are unable to elaborate.

We know we were born because we were told so and we know we are going to die because we are told so over and over again. It is part of the narrative of the person, of a conditioned construction. In reality, we were never born and thus we cannot die. The simple attentive observer will notice that the body (and therefore its extension, the world) is in consciousness and not the other way around. Everything is consciousness, which continues to contract into multiple forms and to relax, in a game of forgetting and recognition of its divine state, total, at the same time first, last, and permanent.

Real death is not the death of the body but the oblivion and stagnation in duality that makes us dead to ourselves, dead to our own divine nature. Rebirth into nonduality is the movement back to our original, divine state. We have already seen how this movement is inscribed in respiration.[112]

What is shown in duality is the destruction of the body. What is perceived from nonduality is the permanent creation and self-realization of oneself in its true nature, a liberation.

If the early Christians were known as the "Living," it was to indicate their inscription in the Presence. "Here and now," no one can die because there is neither before nor after, only total Consciousness.

In Hebrew, the word *mavet,* "death," and *meod,* "very good," are made up of the same letters, which suggests that death is favorable. Indeed, it is an old friend when it reminds us of our condition and invites us to come out of the oblivion in duality to reconquer the citadel of Being, to rejoin ourselves in our true nature. This is what the myths of rebirth want to recall with insistence, whether that of Osiris, of Christ, or of Hiram.

The word *mavet* begins with Mem, a letter that begins and ends with itself, folded into duality. It is associated with the number 40 that we find alike in the forty days of Elijah's walk to Mount Horeb, the forty days spent in the desert by Jesus, the forty days of preparation by Jesus' disciples before leaving for their mission, as well as in Cagliostro's retreats. This withdrawal is an alchemical place-state that allows, within the crucible of duality, for the emergence of the "immortal" of nondual nature. Therefore, the ordinary Mem is open while the final Mem (at the end of the word, therefore at the end of history) is closed. Death is a renewal, a restoration of the Hidden King, the Self, in all its fullness, an inclusion of the duality of Appearance within the Real of nonduality.

In ancient Greek traditions, it was Persephone and her descendants, including Hermes, her grandson, who ensured the immortality of initiates. While we might expect an immortality acquired through the consumption of ambrosia, which suspends time, it is the water of Mnemosyne, memory, that is the determining factor. But this is not a matter of personal memory since it washes away all stain, all conditioning; it is a question of total memory, of all knowledge born from the totality of past, present, and future experiences, which are experiences of the recognition of one's own divine nature.

With Dionysus, initiation results in immortality, whether one is in a body of flesh or not. With Orpheus, we have a process announced in the Orphic inscriptions accompanying the dead on slats of gold: *They will give you to drink (water) from Lake Mnemosyne / And you, when you have drunk, you will walk the sacred way...*[113] In all cases, as in the Isiac rites (Osiris is identical to the water of the Nile), water, the vehicle of information, of the original code, once again is essential. The water of the Styx, like the water of Mnemosyne, makes it possible to distinguish the initiate from the non-initiate, but the first concerns absolute immortality and the second relative immortality, even for the gods. The living waters are beneficial, the swampy waters toxic; the first go from the Source to the Divine Garden, the others stagnate. This informational alchemy is indicated by Aetius:[114] *By Zeus, he designates effervescence and ether; by Hera, mother of life, the air; the earth by Aidôneus; and by Nestis, the tears from which mortals drink, the seed, and the water.*

We will find some representations of the Greek Hades in the Jewish Sheol. The Greek conception of nature and the journey of the soul is found among the Essenes. There were probably shifts in mythemes from one culture to another. The quasi-protocol reported by Aetius corresponds to the knowledge conveyed by the construction of the temple of Solomon as the Body of Glory.[115] Among the common mythemes we find, in almost all the traditions of immortality, the serpent (both a symbol of immortality and a symbol of fertility by its phallic form). The Serpent,[116] as much at ease in Water as on Earth, equips itself with wings to conquer Heaven. The same is true of the peacock,[117] symbol of the psychopomp Hermes (who became at the same time Dionysian, Herculean, and Christic), passed from the Orphic and Pythagorean traditions to Christianity as a symbol of immortality and resurrection. It is the vehicle of the spirit like the griffin or the almost universal phoenix.

If the object of initiation is to become a New Adam by the path of Reintegration, Adam being immortal, it is a question of recovering this immortality, lost by the voluntary plunge into the Appearance of duality. Adam being one, he was not aware of his feminine part and consequently of his masculine part and was thus sterile. The plunge into duality allows him to become aware of his double feminine and masculine nature (the two *Hé*'s of Tetragrammaton). The New Adam thus has an increased awareness of his own nature which enables him to create. What he actually conquers by knowing himself is Freedom.

In Hebrew, the fall, this exile in duality in order to recognize oneself, is represented by the letter Nun. Like the Mem, the Nun has two forms, ordinary and final. The ordinary Nun is the Man of the Stream, the bent man of Judaism, and the final Nun is the New Man, the accomplished initiate, the man straightened by the serpentine restoration of *Nachash* (see the 2nd Letter of the first series, dedicated to the Garden of Eden).

We find this paradoxical letter associated with the word *Mashiach,* the Messiah (see the 8th Letter of the first series, dedicated to anointing). Josy Eisenberg and Adin Steinsaltz[118] remind us that "Messiah" also means "stillborn," aborted. Several interpretations are possible. We can say that the Messiah is in the world carrying eternity and light but remains dead to the world or unidentified with the world.

In a very operative way, as each are Messiah, we can also say that with each breath, in the movement of birth (inbreath), the return to the divine Source (interval), and the death or Reintegration of the Source (outbreath), we can remain in Source if we are already stillborn at the inbreath, unidentified in form, with the world, and so Messiah, New Adam, unborn and therefore immortal.

JOY

TWENTY-FIRST LETTER TO FRIENDS OF THE SPIRIT • SECOND SERIES

OY IS A PARTICULAR WISDOM, A UNIQUE expression of the Recognition of oneself as being the Lord. We are talking here about nondual Joy, without an object, which is born of non-separation and which we can also call Love or Freedom, as these three "dimensions" are inseparable.

We will distinguish nondual Joy from dualistic joy which involves a subject and an object by remembering that these two joys are one. Indeed, dualistic joy points to nondual Joy: it is a memory of it, an echo within duality and also a promise of future realization.

Dualistic joy in fact always points to non-separation. It is the joy of finding a companion after a temporary separation, the joy of sharing a moment of intimacy with your favorite animal, the joy of finding a book that you thought was lost in your library, the joy of contemplating an inspiring painting… The "object" brings us closer to ourselves and tends to merge with the subject in the interval of communion. It is a matter of attention. Every joy experienced in duality is a spark of nondual Joy, Freedom, and Love, usually immediately engulfed in the stream of commentary and comparison.

In Hebrew, dualistic joy is generally expressed by the word *simcha*, which evokes celebrations inscribed in causality. However, this same word also evokes nondual Joy, the joy of God thus qualified as eternal as in Isaiah 51:11: "Therefore the redeemed of the Lord shall return, and come with singing unto Zion; and everlasting *joy* shall be upon their head..." The Aramaic word *chedvah* also carries the idea of a dualistic joy (in Ezra 6:16), or nondual as in Chronicles 16:27: "Splendor and majesty are before him; strength and *joy* are in his place." The Greek word *chara,* which we find in many Bible verses, generally designates causal joy, "the joy of," but it too can designate another form of joy, nondual, acausal. In John 15:11, it is a matter of a perfect joy, one that can only be without cause, independent of the context, nondual: "These things have I spoken unto you, that my *joy* might remain in you, and that your *joy* might be full." Only in joy can there be revelation, deep knowledge, and grasp of the arcana, never in sorrow.

If the most banal joy leads us to Freedom and reminds us of our original state, we can easily understand why states and religions seek to deprive the people of joys in order to keep them in sadness. None other than Baruch Spinoza[119] identified the issues and the mechanisms at work.

For Spinoza, sadness decreases the creative power or "power to act," while joy increases it, but the reverse applies simultaneously: the decrease in the power to act generates sadness, while its increase provides joy. We can already imagine the toxic closed loops that we can be locked into.

In Spinoza's *Ethics,* we encounter two words, *affectio* and *affectus,* often unfortunately translated by the same word, "affection." If *affectus* is in Spinoza the permanent variation of our power to act that results from our degree of orientation towards sadness or towards joy, *affectio* is a category or type of ideas that he distinguishes from notion and essence.

The affection-*affectio* is the response of the body-object or the self-object to a stimulus from an object considered to be external. One object acts on the other within consciousness, for example, a light that dazzles and makes it impossible to see for a few seconds. The affection-*affectio* is this new 'affected object – affecting object' system polarized on the affected side. Its analysis provides information on the nature of the affected object rather than that of the affecting object. For Spinoza, this is the first kind of knowledge, that of relations with external objects. It is resolutely dualistic.

Joy

With "notion," we place ourselves as a witness to the object-object system, that is to say the self-object, often designated as "subject" or the self-body-object, and an "external" object: light, sound, speech, heat, etc. The notion, according to Spinoza, is the idea measuring the adequacy or the inadequacy of the relationship between the two objects: the self-body-object and the "external" object. I can understand the action of cold on my body and establish the adequacy or inadequacy of it. The action may be adequate if the cold soothes the pain from a blow, or inadequate if it causes my body to die. Adequacy is associated with joy and inadequacy with sadness. It is a second kind of knowledge, that of the knowledge of causes. In Spinoza, there is the idea of a common notion, shared by the collective which has itself become an individual entity or system.

With "essence," we touch what is not measurable, an ineffable that totally characterizes us and merges with the infinite power of God. It is the third mode of knowledge which is nondual and arises from the non-separation of the subject-object, which is to say the object-object, since everything that appears in consciousness (such as the ego) is an object. "Here and now," in the infinite interval of Being, there is only Joy, nondual Joy, without subject or object.

The three modes of knowledge echo the journey that goes from the Man of the Stream to the New Man by way of the Man of Desire, in the terminology of Louis-Claude de Saint-Martin.

For Spinoza, it is not we who have successive ideas but ideas that assert themselves in us. He speaks of an *automaton,* as does Aristotle. Individuality, according to Spinoza ("the person," in our frame of reference), is a set of complex relationships, reminiscent of the Buddhist aggregates. We cannot know ourselves since we are tossed about at random by encounters that establish relations. Spinoza thus considers evil as a bad encounter that alters the relations that constitute us.

That we are spiritual automatons evokes the man-machine of

Gurdjieff or the postponed corpse of Pessoa or the words of Martinez de Pasqually: "People in the street do not know why they are walking, but you, you will know." For Martinez too, ideas arise. They are offered by the Good Companion Spirit or on the contrary by the Bad Companion. For Saint-Martin, since the Fall, we thinking beings have become thought beings. We are lived by ideas.

Martinez de Pasqually, like Baruch Spinoza, originated from Marrano culture. Note that the Marranos[120] were very similar to the first disciples of Christ, Jewish protesters within the Jewish community, whom they wished to "rectify," and were very often forced to hide. The Marrano, crypto-Jew and proto-Christian, regardless of the anachronism, is a type of the initiate. Any accomplished initiate is a "marrano" within the world of duality. Realizing his nondual essence, he conceals it in the crypt of the world of duality.

According to Spinoza, religions and states seek to orient us, repeatedly and systematically, towards the pole of sadness in order to keep us in a form of dependence or even servitude vis-à-vis the powers by extinguishing or controlling our power to act. The mechanism works thoroughly nowadays, including in the so-called "democracies." The orientation towards joy frees creativity and affirms the need for realization by liberating from the basic search for the satisfaction of physiological or security needs, as well as the needs for recognition and belonging. Joy is eminently subversive and initiatory. Dualistic joy leads to nondual Joy and, conversely, nondual Joy animates the simplest dualistic joys by recalling our origin and our destination, by calling for the release from the prison of having and doing, or by calling to the fullness of Being. The initiatory process leads from dualistic joy with an object to nondual Joy without an object, just as it does from dualistic love with an object to nondual Love without an object. As a member or leader of an initiatory, research, or (artistic or scientific) creative group, we must, through solarity, increase the power to act of those with whom we work; we must bring joy, a joy first linked to the creative idea, then in the interval, the Joy without idea, the Joy in itself, or the Joy of the Self.

To witness this game of conditioning is to extract oneself from it, to learn to "know oneself" and to rejoin Being, our own nature. But to accomplish this movement of recall and witnessing, we are going to use the power to act, the joy prior to grasping the interval. To grasp the interval is to live on the borderline between the field of sadness (Bad Companion Spirit) and the field of joy (Good Companion Spirit) in duality and to turn to nondual Joy. This is the place-state of rectification, of adjustment, the setting up of the *tikkun*. There is a double nature of *tikkun:* one, ordinary, which results in respect for rites and rules; the other, secret, which leads to the realization and revelation of the Spirit. The process arises in ordinary joy and is realized, fulfilled, in nondual Joy.

Rites and traditional practices bring this joy, this affect that envelops a growing power to act, and orients it towards Being. By localizing joy in sadness and sadness in joy within duality, just as in Portuguese *saudade,* we grow out of the (dualistic) game and out of existence, since existence is an oppositional game, and we switch to the (nondual) Great Game. We grow out of time also, to Eternity rather than the immortality that requires a before and an after. Strictly speaking, it is a "reversal" that erases all opposition. Initiatory praxes are based on this power to act for the attainment of the infinite interval, where Being and its Happiness, Beauty, and Freedom dwell.

FROM THE PEOPLE OF LETTERS TO THE PEOPLE OF BEING[121]

TWENTY-SECOND LETTER TO FRIENDS OF THE SPIRIT • SECOND SERIES

SIDELONG GLANCES AT THE CONNECTIONS BETWEEN TRADITION AND LITERATURE[122]

AS THE TITLE OF THIS LETTER INDICATES, WE will not speak with you about Tradition and Literature as specialists, experts, historians, or academics, but rather as nomads, nomads in voluntary wandering, nomads who have made the choice of motionless drift. No truth, therefore, but touches of paint affixed almost at random on a canvas which we would have preferred white, or black and luminous, but which could not be so.

Let's explain the title:

Sidelong glances. Can it be otherwise? Human beings do not have access to objectivity. They always look at an angle, subjective by nature and unfortunately unconscious of being, except perhaps for the madman who, being master of the diagonals, sees his sidelong glance resting, straight, and inflexible on the Real.

Connections maintain, so as not to forget, that Eros is at the center of Tradition as well as Literature. Connections: romantic, fusional, violent, sulfurous, dangerous, ambiguous… Literature especially speaks to us in all these cases, as well as the mathematical, the geometric, even the chemical.

Tradition and *Literature,* singular or plural, singular and plural. We are talking about the great Tradition, which we call primordial, and the great Literature, which we call eternal, but also of all the garments, all the hand-me-downs, sometimes even the many rags, in which traditions and literatures are covered in the times and spaces of man.

Where to begin? A few loose remarks, to start our ramble.

The title and theme of this conference: *Tradition and Literature.* What is meant by that, and in particular by *Tradition*? Is it the primordial Tradition dear to René Guénon; *esotericism,* a catch-all term despite the efforts of Antoine Faivre; or *occultism,* a more precise and more suitable term thanks to the work of Robert Amadou, but always accompanied by a smell of sulfur? (And then Robert Amadou whispers to me: literature, real literature, doesn't it also smell of sulfur?) Is it *hermetism,* a term that I would prefer, but which would require moving some distance from its strictest meaning and ultimately betraying Hermes? Françoise Bonardel, in her *Que-sais-je?* on Hermes, has further proposed to create the adjective *hermesian* to avoid confusion with the regular meaning of *hermetic.*

Esotericism, occultism, and *hermetism* have Tradition as their central notion. This is undoubtedly more true for occultism and hermetism, which are two traditional doctrines, than for esotericism, certain forms of which have nothing to do with the traditional. In fact, the word *Tradition* signifies *transmission.* The etymology implies a deposit to be transmitted or given. *Tradition* derives from the Latin word *traditio,* the action of transmitting, itself formed from *trans,* through, and *dare,* to give. The Greek παραδοσισ is composed like the Latin *traditio* of a root word expressing the idea of a gift and a prefix inducing passage.

Give what? Through what? What is this fair passage we've outlined? We will evoke two traditional ways of transmitting that we find, transposed, in literature.

There is, on the one hand, a traditional legacy transmissible over time along uninterrupted lines which are differentiated from one another by a particular corpus, a given culture, a cosmogony, a mythology, a metaphysics, and sometimes a theosophy, that are the basis of beliefs and behaviors. These lineages are more or less identifiable historically, made up of influences, of desire, as Louis-Claude de Saint-Martin (1743–1803) says, of meetings, but sometimes also of institutions (initiatory orders, cenacles, fraternities, assemblies, and churches, not to mention magazines, bookstores, publishing houses, sometimes university conferences...).

On the other hand, there is a direct access to the object of Tradition, here and now, freed from time and human representations, an access that traditions veil or unveil, or veil and unveil, to their adepts. Any traditional system is supposed to teach the praxis necessary for the discovery of this passage inscribed in the singular verticality, which is distinct from (without necessarily being opposed to) the serpentine transmissions inscribed in the horizontality of time. Behind the traditions, an absolute, informal, and non-human structure will constitute this passage, this interval towards the Real, towards God, or towards the Absolute, depending on the term that is judged to be the most adapted to one's model of the world. Let us quote Martin Heidegger (*Letter to Sartre*, 1945): "It is a question of seizing in its greatest seriousness the present moment of the world, of holding it to its word without taking into account the spirit of party, the currents of fashion, or the scholarly debates—so that the decisive experience (in which we can learn with what abysmal depth the richness of being is sheltered in essential nothingness) finally awakens." Already the path is emerging that goes from silence to the written word, including the spoken word.

More generally, any transcendent experience, any quest for awakening, for freedom, for the absolute, any conquest of oneself, of one's own most ultimate reality, whether expressed in a religious form or a non-religious form (philosophical or artistic, for example), would thus belong to the essence of tradition. In absolute terms, there would be no transmission because of... Being. Being does not require transmission. It abides. It just has to be unveiled or perhaps allowed to unveil itself.

And in that case, are we not getting closer to Marcel Proust's definition of Literature as the "translation of an inner book"? The word that translates the silence, the writing that translates the word.

Tradition is often qualified as oral. Robert Amadou remarked in his book devoted to the occult that "the term 'oral,' which can characterize the traditional mode of transmission, is especially used in opposition to the term 'material.' We mean that Tradition is not given in the form of written texts that would deliver it whole and unveiled." Does this mean, however, that it is only given orally, through the word? Tradition is delivered only in silence, assert the adepts of the West as well as the East, and silence is underscored by the word, and the word can be quickened in stone. Tradition is given only in a zone of non-concepts, a zone without words and without evils. Oral Tradition is already a secondary representation of the pure experience of the Real. It is no more than the translation of the experience that it wants to perpetuate in a possible double: that of memory, which prolongs the first experience like an echo, of a return to the first experience, of a possible path towards Being. But more than words, more than ideas, it would then be the intervals between the words, the intervals between the ideas, that would constitute the path, that would indeed be Tradition. The Tradition of Nothing. The Fullness of Nothing. (Heidegger makes Being the lieutenant of Nothing, a magnificent intuition.)

Tradition and Literature take us back to the relationship between a Tradition that we call oral (sometimes even abusively) and the written word. Now the Book of Enoch tells us that it was the evil angels who taught men to write. However, very early on, writing made it possible to codify traditions, rites in particular, to convey doctrines, cosmogonies, philosophies, theurgy, and magic so that they would not be lost. There is a concern to preserve, a concern to transmit, even if the traditional writings remain subject, in almost all cases, to the necessarily direct lighting of the word, of the commentary, of its operative staging in consciousness by the play of memory. Let us recall the importance of the art of memory in hermetism and the definition of magic by Giordano Bruno: Magic is the art of memory and the manipulation of fantasies. Far from opposing each other, the oral and the written complement each other and combine in a subtle alloy (in most traditions) to serve Tradition. We know today the disaster of the disappearance and destruction of the traditional texts.

But we are talking here about literature, not writing. Not all traditional texts belong to literature, especially when these writings are memory aids, practice manuals, or functional guides allowing the practitioner to live his spirituality within a given and shared tradition. On the contrary, some traditional texts do come under great literature: the Bible, the Koran, the Torah, the Mahabharata, the Upanishads, the Egyptian Book of the Dead, the Bardo Thödol, the Popol Vuh... among many others, but also all the crepuscular poems that seek to transcribe the ineffable or reveal the arcane by veiling it, and also the tales and metaphors conveying traditional teachings, even techniques and especially salutary paradoxes.

If silence is not established as a true mode of transmission then the word will be the approved mediator for transmitting: the word as a sign, then the word as a symbol.

With Aristotle, the word becomes the collective representation attached to the word, a representation that linguists and other grammarians will only narrow through defining it. The word becomes a symbol of this collective representation. Alfred Korzybscki, the founder of General Semantics (hailed notably by Bachelard), had called at the beginning of the last century for a non-Aristotelian revolution to get out of the trap of language, which freezes the word and turns a living process into a dead crystallization. Everyone remembers the first axiom of General Semantics, "The map is not the territory": the word is not the object designated by the word, but we confuse the word and the object, and this is the source of most of our problems.

After Aristotle, who remains an authentic mystagogue of the great ancient tradition and who, apart from a few deviations, remains very Platonic, the Aristotelian theory becomes anti-traditional. Plato, but also the pre-Socratics and, following Plato, a number of philosophers (first of all the occultists and the hermetists), have another relation to the word that the *Cratylus* addresses in these terms:

> Cratylus is right in saying that things have natural names, and that not everyone is a craftsman of names, but only someone who looks to the natural name of each thing and is able to put its Idea into letters and symbols.[123]

Here we find the principle of the "Lost Word" of the Freemasons, or of the "Wise Geometry of letters and numbers" of the old traditional Rosicrucian lineages, of advanced Shaivite metaphysics, or of Iranian Islam. Here too we find, more simply, Arthur Rimbaud (1854–1891) and his famous vowels. An intrinsic link between the word and the Idea existed long before Korzybski. Saint-Martin defended the thesis that "the disorder of the world perhaps comes from the ignorance—or the forgetting—of the real name of any object."

We have already said that we do not remain in the pure experience of the Real but that we live in its sensory transcription, of which language is yet a secondary representation. These three degrees can be found in the transmission, the silence which is elaborated in sign (the living word, at the same time flesh and spirit, the perceived world) which is elaborated in symbol (the frozen word, the conceived world). As Stéphane Mallarmé (1842–1898), wrote to Victor-Emile Michelet: "Occultism is the commentary on the pure signs that all literature obeys, the immediate stream of the mind." Here then is the link established between Tradition

From the People of Letters to the People of Being

and Literature: both are born *immediately*, without mediation. This *immediate* word is fundamental because it indicates the outflow of time which is a major traditional problem, *the* problem, because the word *time* is in Tradition synonymous with *death,* that Tradition whose object is indeed immortality or eternity, or internity.

These few remarks, on a difficult subject (very difficult, no doubt), naturally lead to the presentation of two types of traditional authors:

- the philosopher, the thinker, who will try to identify and rationalize the primary experience, Being itself, of which he will have the memory or intuition, and to describe the means (*media*) to reach this experience or to renew it. The word will be a symbol. The difficulty will lie in the author's capacity, always very relative, to make a sign of the symbol, rendering it lively and operative, and to set aside the didactic commentary, however brilliant it may be;
- the poet (poetry must be distinguished as a priority within literature as its essence) will on the contrary seek to play with, and to be played upon by, the magic of words in order to thwart the traps of language and to tip the reader into this zone of non-concept, the noumenal zone, that of pure Ideas. According to Saint-Martin again, "The poets had to become aware of what Adam was before he slept, that is to say that, like him, they knew how to awaken life in beings, instead of talking to us about what is in a way only the anatomy of these beings, or even their external figure." This is the choice of hermetic or occult poetry.

In the world of Tradition, many of the leading thinkers of the traditional scene have written. Some were poor authors, others showed a surprising facility, and sometimes the men and women of Tradition were also real writers. We could have fun detecting ideological chains, paths of influence, or even (although it is not without risk) filiations. We might even get angry about one link or another that is out of place. Some examples: Pythagoras, Plato, Virgil, Apuleius, Dante, Fabre d'Olivet, or Martinez de Pasqually, Jacob Böhme, Saint-Martin, Cazotte, Joseph de Maistre, Balzac... Some of them took the poetic route.

Still other names, closer to us in time:

We meet in the Chaldean-Egyptian current, which is often referred to as the Osirian current, several Italian authors who transmitted the main arcana of internal alchemy through Hermetic poetry or Hermetic poetic prose. I am thinking for example of Domenico Bocchini or Giustiniano Lebano, who were the precursors of Giuliano Kremmerz, the founder of the Therapeutic (or Templar) and Magic Brotherhood of Myriam, antechamber of the Order of Osiris, and of Prince Caetani. Their crepuscular poems are almost untranslatable into another language, so much do they play on the different logical levels of each word.

In France, Villiers de l'Isle-Adam (1838-1889) made explicit reference in his novels, *Isis, L'Eve Future,* and *Axël,* to a particular path for which certain families in Florence and Venice were responsible. He uses poetic signs, symbols, and metaphors. Stanislas de Guaita, the founder of the Kabbalistic Order of the Rose-Croix, like Joséphin Péladan, used a similar process.

Herman Hesse was a member of a lodge of the Order of Brother-Initiates from Asia. Gustave Meyrink was a member of the same lodge, and perhaps C.G. Jung. All three produced remarkable writings from the hermetic point of view.

Closer to us still, a text like the *Nabelkos* constitutes the poetic compendium of the doctrine and the practice of the Order of the Silver Ermine, an ancient Celtic current. As well, we will obviously think of Louis Cattiaux and his magnificent *The Message Rediscovered.*

The literary tradition of hermetic poetry is therefore not dead, even if it is not at its best today. Three decades ago now, the Italian magazine Sorgente launched a hermetic poetry competition in three languages: Italian, English, and French. It was not a success.

From the People of Letters to the People of Being

We could spend hours talking passionately about the works of one another's traditional authors. We would like to retain, in a completely arbitrary way, three big names who, it seems to me, can form categories: Cervantes, Dante, and Rabelais, in order to come back to this key theme of Tradition and Literature: time, death, immortality, and the erotic that is inseparable from them.

We have stated it many times and written: "The question of immortalities is difficult to broach because it cannot successfully fit into an Aristotelian world model, which is why it is not uncommon that the search for *super-humanity, supra-humanity,* or *non-humanity* unfortunately leads to inhumanity. Furthermore, it is very well possible to have an excellent intellectual grasp of non-Aristotelian models, as traditional models are, without having integrated this particular non-Aristotelian a-logic into any approach to Awakening, to any Tradition. *Super-humanity* could be symbolized by Heracles, thus signaling the Hero's magical path, which Rabelais was able to express so beautifully. The *supra-humanity,* symbolized by Christ, or even by Orpheus, seems to me to inhabit the work of Dante, and the *non-humanity,* symbolized by Osiris or even by Dionysus, seems to me to correspond to the controlled madness of the *Don Quixote* of Cervantes. We could find other references both in the West and in the Eastern traditions to try to capture what is in fact a difference in metaphysical orientation and operativity."

In Dante, Cervantes, and Rabelais, we find three different types of ways to immortality, which will generate techniques, similar in their principles, but different in their forms.

We would now like to draw your attention to a very important point. Today, the great initiatory orders, large in terms of the number of members, the Masonic obediences foremost, tend to neglect classical and literary culture. Strictly speaking, we read traditional authors, and few enough of those (Freemasons are often poor readers), but we scorn the great names in literature. And yet, there is no Literature without metaphysics, and the literary corpus can be understood as a traditional corpus.

Earlier in this letter, we quoted Proust. The very definition of Literature according to Proust implies a philosophy of awakening, since it is the translation of an interior book whose pages we must not stop turning, just as Tradition is the translation of Being to which we must not cease to draw close. Proust's strength lies in having identified "the adversary," which is also the vector of liberation. We want to talk about the times. Our friend Claude Tannery wisely pointed out to us that at the end of *Time Regained,* the narrator says that he has reached the stage where one can contemplate the essence of things. He also recalls the "sign" of the three trees that he had previously not known how to decipher and from which he had moved away with the sadness of one who failed to recognize a god.

Tradition and Literature seek by multiple and apparently contradictory means to kill time—even all time—which ultimately imposes itself as the last, as the only, obstacle, the only veil, the "veil of veils," which prevents access to the Real. Certainly Western (mainly academic) philosophy has demonstrated the impossibility of living in the present, but it is a present thought that philosophy speaks to us about and not a present perception. *Hic et nunc* is not the present thought, conceived, but is rather a non-time which turns out to be the primary obsession of Tradition and Literature. What does Marcel Proust show us?

In Search of Lost Time stages a true recapitulation, a re-appropriation of Being stretched out in time and in history. Personal history is a pathology, Tradition tells us, just as History, as a more or less scientific discipline, is a pathological form of Literature. Both are only lies about lies, born from the same inability to unravel language (and therefore time) in order to perceive the world instead of thinking it. Proust's literary recapitulation is not technically far from a shamanic recapitulation. Both go against the tide of the temporal disintegration that inexorably leads to death. Like Dante, Proust descends to hell and returns. The work and the life of the author become no more than a single allegory that it is then a question of grasping. Nothing is to be rejected. Everything is material for the quest, everything can be brought to light: "Anything that can help to discover laws, to shed light on the unknown, to make life known more deeply, is also valid," insists Proust, whose work is an anticipation of the book *Being and Time* by Heidegger.

There is in Proust an idea that was already present in Baudelaire. There would be only one author, who would manifest himself through different writers, and a single literary work despite its multiplicity. This is not without evoking the recurring prophet who appears regularly under various names: Abraham, Elijah, Moses… all one, like Proust, Joyce, Céline, Borges, Genet, Kafka, Kazantzakis, Pessoa… all one also. If we accept this presupposition, Literature becomes Tradition. A writer no longer has to be placed in his time; on the contrary, through his daily life it is the timeless in which he invests, which Malraux has perfectly identified in the third volume of *The Metamorphosis of the Gods,* appropriately entitled *The Timeless.* This is why some people rightly take themselves for the Messiah.

Kafka, who is a Cervantes-type author, wrote to Milena:

> One has just been sent out as a biblical dove, has found nothing green, and slips back into the darkness of the ark.[124]

Jean Genet said of the mission of the poet:

> The poet deals with evil. It is his role to see the beauty in it, to extract it and use it. Error interests the poet, since error alone teaches truth.[125]

Borges, in a text entitled "The Desert," declared the art of magic:

> A few hundred feet from the Pyramid, I bent down, scooped up a handful of sand and then, a little farther away, let it silently spill. Under my breath I said: I am modifying the Sahara. The deed was minimal, but the words, which were scarcely ingenious, were exact, and I considered that I had needed my entire life to say them. The memory of that moment is one of the most significant of my stay in Egypt.[126]

Ezra Pound declared:

> I have tried to write Paradise
> Do not move
>   Let the wind speak
>   that is paradise.
> Let the Gods forgive what I
>   have made
> Let those I love try to forgive
>   what I have made.[127]

Nikos Kazantzakis, throughout his life, attempted the four great reconciliations, which he expressed thusly in *Report to Greco*:

> Therefore, reader, in these pages you will find the red track made by drops of my blood, the track which marks my journey among men, passions, and ideas... The decisive steps in my ascent were four, and each bears a sacred name: Christ, Buddha, Lenin, Odysseus. This bloody journey from each of these great souls to the next is what I shall struggle to mark out in this Itinerary, now that the sun has begun to set...[128]

From the People of Letters to the People of Being

It was Robert Kanters who had this very apt comment on Kazantzakis' work:

> Kazantzakis (…) seems to have to relived in the space of a few years all the spiritual adventure of humanity… Perhaps it should be said that with Christ, Kazantzakis wanted to save himself against the world; with Buddha, to escape from the world; with Lenin, to save himself through the world; with Odysseus, finally, saving himself, and the world at the same time, by reinventing a paganism commensurate with man.[129]

We have already recalled the importance of Catherine Pozzi in our seventeenth letter of this series: 17, the number of the Hidden King. We will not press the point.

And Jacqueline Kelen, bearer of a Tradition of Love, noble adventurer of the Spirit, who demonstrates in her work, as in her life, that the writer and the quester share the gift of sacred Solitude:

> To be lonely, like a sparkling diamond or like a wild boar hidden in the forest, is:
> - to be unique, singular,
> - to be gathered, unified, one, whole,
> - to be free and available, guarantor of one's existence, creator, capable of loving without monopolizing or harming,
> - to be open to everyone living, to feel connected, to fraternize with all of creation,
> - to become vertical, spiritualized, to attest to the Unique, to approach divine Solitude, or even merge into it.
>
> By the solitary way, each human being is invited to pass from the egocentric "little I," who complains of being isolated or else believes himself independent, to the divine "Big I," creator, infinitely free. (…)

> When the soul has made contact with this solitude of the Spirit, the human being can then live alone or coupled, in family, in community, in the city, or in the desert. He never feels isolated again since he has awakened to a sovereign dimension, unbreakable and imperishable.[130]

There is with all these authors a power that appears in a few words. The power of the Real, the power of shedding, of lifting, an unshakable will that the unveiled finally appears.

Let us resume: Time – death – immortality… Woman! Always, the woman and the erotic, without which no path is possible. Literature, sometimes better than Tradition, as far as the Christian and especially the Catholic West is concerned, has been able to approach the arcanum of the Eternal Feminine, with which the quester must be confronted, whether through the flesh or the spirit (which are inseparable in any case). The flesh teaches the spirit, the spirit teaches the flesh. The erotic and eroticism merge.

This question of Femininity, which deserves a very long elaboration, impossible in this context, leads me to approach a last important point: that of the relations between Tradition and the avant-garde. Woman was in fact recognized by the artistic avant-garde and by the initiatory traditions as both key and guardian of Initiation, as both mediator and crown, even if this was not without confusion, without repression, nor without ulterior motive, as much on the side of the avant-garde as on the side of the traditions. This led the traditions and the avant-garde to state the foundations of a metaphysics of sex, which sometimes had its natural extension in a metaphysics of madness.

A few years ago, we had a long conversation with Lima de Freitas who by himself could, through his life and his literary or pictorial work, illustrate the whole of what I am saying today. The question of the relationship between Tradition and the avant-garde quickly came to the fore.

From the People of Letters to the People of Being

Winnicott had already stated that "in any cultural field, it is impossible to be original without relying on tradition."[131] We wanted to go further. We agreed to say that Tradition and the avant-garde were inseparable, that what was new was so only because it was very old, older than the old, that what was very old remained revolutionary, and that if Tradition revealed the immutable, the immutable could only be avant-garde. We ended up stating the principle of a natural alliance between Tradition and the avant-garde, between the traditions and the avant-gardes, although this alliance remains incomprehensible to most minds, quite incapable of escaping their narrow representations. This alliance makes sense especially in times that demand intensity.

At the end of the 19th century and the beginning of the 20th century, Joséphin Péladan (1858-1918) and the famous Salons of the Rose-Croix disturbed, bothered, and perturbed. It must be said that Péladan mocked contradictions and went from provocation to provocation. He was uneven and unpredictable, and he elegantly passed from an almost superstitious Catholicism to offbeat, libertarian[132] attitudes, we might say. He founded an Order of the Catholic Rose-Croix and the Grail, itself conceived as a work of art, which should be characteristic of all initiatory orders. His writings (he was above all a writer) were totally original. Towards the end of his life, he warned:

> Don Quixote also wanted the Grail, I believe. He wanted it with a pure and mad heart; and his name serves as an epithet to discredit chivalry.
>
> After having laughed at the knight with the sorry face, you have to wonder if you haven't had your own hour of don-quixotism. If you don't find it in your past, you should bow your head, because this hour is perhaps the one when man reaches the highest degree of consciousness.[133]

Since Péladan, this alliance has been repeated over and over again. Certainly in and through surrealism with André Breton (1896-1966), Robert Desnos, but also with Victor Brauner,[134] the painter of high magic and internal alchemy of which he, like Desnos as well, had a keen intuition. Many surrealist writings, especially those of Breton (and he was reproached for this), are tinged with hermetism or occultism. It was the same also with the movement of the *Grand Jeu*, in which we find an essential author René Daumal, or with Georges Bataille and the review *Acéphale,* followed by his College of Sociology. On the fringes of surrealism, we should talk about Charles Duits and *La seule femme vraiment noire* or Malcolm de Chazal, the Mauritian poet who was fortunately rehabilitated by our friend Sarane Alexandrian and his very beautiful surrealist review *Superior Inconnu*. Sarane Alexandrian explained regarding Malcolm: "His unpublished work, *L'Apocalypse du vivant,* also included a chapter *La volupté, premier parvis de l'âme et portique d'immortalité,* which was to develop this notion in the same direction. But voluptuousness exists only as a function of sex and nudity, of which Malcom de Chazal has made analyzes no less extraordinary: 'Sex—complemented by nudity, its agent of undressing and connection—this is the sole source of Beauty. There is no aesthetic form that does not owe everything to it... Desexualize the painting: all that will remain is colored ashes. Desexualize harmony and you will only have a shapeless cry. The statue for which sex does not drip down its form is a marble corpse. Sex is so religious that it is the propulsive source of mysticism.'"

And how do we respond in turn to Georges Bataille in *Les Larmes d'Éros,* published by Pauvert? This beautiful book sees Georges Bataille exploring time from antiquity and space from East to West, to capture the tears of Eros, those flashes of light that make men and women transcend themselves. Georges Bataille is one of those who have perceived, sensed, and tracked down the possibility of a sacred, religious or non-religious, eroticism in which art has a central function. From pleasure to ecstasy, Georges Bataille seeks the link, sometimes to his own discomfort, between eroticism and death, and even more between eroticism and sadism. Georges Bataille, poet-warrior, had intuitions often remarkable, sometimes terrible. This book bears witness to that. Let's listen to him:

> The foundation of eroticism is sexual activity. However, this activity falls under the blow of a prohibition. It is inconceivable! It is forbidden to make love! Unless you do it in secret.
>
> But if, in secret, we do it, the prohibition transfigures, it illuminates what it prohibits with a glow that is both sinister and divine: it illuminates it, in a word, with a religious glow.[135]

This alliance between Tradition and the avant-garde also takes other forms. André Breton harangued the university and invited it (to put it mildly) to turn to occultism by a formal notice published in 1948 in *La lampe dans l'horloge*:

> It is high time you realize what you have done along the way with the major interrogation of mankind. How can you hand us those corny pictures depicting the tedious saga of your kings and the even more insipid tribulations of your wretched Sorbonne? Enough elementary history, what are you hiding from us? Gnosticism, badly misunderstood, is still today such a catchall word. Let us not even go so far back; you have decided to make us cry over André Chénier's fate: we don't care. What would interest us in that same period is to know where Martinez de Pasqually was coming from and where he was going. Even closer to our time, we hear you dwelling at length on Renan: why do you keep silent about Saint-Yves d'Alveydre? Enough flimflam.[136]

After the Second World War, the alliance ran out of steam but reappeared where we did not expect it. Two cases seem surprising to me: Guy Debord and Dominique de Roux. Everything about them seems opposite. The first founded a Situationist International and denounced the society of the spectacle that everyone understands to be the mediated society, whereas for Debord, all representation is spectacle, and the political becomes a way of awakening. The second called for a Gaullist International, referring to Lautréamont, to Bloy, and to Hello. Both are victims of the "terrible simplifications" that suit too many people because they are excuses for us to not think, to not question, to not look behind the curtain of our prejudices. For Guy Debord, as for Dominique de Roux, politics could be an ascesis at the same time as an art. They are not very far from Agostinho da Silva's art of doing nothing. Undoubtedly, the most important thing for both is unconditionality, a fundamental quality of aristocrats and libertarians. This is also what makes them (especially!) incomprehensible to most intellectuals, almost all of whom have a price. They are not for sale. This is what allows them to converge, even if this convergence undoubtedly remains without formal result. Let us quote on this subject Pétrus Batselier: "But we do think that this connection was deeper. It should be noted that the 'site' felt in a way like an exile on this planet. They believed in the role of small groups, if not an individual, to overthrow the order of the world; hence their common interest in the Brothers of the Free Spirit, the Rose-Croix, but also the Order of Assassins. De Roux and Debord, they are both Gnostics, it is the basis of their relationship. On the political level we can only treat them both as aristocrat-libertarians."[137]

Here are the two words spoken, linked by this magical hyphen. Aristocrat and libertarian. Tradition and Literature. Tradition, which is essentially aristocratic, in the sense that nothing is acquired, that everything, and the Whole more than anything, must be conquered, and Literature, which is essentially libertarian, freed from all rules, without

From the People of Letters to the People of Being

limit. But is not this same Literature aristocratic, even elitist (although it does not claim to be either), which does not sell, and which demands to be conquered, by force or by seduction; even as Tradition is revolutionary, libertarian, the ultimate emancipation that Kazantzakis identified with this magnificent phrase: "We must free ourselves even from freedom," which echoes this superb confession, this time from Meister Eckhart in his sermon 52, "I pray God to rid me of God…"

And today? For four or five decades this alliance between Tradition and the avant-garde has been trying to renew itself, in surrealism and in 'Pataphysics, among others. This was particularly the case at the end of the last century thanks to Sarane Alexandrian and his review *Superior Inconnu,* but also elsewhere and otherwise.

The title of the review *Superior Inconnu* is an explicit reference to Tradition. Sarane Alexandrian explained to us in a letter the reason for this deliberate choice which may surprise:

> It was André Breton, on the advice of Jean Paulhan, who in 1948 wanted to title the first post-war surrealist review *Superior Inconnu,* which Gaston Gallimard was to publish. For André Breton, this magnificent term could be detached from its Martinist context and designated the ideal objective of the poetic research of the future.
>
> This project, due to the internal dissensions of the surrealist group, did not see the light of day as planned. Almost fifty years later, we take up the title again: this same eternally modern title, as an expression of our *fin de siècle,* where writers and artists should unite to seek the new gnosis.

At the end of the last century, after long discussions with Robert Amadou, an old companion on the road to Ithaca, and after long work continued with several traditional initiatory orders and circles in Europe, we developed the first *Incoherist Manifesto*[138] in order to renew the alliance between traditions and the avant-garde.

To conclude, if "conclusion" has an other-than-formal meaning, a few words from Heidegger and then from Pessoa.

Martin Heidegger first:

> Being is.
> Non-being is not.[139]

Perfect traditional metaphysics and a remarkable literary achievement. But for these few words to slice the veil of representations and reveal the Absolute, a particular posture is necessary, to avoid causing only a shrug of the shoulders. This posture is that of the man or woman of Tradition. It is also that of the man or the woman of Literature.

Finally, Fernando Pessoa in *The Book of Disquiet:*

> Everything that man exposes or expresses is a note in the margin of a completely erased text. We can more or less, from the meaning of the note, deduce what the meaning of the text should be; but there is always a doubt, and the possible meanings are multiple.[140]

BIBLIOGRAPHIES AND MALLARMÉ[141]

This twenty-second letter closes our discussions and, we hope, opens up the Adventure, initiatory and amorous.

We choose not to offer a bibliography. Indeed, these Letters to Friends of the Spirit do not have an academic character and do not warrant academic rigor. They are part of spiritual friendship and intimacy. Even if we have pointed out a few references here and there, the Friend is invited to seek sources and influences for himself, rather by constellations of authors than by lists of scholarly works.

Thus, the constellation which is most familiar to us is undoubtedly that formed by Martinez de Pasqually, Louis-Claude de Saint-Martin, Jean-Baptiste Willermoz and, by extension, Jacob Böhme, Emmanuel Swedenborg, Karl von Eckartshausen... all the way to Meister Eckhart.

Let us follow thinkers, even by wandering paths, rather than with precise books, in order to weave, in our own style, in an original way, the web of Tradition. This sometimes presents itself as a library organized according to the rules of the art of memory.

Another constellation, relating to our subjects, would be formed, in a non-exhaustive way, of the great texts of the Kabbalah and of its excellent commentators or explorers such as Abraham Abulafia or Isaac Luria and, near us, Georges Lahy-Virya, Josy Eisenberg, Adin Steinsaltz, Gershom Scholem, Marc-Alain Ouaknin... crossing with another constellation of atypical but equally fascinating authors: Dominique Aubier, Jean-Charles Pichon, Carlo Suarès, António Telmo, A.D. Grad...

The constellation of the great nondual masters of Kashmir,

Abhinavagupta, Ksemaraja, Utpaladeva… will bring us closer in essence to that formed by Rumi, Shams-i Tabrīzī, Suhrawardi, Ibn Arabi… but also to that of a Meister Eckhart.

The constellation of the authors of the Beat Generation or that of the figures of the anti-psychiatric movement of the 1960s and 1970s are also vehicles of a way of awakening.

We can learn to navigate by following the constellations of stars that are the thinkers (and not the lost-in-thoughts)[142] or lineages of influences, real or perceived. This does not exclude methods.

Here is an example, concerning the reading of Mallarmé:

The question arose in our discussions with Robert Amadou about a possible parentage: Mallarmé, Bloy, Ducasse, and De Roux.

Robert Amadou took the time to answer us by letter:

"Mallarmé! We're getting started,[143] and the term isn't that literal!"

Behind the alert, a real initiation indeed:

"Impossible or criminal to speak at the outset of its metaphysics. She does have the two characters you speak of.[144] But let me direct you. First by confusing you."

Robert then offers us his initiation to Mallarmé, poetic initiation (and more, we discovered much later), in four stages, as follows:

Stage I. *Vers de circonstance* by Mallarmé, Poésie collection (Paris: Gallimard, 1996).

"Read the verses skipping the preface. Then with the verses read, come back to the preface. Bonnefoy is a bad poet, he adds, but he says just and profound things about the *Vers de circumstance* that will bring you back to the edge of the path. Nothing more."

Stage II. *Selon Mallarmé* by Paul Bénichou, Folio essais collection (Paris: Gallimard, 1999).

Paul Bénichou, Robert's friend, had just died.

"No metaphysics but more glimpses of 'trivialities and some errors that will shower you a little.'"

Stage III.

"The small various writings devoted to Mallarmé by Valéry. Find the references in 'La Pléiade' then refer to the current editions."

Stage IV. *Mallarmé* by Guy Michaud (Paris: Hatier-Boivin. 1957).

"To get a glimpse of the essential (at a first impression, make no mistake!)"

Robert added this salutary advice:

"While you're preparing, don't read anything about Mallarmé other than each book (or anthology in Valéry's case), one after the other. No chatter in all of this."

We are therefore transmitting to you the "initiation" as we have received it.

With hindsight, it seems that this is not only a first, but an essential initiation to Mallarmé. It is also, above all, an initiation into poetry and reading.

Among all that Robert Amadou, magnificent "Elder Brother," has confided to us, this "time of Mallarmé" remains, in its apparent simplicity, a pure jewel.

A painter, who also devoted himself to poetry, told Mallarmé of the difficulties he was having in writing a poem despite having determined its ideas and sentimental atmosphere.

Let us add, to close the work, this anecdote reported by Paul Nougé, an essential figure of surrealism:[145]

"I lack nothing," he repeated, "and yet…"

"But, dear friend," replied Mallarmé, "a poem is not made with ideas, any more than it is with feelings—a poem is made with words."

I don't know if I should add that the listeners burst out laughing.

Undoubtedly, they took as a jest what nevertheless, from the lips of Mallarmé, took on the most serious meaning.

Endnotes

1. *Diaboles* (Fr.): diabolicalities, devils. – Trans.
2. *St John Chrysostom, Complete Works*, Vol. 3, trans. M. Portelette (Bar-le-Duc, Fr.: L. Guérin, 1869).
3. Raymond Abellio, *La structure absolue* (Paris: Presses du Châtelet, 2014).
4. Joachim de Fiore had fixed this descent of the Holy Spirit in 1260.
5. Robert and Catherine Amadou, *Les leçons de Lyon aux élus coëns. Un cours de martinisme au XVIIIe siècle par Louis-Claude de Saint-Martin, Jean-Jacques Du Roy D'Hauterive, Jean-Baptiste Willermoz*, first complete edition published from the original manuscripts (Paris: Dervy, 1999).
6. Subject covered in Rémi Boyer, *The Rectified Scottish Rite, from the Doctrine of Reintegration to the* Imago Templi, prefaces by José Anes and Serge Caillet (Bayonne, NJ: Rose Circle, 2023).
7. *"Trois pas"* (Fr.) = three steps, *"trépas"* (Fr.) = death. – Trans.
8. Louis-Claude de Saint-Martin, *Man: His True Nature & Ministry*, trans. Edward Burton Penny (London: William Allen and Co., 1864) p. 34.
9. Josy Eisenberg and Adin Steinsaltz, *L'alphabet sacré* (Paris: Fayard, 2012).
10. The caparison as the armor of the horse (there are also gala caparisons of fabric) represents horizontality, while the armor of the knight represents verticality.
11. The phallus symbolizes not only the divine Fires that generate the Light but also the Word.
12. Rémi Boyer, *Mask Cloak Silence: Martinism as a Way of Awakening*, preface by Serge Caillet (Bayonne, NJ: Rose Circle, 2021).
13. Rémi Boyer, *The Rectified Scottish Rite, from the Doctrine of Reintegration to the* Imago Templi, prefaces by José Anes and Serge Caillet, cover painting, *Maria Madalena or Sophia* by Carlos Barahona Possollo (Bayonne, NJ: Rose Circle, 2023).
14. To study the relationship between the brain and the Hebrew alphabet, refer to the remarkable work of Dominique Aubier, particularly *La face cachée du cerveau* (Paris: Dervy, 1990). https://www.dominique-aubier.com/
15. The expression *"Notre Dame"* ("Our Lady") also evokes *"Notre Damier"* ("Our Checkerboard") and the parvise (or forecourt) of the Temple of Solomon. *"Notre Damier"* also means "Our Calculation" and refers to the science of the measurements of the Temple.
16. *Fin'amor* (courtly love) = *la fin de la mort*, the end of death. *Finistère* = *la fin de la Terre*, the end of the earth and the beginning of infinity. There are several *finistères* facing the Atlantic, including those in Brittany and Portugal. Usually these are lands of dragons in local lore, and dragons are associated with chivalry and the goddess. – Trans.
17. A reference to the Song of Songs.
18. Paris: Gallimard, 1984.
19. 515 is found on the 32° tracing board in the Ancient and Accepted Scottish Rite,

often underestimated in its operative dimension.
20. *515, Le lieu du miroir* by Lima de Freitas (Paris: Albin Michel, 1993).
21. *Correspondance imaginale. Lima de Freitas & Gilbert Durand,* preface by Michel Cazenave, ed. Rémi Boyer (La Bégude de Mazenc, Fr.: Arma Artis, 2016).
22. The first masterpiece of Iberian painting, the six-panel polyptych by Nuño Gonçalves, dated 1445, is as important as *Os Lusíadas* by Camões to Portugal, which designates them both as of *Ínclita Geração, the illustrious generation.* Fernando Pessoa drew inspiration from this in *Message.* The controversy over the meanings continues and feeds the Lusitanian mysteries.
23. Lima de Freitas refers to an inscription carved in a stone phylactery at the Convent of Tomar: "1. 515". He connects this with a painting by Jorge Alfonso that bears a curious inscription mixing numbers and letters: "1SIS".
24. A synthetic presentation of Sebastianism can be found in Rémi Boyer, *Hymnaire au Roi Caché, 17 Hymnes Sébastianistes. Hinário ao Rei Encoberto, 17 Trovas Sebastianistas,* French-Portuguese bilingual edition, accompanying text by Maria Luísa Martins da Cunha (Sintra, Pt.: Zéfiro & Arcano Zero, 2013). *L'hymnaire au Roi Caché* was recently republished in French in Rémi Boyer, *La voie des sans maîtres* (Aubagne, Fr.: Editions de la Tarente, 2021).
25. For a more in-depth look at the text of the Apocalypse of John, it will be helpful, if not necessary, to refer to the remarkable work of our friend Georges Bertin, *Mystères de l'Apocalypse de Jean* (Lyon: Cosmogone, 2021).
26. By "Book of David" we should understand the psalms written by David and by extension the entire Book of Psalms, but a detour through the first and second Books of Samuel as well as the first Book of Kings would also be useful.
27. See the text by Victor Tibika, *La Trisection vaincue* (Paris: printed by the author, 1973).
28. For more on the subject, see Rémi Boyer, *Mask Cloak Silence: Martinism as a Way of Awakening* (Bayonne, NJ: Rose Circle, 2021).
29. *Mishnat ha-Middot* — Trans.
30. Practice detailed in Rémi Boyer, *Éveil et incohérisme* (La Bégude de Mazenc, Fr.: Arma Artis, 2005), also *Mask Cloak Silence: Martinism as a Way of Awakening* (Bayonne, NJ: Rose Circle, 2021).
31. The National Library of France maintains an archive collection of Louis Boutard collected by M. Hatinguais. You can also consult the site: http://louisboutard.com/.
32. Adin Steinsaltz, *The Thirteen Petalled Rose: A Discourse on the Essence of Jewish Existence and Belief* (New York: Basic Books, 1985).
33. Dominique Aubier, *Le principe du langage ou l'alphabet hébraïque* (Lausanne, Fr.: Mont-Blanc, 1970), p. 297.
34. Fr.: *mesure* — Trans.
35. Fr.: *justement* — Trans.
36. Fr: *Attention. Attends Sion. A-temps Sion.* — Trans.
37. Fr: *« Aimez votre prochain comme vous-même. » | Aimez votre proche-UN.* — Trans.
38. Fr: *Apprendre c'est A-prendre.* — Trans.
39. Fr: *Affaire (ou A-faire)* — Trans.
40. Fr: *l'enfer, l'en-faire* — Trans.
41. Gr.: χατζη-, prefix meaning 'pilgrim'. Derived from Arabic: *hajji.* — Trans.
42. António Telmo. *Philosophie et Kabbale* (Aubagne, Fr.: Editions de la Tarente, 2021).
43. Marc-Alain Ouaknin, Philippe Markiewicz, and Mohammed Taleb, *Jérusalem, trois fois sainte.* Arpenter le sacré collection (Paris: Desclée de Brouwer, 2016).
44. We must, I believe, remember the three temples of Solomon: the Temple of stone, the Temple of paper, and the Temple of man. In 586 BC, the first temple of Sol-

Endnotes

omon, a stone temple, was destroyed by Nebuchadnezzar. This is the Babylonian exile, for 70 years according to the Jewish tradition, until the Persian victory over the Babylonians. Freed, the Jews return to Judea and rebuild the Temple.

In 70 AD, Vespasian, then a Roman general, surrounded Jerusalem with his troops. The besieged city is close to defeat when a chief rabbi, Yohanan Ben Zakkai, escapes from the city, joins General Vespasian's encampment, introduces himself and salutes him by bowing to him as Emperor. While Vespasian, offended, is about to punish him, a messenger, just arrived from Rome, announces to him that he has just been named Emperor. Impressed by the rabbi's foreknowledge, Vespasian asks him what he wants. Instead of demanding the end of the siege and the protection of Solomon's Temple, Ben Zakkai asked him for permission to found with a few disciples a Talmudic school in a small town, Yavne. Vespasian agrees, somewhat surprised by this unexpected request. This event is considered to be the founding of Judaism. This school will produce a remarkable teaching: Mishnah, midrash, gematria, Zohar, Kabbalah, philosophy, wisdom texts, poetry, Jewish literature, etc., a culture of paper succeeding the culture of stone. The invisible temple of paper supplants the temple of stone which will again be destroyed and heralds an even more elusive temple, the Temple of the Spirit, Inner temple, Temple of man and Temple in man to be paralleled by the Primordial Cult of the doctrine of Reintegration, the prototype of all cults.

45. Fonds Z.
46. Letter from Robert Amadou addressed to Rémi Boyer, dated September 22, 1994.
47. Of course the Spirit is absolutely free, and sometimes archetypes breeze in from the Imaginal that inspire beyond the consciousness of the author.
48. Catherine and Robert Amadou, *Angéliques*, 2 vols. (Guérigny, Fr: CIREM, 2001).
49. Letter from Robert Amadou addressed to Rémi Boyer, dated June 24, 1997.
50. Jérémie Koering, *Les iconophages. Une histoire de l'ingestion des images* (Paris: Actes Sud, 2021).
51. He who is chaste, who is pure, is without thought. The sexual act is chaste when it is performed in silence (in the interval) as a celebration of divine union. The couple are united like a god and their consort, like Christ and Mary Magdalene. It is a sacramental act.
52. The first cup is a cup of wine, while the second cup is a cup of organic grape juice. Similarly, the bread intended for the Eucharist is made from wholemeal flour, salt, water, and olive oil, the last of which is the symbol of Love.
53. Isis, Mary, Magdalene, Yemaya… manifest the same archetype through a constellation of common mythemes.
54. More commonly known in English as "Elizabeth of Portugal." – Trans.
55. Rémi Boyer, "Hymnaire au Roi Caché" in *La voie des sans maîtres* (Aubagne, Fr.: Editions de la Tarente, 2021).
56. *Inès*: more commonly known in English as "Agnes of Rome." – Trans.
57. Louis-Claude de Saint-Martin, *Le Crocodile ou la guerre du bien et du mal arrivée sous le règne de Louis XV* (Paris: Triades, 1962).
58. Philippe Muray, *Le XIXème siècle à travers les âges* (Paris: Denoël, 1984).
59. Louis-Claude de Saint-Martin, *Controverse avec Garat, précédé d'autres textes philosophiques* (Paris: Fayard, 1990).
60. Louis-Claude de Saint-Martin, *Mon portrait historique et philosophique* (Paris: Julliard, 1961).
61. For more information, refer to the work by Jean-Louis Ricard, *Initiation par l'intime:*

Louis-Claude de Saint-Martin, *Le Philosophe Inconnu, une voie alternative entre Théurgie et Alchimie* (Aubagne, Fr.: Editions La Tarente, 2020).

62. This text was published in a slightly different version in Rémi Boyer, *Soulever le voile d'Elias Artista, la rose-croix comme voie d'éveil, une tradition orale*, (Cordes sur Ciel, Fr.: Rafael de Surtis, 2010) [Published in English as *Beneath the Veil of Elias Artista: The Rose-Croix as a Way of Awakening, An Oral Tradition* (Bayonne, NJ: Rose Circle, 2021)] and then repeated in Rémi Boyer, *Essais et discours de Sintra* (La Bégude de Mazenc, Fr.: Arma Artis, 2015).

63. See the very beautiful work by André Coyné, *Portugal é um ente — De l'être au Portugal* (Lisbon: Fundação Lusiada, 1999).

64. Coyné, *Portugal é um ente*, p. 153.

65. At the beginning of the 17th century, libertines, Spanish Alumbrados, and Rose-Croix were denounced and stigmatized in the same way by the Church. It is, improbably, this stigma and these amalgamations of disjointed movements that would bring about a rapprochement between these three currents, devoted (each in their own way) to freedom.

66. Lima de Freitas, "Fernando Pessoa and the Tomb of Christian Rosenkreutz," in Rémi Boyer, *Beneath the Veil of Elias Artista: The Rose-Croix as a Way of Awakening, An Oral Tradition* (Bayonne NJ: Rose Circle, 2021).

67. This text was also published in a slightly different version in Rémi Boyer, *Soulever le voile d'Elias Artista, la rose-croix comme voie d'éveil, une tradition orale*, (Cordes sur Ciel, Fr.: Rafael de Surtis, 2010) [Published in English as *Beneath the Veil of Elias Artista: The Rose-Croix as a Way of Awakening, An Oral Tradition* (Bayonne, NJ: Rose Circle, 2021)] and then repeated in Rémi Boyer, *Essais et discours de Sintra* (La Bégude de Mazenc, Fr.: Arma Artis, 2015).

68. In 1992, an inner college was set up bringing together custodians of initiatory traditions and specialists for a triple mission of the conservation of rites and ways, theurgic and alchemical laboratories, and oratories for internal practices of completion. This college, like Janus, always presented two faces, one Western, and the other, more discreetly, Eastern. It borrowed several names including, generically, that of ORDO, which became an acronym developed by Robert Amadou in three forms: *Ordo Rosicrucianus Divorum Ordonum* for the first order, *Ordo Rosicrucianus Divini Operis* for the second order, and *Ordo Rhodostaumoticus Divini Operis* for the third order. Robert Amadou (1924–2006) was the principal guardian of the Western temple from 1992 to 2002, when he suspended his vigil. Lima de Freitas (1927–1998) was also one of the ORDO guardians. He could only assume this function for a few weeks because of his departure to the Eternal East.

69. Among others, consider the famous vignettes of the *Rosarium philosophorum*, dated 1550, a very important work in the alchemical corpus. It contains a relevant collection of twenty-one engravings which are among the most famous examples of alchemical symbolism, many of which depict unions between a queen and a king.

70. For Baruch Spinoza, in his *Short Treatise on God, Man, and His Wellbeing*, chapter 8 of the first part, in the translation by Abraham Wolf (London: A. and C. Black, 1910): "By *Natura naturans* we understand a being that we conceive clearly and distinctly through itself, and without needing anything beside itself (…), that is, God. The Thomists likewise understand God by it, but their *Natura naturans* was a being (so they called it) beyond all substances," and "The *Natura naturata* we shall divide into two, a general, and

a particular. The general consists of all the modes which depend immediately on God... the particular consists of all the particular things which are produced by the general mode. So that the *Natura naturata* requires some substance in order to be well understood."

71. Read Kandinsky on this subject, particularly *Du spirituel dans l'art, et dans la peinture en particulier* and *Point ligne sur plan*, (Paris: Denoël/Gallimard, Folio Essais, 1989 and 1991).

72. Jean-Luc Leguay, *Le Tracé du Maître* (Paris: Dervy, 2008).

73. Rémi Boyer, *The Rectified Scottish Rite, from the Doctrine of Reintegration to the Imago Templi* (Bayonne, NJ: Rose Circle, 2023).

74. Jean-Claude Sitbon, *L'aventure du Rite Ecossais Rectifié*, Volume 1: *Approche historique*, Volume 2: *De Tubalcaïn à Phaleg*, (Aubagne, Fr.: Editions La Tarente, 2015).

75. Rémi Boyer, *Mask Cloak Silence: Martinism as a Way of Awakening* (Bayonne, NJ: Rose Circle, 2021).

76. Visible at the Rossio Railway Station in Lisbon.

77. Paul Sanda, *Puits obscur Puits lumineux: hommage à Kernadec de Pornic*, preface by Rémi Boyer, drawings by Didier Serplet (Cordes sur Ciel, Fr.: Rafael de Surtis; Mellac, Fr.: Les Chemins bleus, 2014). – Trans.

78. Rémi Boyer, "Initiation au Jardin et Initiation dans la Cité" in *L'Ordre des Francs-jardiniers. Rituals*, ed. Rémi Boyer and Howard Doe (Aubagne, Fr.: Editions de la Tarente, 2019).

79. George Steiner, "Langage et gnose" in *Œuvres* (Paris: Quarto Gallimard, 2013).

80. Johann Ambrosius Siebmacher, *Wasserstein der Weysen* (Frankfurt: 1619). First translated into English by A.E. Waite as *The Sophic Hydrolith* in *The Hermetic Museum* (London: J. Elliot, 1893), pp. 69–120.

81. See on this subject: Philippe Guillemant and Jocelin Morisson, *La physique de la conscience* (Paris: Guy Trédaniel, 2015). Philippe Guillemant, physicist at the French National Centre for Scientific Research, "offers us, through a cybernetic model of consciousness that asserts the quantum control of space-time, a vast reversal of perspective that completely transforms our vision of the world. Finally freed from the primordial machinery, we would have an essential role to play in individually and collectively shaping our reality, due to the capacity that we have to consciously stir the water of a veritable ocean: that of the void, which is to say, that of the invisible worlds."

82. This is not the case in the USA where the New Church is radiant, nor in Great Britain with the important cultural activities of the Swedenborg Society.

83. Claude Bruley, *Le Grand Œuvre comme fondement d'une spiritualité laïque*, then *Sur le fleuve infini des mythes* (Cordes sur-Ciel, Fr.: Rafael de Surtis, 2008 and 2011).

84. Louis-Claude de Saint-Martin, *Controverse avec Garat: précédée d'autres écrits philosophiques* (Paris: Fayard, 1990).

85. *L'Esprit des Choses* n°4, new series (Guérigny, Fr: CIREM, 2009).

86. Read on this subject the remarkable work of François Trojani, *L'orgone. Théories, notes et expériences* (Saint-Nazaire-en-Royans, Fr: Energeia, 2021).

87. Serge Caillet, *La Franc-maçonnerie swedenborgienne* (Aubagne, Fr.: Editions de la Tarente, 2019).

88. A longer version was inserted in the collection *Essais et discours de Sintra* (La Bégude de Mazenc, Fr.: Arma Artis, 2015).

89. On this subject, and other adjacent ones, we refer to the exceptional work, in its entirety and its particulars, of Jacqueline Kelen, guardian of a Tradition whose

most striking expression is undoubtedly the figure of Mary Magdalene.

90. Valentin Bresle, *Thesaurus Magiæ, Encyclopédie du Poétisme et des Sciences Occultes*. 1944–1947. Edition reserved for members of the Jurande Templière founded by Valentin Bresle (1892–1978). This is a remarkable series of booklets, unfortunately forgotten despite the efforts of Editions Ramuel, which in 1999 published the first three booklets, arguably the most interesting ones. All the quotes from Valentin Bresle chosen for this text come from this corpus.
91. Catherine Pozzi, *Peau d'âme*, preface by Lawrence Joseph (Paris: La Différence, "Philosophia perennis" series, 1990).
92. *Anthéos:* from the Greek, "ανθος," blossom, but also the mythological Antæus. – Trans.
93. Rémi Boyer, *Le Fou de Shakti*, Franco-Portuguese edition (Lisbon: Hugin, 1998).
94. Letter from Robert Amadou to Rémi Boyer dated November 23, 1995.
95. Original: *"NU en UN."* – Trans.
96. According to Robert Ambelain, the Black Virgin of the Abbey of Saint Victor in Marseille would always be "the patroness of the Order," hence the repeated pilgrimages of some members of the Order to the crypt.
97. We find these extraordinary hands (as well as the almond-shaped eyes) in the figures of another exceptional church: the Church of the Assumption of Our Lady or Church of Saint Mary in Rieux-Minervois. This Languedoc Romanesque church has particular symbolic characteristics. Some consider that its builders inscribed in stone a "book" of the *Arcana Arcanorum*.
98. The Roma and the Companions of the *Devoirs de Liberté* exchange during meetings at the Church of the Saintes Maries de la Mer.
99. It would be interesting to examine the case of the Cagots, who were authorized to exercise the trade of carpentry. Here we have one of the sources of the carpentry Companions.
100. Text modified from the author's address at the Second Conference of Editions La Tarente devoted to "The Egyptian Rites from Cagliostro to the Sons of Alexandria" on November 4, 2017 in Marseille. The final part of the talk, devoted to water and the internal, is included in the 15th Letter of the second series.
101. Former Grand Hierophant of the Great Adriatic Sanctuary of the Rite of Misraïm and Memphis (lineage: Marco Egidio Allegri, Conte Ottavio Ulderigo Zasio, and Conte Gastone Ventura).
102. To better approach this exemplary school, we point out the work of Karol Axel, *Les Arcana Arcanorum et les rites maçonniques égyptiens de Memphis-Misraïm, une voie pour l'Occident* (Aubagne, Fr.: Editions de la Tarente, 2022).
103. Jean-Pierre Giudicelli de Cressac-Bachelerie, *De la Rose Rouge à la Croix d'Or* (Paris: Axis Mundi, 1988), p. 67.
104. Ibid, p. 79.
105. See the 15th Letter of the second series for references.
106. http://www.lemessageretrouve.net/
107. *Cyprine* (French): vaginal secretion specifically associated with feminine desire. – Trans.
108. Arthur directs the Round Table and leads the sacred hunt. He sometimes leaves this privilege to Gargantua, who then becomes his Grand Huntsman.
109. Pierre Gordon, *Le géant Gargantua* (La Bégude de Mazenc, Fr.: Arma Artis, 1998).
110. Our popular bloodsucking vampire is for Pierre Gordon a degeneration of the divinizing vampire, the giant.
111. Refer to the 15th Letter of the second series.

112. In the 3rd Letter of the first series, dedicated to the Holy Spirit.
113. G. Pugliese Carratelli, *Les lamelles d'or orphiques. Instructions pour le voyage d'outre-tombe des initiés grecs,* Vérité des mythes collection (Paris: Les Belles Lettres, 2003).
114. Aetius, *Opinions, Les Présocratiques,* Bibliothèque de la Pléiade (Paris: Gallimard, 1988.
115. Rémi Boyer, *The Rectified Scottish Rite, from the Doctrine of Reintegration to the Imago Templi* (Bayonne, NJ: Rose Circle, 2023).
116. Rémi Boyer, *La voie des sans maîtres* (Aubagne, Fr.: Editions de la Tarente, 2021).
117. Raphaël Demès, "Autour du paon et du phénix : étude d'une iconographie cultuelle et funéraire dans le Bassin méditerranéen (IVe–XIIe siècle)" (doctoral thesis, Université Bourgogne Franche-Comté, 2017).
118. Josy Eisenberg and Adin Steinsaltz, *L'alphabet sacré* (Paris: Fayard, 2012).
119. To approach Spinoza, the best starting place remains that of Gilles Deleuze. Although exaggeratingly affirming that he does not understand the third mode of knowledge, that of singular essences, Gilles Deleuze has brought Spinoza's work within our reach in his courses, notably available on the site: www.webdeleuze.com/cours/spinoza. There is also a CD of his course *Spinoza: immortalité et éternité* in the *à voix haute* collection, Gallimard, Paris, 2001.
120. Marc Goldschmit, *L'Hypothèse du Marrane. Le théâtre judéo-chrétien de la pensée politique.* (Paris: Le Félin, 2014).
121. A play on words suggested by our friend Jacqueline Kelen. [(Fr.) *Des gens de lettres aux gens de l'Être*—Trans.]
122. This text continues in part a talk given in Lisbon in 2005 and published notably in Rémi Boyer, *Essais et discours de Sintra* (La Bégude de Mazenc, Fr.: Arma Artis, 2005).
123. Plato, *Cratylus,* trans. C.D.C. Reeve (Indianapolis: Hackett, 1998), 390d–e. —Trans.
124. Franz Kafka, *Letters to Milena,* ed. Willi Haas, trans. Tania and James Stern (New York: Schocken, 1965), p. 208. —Trans.
125. Jean Genet, *Pompes Funèbres* (Paris, Gallimard, 1953), p. 190. —Trans.
126. Jorge Luis Borges and María Kodama, *Atlas* (Buenos Aires: Sudamericana, 1984), p. 82. —Trans.
127. Ezra Pound, "Notes for Canto CXX," *The Cantos of Ezra Pound* (New York: New Directions, 1972), p. 803. —Trans.
128. Nikos Kazantzakis, *Report to Greco,* trans. Pier Bien (New York: Simon and Schuster, 1965), p. 9. —Trans.
129. Robert Kanters, "Lettre au Greco. Un grand conteur oriental trace les étapes de son développement spirituel: un paganisme à la mesure de l'homme," in *Le Regard crétois,* no. 33 (December 2006). —Trans.
130. Jacqueline Kelen, *L'Esprit de solitude.* Paris: Albin Michel, 2005. ePub. —Trans.
131. D.W. Winnicott, *Jeu et réalité* (Paris: Gallimard, 1975).
132. Note that in French, the term "libertarian" carries different connotations than in English. It is a political view close to anarchism, supportive of equality and critical of capitalism. —Trans.
133. Joséphin Péladan, "Don Quichotte et Parsifal," in *Le Soleil,* no. 134 (May 14, 1905). —Trans.
134. We owe much to Sarane Alexandrian who was the great biographer of Victor Brauner and who ensured that he was not forgotten. More recently, we would like to point out the magnificent catalog of the exhibition *Victor Brauner. Je suis le rêve. Je suis l'inspiration* by the Museum of Modern Art in Paris, published by Les Musées de la ville de Paris in 2020.
135. Georges Bataille, *Les Larmes d'Éros,* in *Œuvres complètes,* vol. 10 (Paris: Gallimard, 1987), p. 607. —Trans.

136. André Breton, *La lampe dans l'horloge* (Paris: Robert Marin, 1948), p. 57. – Trans.

137. Pétrus Batselier, "De Roux-Debord," in *Politique de Dominique de Roux*, dossier compiled by Pétrus Batselier and Didier da Silva (Clermont-Ferrand, Fr.: Au Signe de la Licorne, 1998).

138. The Incoherist and Sebastianist manifestos are now grouped together in Rémi Boyer, *La voie des sans maîtres* (Aubagne, Fr.: Editions de la Tarente, 2021).

139. This is usually attributed to Parmenides (fragment 6). For an exploration by Martin Heidegger of this passage, see his *Einfuehrung In Die Metaphysik* (Tübingen: Max Niemeyer, 1953), pp. 118–120. – Trans.

140. Fernando Pessoa, *Livro do Desassossego por Bernardo Soares*, vol. 2 (Lisbon: Àtica, 1982), p. 469. – Trans.

141. Note published in Rémi Boyer, *Essais et discours de Sintra* (La Bégude de Mazenc, Fr.: Arma Artis, 2005).

142. In the original French: *penseurs* (thinkers) vs. *pensifs* (those who are lost in their thoughts). – Trans.

143. "started": in French, *initie*. – Trans.

144. This unfortunately we have not recovered.

145. Paul Nougé, *Histoire de ne pas rire* (Lausanne, Fr.: L'âge d'homme, 1980), p. 199.

www.ingramcontent.com/pod-product-compliance
Lightning Source LLC
Chambersburg PA
CBHW082028120526
44502CB00038B/2242